From Ruins to Reconstruction

FROM RUINS TO RECONSTRUCTION

*Urban Identity in Soviet Sevastopol
after World War II*

KARL D. QUALLS

CORNELL UNIVERSITY PRESS
ITHACA AND LONDON

First published 2009 by Cornell University Press

Printed in the United States of America

Library of Congress Cataloging-in-Publication Data

Qualls, Karl D.
    From ruins to reconstruction : urban identity in Soviet Sevastopol after World War II / Karl D. Qualls.
        p. cm.
    Includes bibliographical references and index.
    ISBN 978-0-8014-4762-4 (cloth : alk. paper)
    1. Reconstruction (1939–1951)—Ukraine—Sevastopol'. 2. City planning—Ukraine—Sevastopol'—History—20th century. 3. Urban policy—Ukraine—Sevastopol'—History—20th century. 4. Public architecture—Ukraine—Sevastopol'—History—20th century. 5. Central-local government relations—Ukraine—Sevastopol'—History—20th century. 6. Sevastopol' (Ukraine)—History—20th century. I. Title.

    D829.U4Q35 2009
    307.7609477'1—dc22

2009017877

Cornell University Press strives to use environmentally responsible suppliers and materials to the fullest extent possible in the publishing of its books. Such materials include vegetable-based, low-VOC inks and acid-free papers that are recycled, totally chlorine-free, or partly composed of nonwood fibers. For further information, visit our website at www.cornellpress.cornell.edu.

Cloth printing 10 9 8 7 6 5 4 3 2 1

To Gretchen, Hayden, and Hadley

Contents

List of Illustrations   ix

Acknowledgments   xi

List of Archival Abbreviations   xv

Introduction: Rebuilding as an Urban Identification Project   1

1. Wartime Destruction and Historical Identification   11

2. Local Victory over Moscow: Planning for the Future   46

3. Accommodation: Bringing Life to the Rubble   85

4. Agitation: Rewriting the Urban Biography in Stone   124

5. Persistence and Resilience of Local Identification   157

Selected Bibliography   197

Index   207

ILLUSTRATIONS

1. Map of the city center xviii

2. Destruction in the city center 14

3. Ruins at Khersones Archaeological Preserve 24

4. Girl at Gosbank vault 90

5. Reconstruction on Nakhimov Prospect 98

6. Scuttled Ships monument 134

7. Kazarskii monument 138

8. Crimean War Panorama on Historical Boulevard 151

9. Former Sechenov Institute 153

10. Lunacharskii Drama Theater 153

11. Hotel Sevastopol 154

12. Megasport sporting goods store 179

13. Fete store 180

14. Store and apartments on Bol'shaia Morskaia 181

ACKNOWLEDGMENTS

There are many people and institutions to whom I owe great debts. I have been fortunate enough to study with wonderful mentors who have fostered a love of learning and a multidisciplinary approach to understanding Russia and its history. As a teenager at the University of Missouri I had the honor to study with historians Charles Timberlake and Russell Zguta, political scientist Robin Remington, geographer Robert Kaiser, and Russian visual art and literature specialists James Curtis and Gene Barbatalo. These scholars and teachers helped me to appreciate the country to which I have devoted my professional life. At Georgetown University I had the pleasure to work with many talented historians, and the guidance provided by Roger Chickering, David Goldfrank, and Richard Stites was essential to the early development of this project. I owe special thanks to Richard for urging me to look at "history from the side" so that I could illuminate the "above" and "below." Their encouragement and prodding in the last few years have helped to bring this multidisciplinary study to fruition.

Along the way a number of other scholars, whether they realize it or not, have helped me to expand my approach to this topic and to sharpen my arguments. To name them all is impossible, but I would especially like to thank Blair Ruble, who has given me guidance since this project's inception. Don Raleigh, Don Filtzer, Susan Reid, David Crowley, Marcus Funk, Diane Koenker, Anne Gorsuch, and many others have provided comments at conferences, edited related publications, and/or provided assistance securing funding and preparing the project for publication. Jeffry Diefendorf asked the question that started me on this study. "It would be extremely interesting," Diefendorf wrote, "to know how the Soviet Union dealt with the task of reconstruction."[1] I hope that I have answered some of his questions. The participants in Sheila Fitzpatrick's "Stalin's Last Decade" workshop at the University of Chicago in 2000 provided wonderful critiques at an early stage. The contributors to the "Cities after the Fall" conference hosted by John Czaplicka and Blair Ruble at Harvard's Center for European Studies in 2005 helped me to extend my investigation of the postwar decade to the beginning of the twenty-first century.

A special thanks also goes to a group of young upstarts like myself who in the 1990s started to venture into the postwar period. An even smaller number of researchers began to investigate the Soviet Union outside of Moscow and St. Petersburg. Discussions with Jeff Jones, Per Brodersen, and Heather DeHaan have been especially helpful. In the last few years I have had the pleasure of exchanging ideas with a group of young East-Central European specialists who have forced me to rethink some of my previous conclusions. I will blame all of the above for the lengthy writing process! Their probing questions and scholarly examples made me keep going back to sources with new ideas in mind. Thank you.

Many institutions and organizations have provided assistance and support along the way. Dickinson College's Research and Development Committee has never turned down a request for time or money to pursue research or to travel to conferences. To these colleagues I am indebted. In the early stages I benefited from financial and administrative support from the Center for the Study of Russia and the USSR, the Kennan Institute for Advanced Russian Studies, and the American Council of Teachers of Russian. Generous grants during my sabbatical year provided me with the resources to support my family and to travel extensively while chasing leads across Ukraine, Russia, and the United States. Funding was provided by the National Council for Eurasian and East European Research and International Research and Exchanges Board under the authority of a Title VIII

---

1. Jeffry Diefendorf, ed., *Rebuilding Europe's Bombed Cities* (New York: St. Martin's, 1990), 12.

grant from the U.S. Department of State. A sizable J. Paul Getty Fellowship provided additional funding that allowed me to extend a sabbatical year to nearly eighteen months. An American Council of Learned Societies Library of Congress Fellowship in International Studies, with funding from the Andrew W. Mellon Foundation, the Association of American Universities, and the Library of Congress, provided magnificent facilities in the library for the latter stages of writing, particularly chapter 5.

Of course, wonderful, hardworking, and underpaid archivists make research much easier. I want to give specific thanks to Liudmila Gennadievna Kiseleva at the State Archive of the Russian Federation (GARF II). Not only were she and the rest of the staff exceedingly helpful, but Liudmila Gennadievna's excitement about my topic helped me through some tough days. The staff of the State Archive of the City of Sevastopol (GAGS) went well beyond my expectations. There has been turnover in the decade since I first started working there, but the continuity of service, collegiality, and friendship never changed. Although sometimes I just wanted to focus on work, I appreciated their invitations to the various celebrations hosted at the archive. The motherly attention of the archivists when I was sick or homesick made the long months go by quickly.

I am grateful to the following for permission to use previously published material.

One of the initial ideas in chapter 1 originated from Karl D. Qualls, "Whose History Is 'Our' History: The Influence of Naval Power in Sevastopol's Reconstruction, 1944–53" in *Endangered Cities: Military Power and Urban Societies in the Era of the World Wars,* ed. Roger Chickering and Marcus Funck (Boston: Koninklijke Brill N. V., 2004). Reprinted by permission of Koninklijke Brill N. V.

The ideas in chapter 2 originated from Karl D. Qualls, "Local-Outsider Negotiations in Postwar Sevastopol's Reconstruction, 1944–53," in *Provincial Landscapes: Local Dimensions of Soviet Power, 1917–1953,* ed. Donald J. Raleigh (Pittsburgh: University of Pittsburgh Press, 2001). Reprinted by permission of the University of Pittsburgh Press.

The initial ideas in chapters 3 and 4 developed from Karl D. Qualls, "Accommodation and Agitation in Sevastopol: Redefining Socialist Space in the Postwar 'City of Glory,'" in *Socialist Spaces: Sites of Everyday Life in the Eastern Bloc,* ed. David Crowley and Susan Reid (Oxford: Berg, 2002). Reprinted by permission of Berg Publishers.

Portions of chapter 5 appeared in my chapter "'Where Each Stone Is History': Travel Guides in Sevastopol after World War II," in *Turizm: The Russian and East European Tourist under Capitalism and Socialism,* ed. Anne E. Gorsuch and Diane P. Koenker, copyright © 2006 by Cornell University Press; and in my chapter "Today's Travel through Sevastopol's Past: Postcommunist Continuity in a 'Ukrainian' Cityscape" in *Cities after the Fall of Communism: Reshaping Cultural Landscapes and European Identity,* ed. John J. Czaplicka, Nida Gelazis, and Blair A. Ruble (Baltimore, MD: Johns Hopkins University Press and Woodrow Wilson Center Press, 2009).

Of course, none of this could have happened without the love and support of my family. My parents, Sam and Marilyn, never had the opportunity to gain a college education, but they made sure that their sons knew the value of knowledge, the joy of reading, and the benefits to be gained from hard work. My brother, Sam, always provided an example of academic excellence and inquiry that helped drive me forward. Most important, I need to thank the people to whom this book is dedicated: Gretchen, Hayden, and Hadley Qualls. Gretchen put up with repeated absences of months on end, and she held down the home front and assumed the double burden of providing an income and caring for the children (the model of the new Soviet woman) without a single complaint. Likewise, our son, Hayden, especially through brief phone calls from thousands of miles away, has been a constant reminder to me of why I feel compelled to work hard and to teach well. Fortunately for Hadley, she has had to endure only the last stages of writing. When she learns to read, she will wonder why she is in this dedication. It is for our children and their generation that I seek to explain the past with the hope that they may be able to live in a century more peaceful and humane than the last.

Karl D. Qualls
Carlisle, Pennsylvania

ARCHIVAL ABBREVIATIONS

Gosudarstvennyi arkhiv goroda Sevastopolia (State Archive of the City of Sevastopol): GAGS

Gosudarstvennyi arkhiv Rossiiskoi Federatsii (State Archive of the Russian Federation): GARF

National Archives and Record Administration: NARA

Rossiiskii gosudarstvennyi arkhiv ekonomiki (Russian State Archive of the Economy): RGAE

Rossiiskii gosudarstvennyi arkhiv literatury i iskusstva (Russian State Archive of Literature and Art): RGALI

From Ruins to Reconstruction

1. Artillery Bay
2. Bol'shaia Morskaia Street
3. Count's Wharf
4. Historical Boulevard and Panorama
5. Hotel Sevastopol
6. Kazarskii Monument
7. Lazarev Square
8. Lenin Monument
9. Lenin Street
10. Lunacharskii Theater
11. Nakhimov Prospect
12. Nakhimov Square and Monument
13. Pobeda Cinema
14. Pokrovskii Cathedral
15. Scuttled Ships Monument
16. Sechenov Institute
17. South Bay
18. Soviet Street
19. Suvorov Square
20. Ushakov Square
21. Vladimir Cathedral (city center)

Northern Region due north
Shipside Region across South Bay
Black Sea outlet northwest

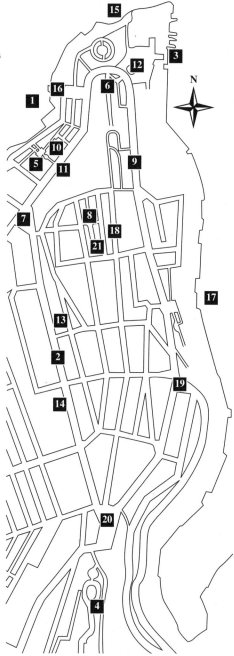

Figure 1. Map of the city center. Designed by Karl D. Qualls and Amanda Delorenzo.

Introduction

Rebuilding as an Urban Identification Project

When Sevastopol municipal officials filed their first report about life in the city after the Red Army had reversed the two-year Nazi occupation, there was little positive to say. Everywhere one looked, there was tragedy. Enemy bombers and artillery had laid waste to the home port of the Soviet Black Sea Fleet. People lived in elevator shafts, the vault of a destroyed bank, earthen dugouts (*zemlianki*), caves, basements, stairwells, and the open air. Only 3 percent of the city's buildings were still intact.

Daily survival in the rubble that once comprised a beautiful seaside was nearly as arduous as the war itself. Vehicles, fuel, and horses were scarce on the cratered streets and sidewalks. The cutters that had once shuttled residents across the city's bays now rested in ruins. Unexploded shells hid throughout the city waiting to claim a victim. The stench of the city, with death and disease everywhere, was unimaginable. Dead bodies rotted in the open sun both in the water and on land; human feces and animal carcasses polluted streets and waterways; rabid and diseased animals (those that had not been eaten or died from starvation) wandered the city. As the

Nazis retreated, they destroyed the sewage and water systems. With no clean water and a lack of soap and disinfectants, Sevastopoltsy quickly succumbed to typhus, dysentery, diphtheria, malaria, tuberculosis, and many other maladies. The prevalence of gastrointestinal ailments and skin infections testified to the utter lack of hygiene and sanitation in the first postwar months. Daily physical survival was the first priority, but the demands that everyday life put on the body and the psyche created an equivalent need to escape from the daily grind, either in the cinema or to a park or beach spared of the ordnance. None of these retreats remained.

How did people survive the horrors of war and an annihilated city, and from where did a new sense of community come as the few remaining longtime residents mingled with newly arrived construction workers and sailors? This book is about rebuilding Sevastopol during the first postwar decade and the conflict of competing visions for restoration. I focus on how local officials in Sevastopol hijacked Moscow's rebuilding plans in order to both better meet the everyday needs of the population and forge stronger local and national identifications. It touches on how people on the ground fought for survival in a provincial city that had all but ceased to exist and provides a window into daily life, bureaucratic infighting, the power of built space, and the points of agreement and contestation between regime and people. The work, therefore, reaches beyond the boundaries of Sevastopol to contribute to the political and social history of the attempts to regain control of the population during the first postwar decade.

With the war over, a center-periphery battle ensued to control the planning of the city. Life in the rubble was harsh, but local officials, conscious of the city's past and future importance as a Cold War naval base, consistently flouted the law to accommodate the local population with the few resources at hand. With so much of the prewar population evacuated, at the front, or killed, access to labor became a major bottleneck for reconstruction.[1] In repopulating the city, planners also realized that they needed to redefine the city's urban biography and to provide a sense of place for war-weary

---

1. G. F. Krivosheev, *Soviet Casualties and Combat Losses in the Twentieth Century* (London: Greenhill, 1997), 107, 142–43, suggests that the defense of Sevastopol, 30 October 1941–4 July 1942, had the following results: irrecoverable losses, 156,880; sick and wounded, 43,601; total losses, 200,841; average daily loss, 808. For the Crimean Strategic Offensive, 8 April–12 May 1944, he calculates: irrecoverable losses, 17,754; sick and wounded, 67,065; total losses, 84,819; average daily loss, 2,423.

residents. A clear narrative eventually emerged, but it was not without debate and challenges. My research focuses on a process, often quite contested, that created the myth of Sevastopol as a "hero-city." As with all myths, this one was flexible and adaptable to changing circumstances.

Dotted as it was by reminders of the city's military feats of protecting the Russian homeland, Sevastopol remained a stalwart presence of Russian identification even after Nikita Khrushchev transferred it from the Russian to Ukrainian SSR in 1954. On the ground, people sought to create their own myth of Sevastopol that was rooted as much (if not more) in the mid-nineteenth century as in the mid-twentieth. This deeper historical connection of the city with heroism and sacrifice for the Motherland allowed it to rather easily transition to a post-Soviet city without the upheavals so common throughout Eastern Europe since 1989. The city had acquired a local mythology that survived throughout the Soviet period and has remained almost entirely intact in independent Ukraine since 1991.

I began working on Sevastopol just as the USSR's postwar decade was becoming a fruitful period of research for historians investigating daily life, state control, bureaucratic behavior, center-periphery relations, and other related topics. Compared with the revolution, the New Economic Policy (NEP), and the 1930s, the postwar years are little known. As one author has noted, it was a period of "hopes, illusions, and disappointments" that we are only now beginning to investigate.[2] With the end of the war, many Soviet citizens felt that their wartime sacrifices should be rewarded with a loosening of the reins. Even in the interior, untouched by battle, people had suffered from shortages of food, fuel, and consumer goods. With approximately 27 million Soviets dead and many more injured, every family felt the war's effects. Family life changed dramatically for the numerous single mothers and orphaned children, but some people also saw positive results from wartime changes. Communist Party authority and discipline declined during the war as tens of thousands of new and ideologically impoverished people became Komsomol and party members, particularly in the military. Collective farms had collapsed, and the Russian Orthodox Church again operated legally.

---

2. Elena Zubkova, *Russia after the War: Hopes, Illusions, and Disappointments, 1945–1957,* trans. Hugh Ragsdale (Armonk, NY: M.E. Sharpe, 1998).

When a regime stakes its legitimacy on the monopoly of production and distribution, a crisis of this magnitude can shake the very foundation of its power.[3] Distribution of material goods would have to wait for the reconstruction and retooling of factories, but Stalin's regime could not allow its authority to be challenged. Propaganda, terror, and privileged treatment for key groups were all dominant strategies in the campaign to overcome the crisis of confidence.[4]

Destroyed cities were another central concern as the regime sought to redefine its relation to society and repair its image in the eyes of the population after nearly thirty years of revolution, civil war, famines, and purges. Reconstructed buildings and reborn cities became new symbols of progress and economic strength. New structures rising from and above the ruins offered more than space for housing, production, convalescence, and education. Each new building was a marker of progress, healing, and recovery. Because city building throughout the Soviet Union was an all-Union affair without international support like the Marshall Plan, it became a leading symbol for the Soviet system until the Korean War and beyond. Whereas Western Europe recovered with billions of dollars from the United States, the Soviets boasted of overcoming destruction with hard work, ingenuity, and collective effort in a do-it-yourself-project on a national scale. In the Soviet Union, perhaps only the space race and Nikita Khrushchev's "virgin lands" campaign to expand crop farming to new regions of the USSR could claim the same level of national importance in the postwar decades. Urban recovery was a national project, and its success was essential to prestige at home and abroad.[5] But each of the destroyed cities had its own history and tradition, which also made the rebuilding process intensely local.

The number and variety of destroyed cities led to a complex and contested process of rebuilding. When one looks at the problem from the periphery, decision making in Moscow appears to have been more a process than a dictate. Heterogeneity of opinion was more common than homogeneity.

3. Katherine Verdery, *What Was Socialism? And What Comes Next* (Princeton: Princeton University Press, 1996), chap. 1.

4. These strategies are detailed in Vera Dunham, *In Stalin's Time: Middleclass Values in Soviet Fiction* (Durham, NC: Duke University Press, 1990); Elena Zubkova, *Obshchestvo i reformy 1945–1964* (Moscow: Rossiia Molodaia, 1993); Eric Duskin, *Stalinist Reconstruction and the Confirmation of a New Elite, 1945–1953* (New York: Palgrave, 2000).

5. Lawrence J. Vale and Thomas Campanella, eds., *The Resilient City: How Modern Cities Recover from Disaster* (New York: Oxford University Press, 2005), 342–45.

Center and periphery debated and contested policies, but they were often complementary and not merely oppositional. Differences were often a matter of degree and priorities. To be sure, Stalin and his inner circle could and did intervene arbitrarily. But the formula of traditional totalitarian studies and its focus on command authority from above has been revealed as a half-story. Even after the 1946–48 campaign against the intelligentsia, known as the *zhdanovshchina,* specialists asserted their authority over the form of reconstruction. Everyday urbanites, with their diversity of backgrounds and training, petitioned local and central officials to improve their standards of living in a multitude of ways. Even at the heart of power in Moscow, residents pressed for greater attention to their desires.[6] In some cases, particularly in Sevastopol, the periphery dictated to the center, which sometimes responded to locals' concerns.

Agitation and Accommodation

Faced with utter destruction and the sufferings of the population, officials in Sevastopol fought back against Moscow's triumphal socialist designs for the postwar city and instead crafted human-scale projects that both met the people's material needs and revived their sense of place and willingness to sacrifice for its future. Local officials refused to allow the construction of massive "wedding cake" buildings like Moscow State University that soon proliferated in the capital. The local planning approach is what I call "agitation and accommodation." Agitation (re)created myths of a glorious past and present and combined them with the future promise of the great Soviet utopia. Accommodation was an attempt to meet the immediate needs of the city and residents.

Strategies of agitation and accommodation often intertwined as Soviet planners adopted prewar and prerevolutionary models of modern urban design. For example, green areas in cities accommodated demands for recreation, relaxation, and communing with nature and fellow citizens. Parks also occupied a central place in public health (*zdravookhranenie*) plans by providing fresh air and opportunities for exercise to urban dwellers who

---

6. Stephen V. Bittner, *The Many Lives of Khrushchev's Thaw: Experience and Memory in Moscow's Arbat* (Ithaca, NY: Cornell University Press, 2008;), especially chap. 5.

could not escape to dachas. But parks served important agitational purposes, too. Evening strolls in parks dotted with historical monuments allowed passers-by to link the present with the heroic defenders of the Motherland who had lost their lives on battlefields past. Parks and monuments helped to further the local population's identification with a familiar urban biography and encouraged them to view the central regime as accommodating and attentive to local needs for relaxation and health. Using the awe-inspiring architectural forms and scale of the city's ancient Greek heritage, designers combined images of patriotic heroes with the legendary martyrs of two revolutions and a civil war. By incorporating an existing set of myths in the design of new construction, officials accommodated the residents' desire to live in a city that was familiar to them, not one radically changed as Moscow had prescribed.

Agitation and accommodation in Sevastopol from 1944 (the return of "Soviet power" to the city) to 1953 (Stalin's death) were key strategies for relinking the city and its people to the Soviet project. "[W]here destruction has been brought to bear on places of particularly resonant symbolism," argue Lawrence Vale and Thomas Campanella, "a disaster exposes and unleashes the contested politics of local power struggles and global interconnections."[7] The destruction of the Black Sea Fleet's home base was more than symbolic, and the urgent need to rebuild created a cacophony of opinions on what the new city should look like. There was a great deal of debate over Sevastopol, but both center and periphery realized the importance of its rebuilding: the population needed to vastly improve its living conditions, and both Moscow and Sevastopoltsy wanted a symbolic and unifying urban setting, although for different reasons.

Memory and Identification

Much of Sevastopol's agitational plan sought to shape the memory of the local populace in a manner that would ensure its identification with both the city's emerging mythology and the larger Soviet project. The literature on memory has increased exponentially in past decades, and definitions of

---

7. Vale and Campanella, *The Resilient City,* 8.

"memory" and "collective memory" have proliferated such that they have nearly lost meaning. The present book focuses not on the memories and their accuracy but rather on the processes of their creation as a tool or technique for forging residents' identification with the city itself and simultaneously with Russia and the Soviet Union. In this way, the memory project parallels the process through which central intentions were mediated to accommodate local aims and goals.

The active construction of a population's memories is not a new phenomenon. Groups that seek to maintain, obtain, or delegitimize power have a great interest in reconceptualizing the way the past is presented.[8] The French revolutionaries turned history on its head when the new revolutionary culture erased the past of monarchs, aristocrats, and clergy and instead elevated the Third Estate. A similar rewriting of the past has occurred in every major revolution. Stable regimes also change the presentation of the past by funding new museums, creating new holidays, or drawing the nation's attention to its past during anniversary events. In addition to political leaders, economic interests, interest groups, and mass media all play a part in reconceptualizing the past.

Whereas most histories of national memories focus on the nation as a whole, the present work explores how memory and identification function at the local level. Alon Confino's investigation of "local-national memory" in late-imperial Germany began to focus not on an exclusive and hegemonic national identity that precludes all other groupings but instead on the *inclusivity* of national vis-á-vis local identity.[9] This approach has guided much of my study of Sevastopol's localization and the ways in which the local reinforces identification with the larger polity.

Written texts and monuments have thus far dominated scholarly discussions of collective remembrance, and the role played by urban space in creating national or local identities is usually an afterthought if it is considered at all. I investigate the design process for the resurrected Sevastopol by focusing on the all-Union "mnemonic practices" envisioned by

---

8. Geoffrey Cubitt, *History and Memory* (Manchester, UK: Manchester University Press, 2007), 14, 224.

9. Alon Confino, *The Nation as a Local Metaphor: Württemberg, Imperial Germany, and National Memory, 1871–1918* (Chapel Hill: University of North Carolina Press, 1997), 8 n. 20. For Confino, local-national memory denotes the "memory Germans constructed to reconcile localness and nationhood."

Moscow architects and the resistance to them mounted by local architects, officials, and citizens.[10] One study of the "memory project" of the October Revolution focuses on the revolution and its *"legitimizing function* vis-á-vis the Soviet state."[11] Newspapers, books, and other written texts joined the proliferation of monuments in the postwar years to help define Sevastopol's mythology. But the city's identity derived from much more than these oft-studied sources. Street names, local architectural aesthetics, and space use revitalized local tradition. Rather than redesign the city plan and erect buildings that mirrored the prewar Moscow Plan that was to serve as a model for all Soviet cities, locals preserved the street grid, architecture, and toponyms of prerevolutionary Sevastopol. But localness could and did have a legitimizing function for Moscow because local policymakers consciously linked Sevastopol with Russia and the USSR.

The various strategies of identification employed in Sevastopol were contested, but all of them sought to define the city's mythology for both residents and outsiders.[12] Identification can be relational or categorical. The former comprises the relationship with other people, be they family, friends, or clients. The latter places identifications into groups based on attributes like language or ethnicity.[13] Sevastopol's relational identification has been and remains with Moscow, and its categorical identification is that of a naval power and hero-city defending the Motherland. The city's close tie to Russia's nineteenth-century state building has forged a relational identification with Moscow rather than with the Ukrainian capital at Kyiv. The city's founding as a naval city and the numerous conflicts fought in or from the city have shaped its categorical identification. Various strategies, from Moscow's provisioning of resources to the construction of agitational spaces that honored Russian naval feats, aided the formulation of the city's relational and categorical identifications. Newsreel directors, writers and

---

10. Jeffrey K. Olick, ed. *States of Memory: Continuities, Conflicts, and Transformations in National Retrospection* (Durham: Duke University Press, 2003), 6. Mnemonic practices encompass the diverse ways that people recall the past, whether accurately or not, focusing on process and agency rather than something that is reified, static, or primordial.

11. Frederick Corney, "Rethinking a Great Event: The October Revolution as Memory Project," in Olick, *States of Memory,* 17–42, 36 (emphasis in original).

12. The term "strategies of identification" comes from one of my many conversations with Per Brodersen about his work on postwar Kaliningrad.

13. Rogers Brubaker and Frederick Cooper, "Beyond 'Identity,'" *Theory and Society* 29, no. 1 (February 2000): 15.

journalists, architects and planners, and city officials all employed these strategies in order to construct an urban biography that would provide a sense of place and purpose to postwar residents who more often than not were not native to the city and had no close knowledge of its history and traditions. Long-term residents wanted the restoration of the familiar environment, and, in order to stabilize the workforce, new residents had to be convinced that the city, with its special role within Russian and Soviet history, was worth sacrificing for.

As with memory, urban identifications are both internally and externally manufactured. Local agents construct identification at the local level while outsiders—in our case, Moscow-based authorities—try to manufacture identification externally. Locals posit the alternatives to outsider interference because the inanimate city has little agency of its own. Local leaders and residents in Sevastopol, however, stressed a continuity with past traditions and aesthetics that sometimes challenged the intentions of the central regime. The state, media, local government, and individual residents all contributed to the scripting of an urban biography, essentially "a collective self-understanding," for the city.[14] A focus on the *process* of identification, although limited here to one city, allows us to better understand the Soviet system's attempts to construct a polity, its ideas, and its affinities. The dialogue between central and local officials reveals as much about the former as the latter.

Indeed, although it may appear counterintuitive, robust identification with the local could actually strengthen identification with the center. Local officials and citizens began to prescribe and proscribe history and its remembrance so that Sevastopol's image as a Russian naval capital was nearly as strong in the early twenty-first century as it was in the late 1940s. Because local officials succeeded in wresting control from Moscow, Sevastopol maintained its strong connections to its prerevolutionary naval heritage and became a more livable city, replete with architectural elements that resonated with its past. Although the near total destruction during the war made radical replanning possible, locals argued that maintaining past traditions was essential to the stability and happiness of the population, which in turn would reflect well on the central regime. Since Sevastopol's

---

14. Brubaker and Cooper, "Beyond 'Identity,'" 16.

history focused on military sacrifice in defense of the Motherland, the new localized vision for Sevastopol complemented rather than competed with larger Soviet objectives. The irony is that local officials had to fend off central attempts to change the city's built space and sites of memory and in the process they created a stronger link with the center. The resilience of the postwar decade's localization project, embedded in built space and rehearsed in classrooms and festivals for decades, is now the source of tension with the Ukrainian capital of Kyiv.

Sevastopol shared many of the same problems of physical reconstruction with other destroyed cities, but it is likely a unique case of a city outside Russia that benefited from the turn to Russocentrism during the Stalin years. The power of local history and identification is abundantly clear in Sevastopol in both its built space and its residents' understandings of self and place. Soviet Russocentrism and a revival of localism after World War II created a Ukrainian city that today views itself as Russian.

The following chapters move from Sevastopol's wartime experience to plans for its rebirth to the harsh conditions of the postwar decade in which the core elements of Sevastopol's urban biography were created. Chapter 1 details the massive physical destruction of the German siege, two-year occupation, and Soviet reconquest. During this period Soviet mythmakers began to construct a new narrative linking the city's heroism in the Crimean War with its experience in the latest conflict. In doing so they sought to encourage further sacrifice and heroism for the tasks of rebuilding and to provide a sense of purpose and place to thousands of newly arrived residents. Chapter 2 details the competing architectural visions for Sevastopol and in particular the tension between center and periphery. Chapter 3 focuses on attempts by local leaders to accommodate the housing, health-care, and leisure needs of the city's residents. Chapter 4 turns to the way by which sites of memory and loci for identification were embedded in the built space of the city. Monuments, street names, and a particular neoclassical building style constructed a unique image for the city. Chapter 5 shows how tourism and guidebooks perpetuated the image constructed during the postwar decade and came to pose a challenge for Ukraine, which in 1991 assumed control of a city with a biography and demography that are overwhelmingly Russian.

1

Wartime Destruction and Historical Identification

[O]nly now have the tales of those days of Sevastopol ceased
to be just so many beautiful historical legends for you:
they have become authentic, a fact. You will clearly understand,
picture yourself, the people you have just seen, those heroes who in those
stern days did not lose heart but became even more exalted in spirit
and gladly prepared to die not for a town, but for their motherland.
This epic of Sevastopol, the hero of which was the Russian people, will
leave its deep impress on Russia for a long time to come.

Lev Tolstoy, *Sevastopol Tales*

The selfless struggle of Sevastopoltsy...serves as an example of heroism for
all the Red Army and Soviet people. It is certain that the glorious defenders
of Sevastopol fulfilled their debt to the Motherland with
dignity and honor.

Joseph Stalin, quoted in Zakhar Chebaniuk,
Sevastopol: Istoricheskie mesta i pamiatniki

A century before Hitler's forces invaded the Soviet Union and brought
destruction to Sevastopol, the young writer Lev Tolstoy began to construct
a narrative of Sevastopol and the people who lived there and fought for
it. As he so clearly noted, the retelling of the scenes of battle would make
legends "authentic, a fact." Similar attempts a century later to make the
travails of a small number of people authentic for a mass audience came to
be labeled propaganda. However, at the heart of the narratives of Tolstoy
and Soviet mythmakers of World War II was the search to show that sacrifice mattered. Joseph Stalin and Lev Tolstoy both evoked a battle for the

Motherland, not just Sevastopol. Tolstoy's heroes were "gladly prepared to die," but Stalin's subjects performed a "selfless sacrifice" and "fulfilled their debt." Remarkably, however, over a century between the two wars, Sevastopol's imagined place within the Russian-Soviet empire had changed little. Sevastopol was a city of heroes who would die to protect not only their homes but also their country. This chapter shows both what happened to the city and its inhabitants during the war and the myth that arose from it on paper and celluloid.

During war and rebuilding, the Soviet propaganda machine used various media to create a mythic image of the city and a narrative of its heroic defense and reconquest in order to assure the population of eventual victory. In the postwar period the repetition of heroic images provided a sense of belonging for the new population that came from all corners of the Soviet Union. It provided hope for progress if the postwar population could only sacrifice as it had during the war. Wartime filmmakers and writers echoed the Crimean War reporting of Lev Tolstoy instead of Soviet ideology from the revolution and civil war.[1] Residents and local officials used the wartime examples as the foundation for constructing and reconstructing an urban biography and identification for the transient population. New residents were now told that they were part of a long lineage of heroic sacrifice in defense of the Motherland, whether it be Imperial Russia or the Soviet Union. With the arduous task of rebuilding Sevastopol ahead, propagandists sought to motivate the population by relating their sacrifices to the efforts of warriors past. This effort provided a sense of purpose, place, and motivation.

In a war that brought more destruction to civilian populations than ever before (or since) in human history, stories of survival and heroism were as important as ever for connecting dislocated populations to places. Sevastopol's reconstruction shows that war stories in print and film helped provide a link to the city's past that eventually allowed local officials and planners to recast Sevastopol's biography to favor its naval, military history over its revolutionary past. The Sovietness of Sevastopol was never questioned directly, but the socialist revolutions and civil war feats became

---

1. On the problematic and contested rehabilitation of Tolstoy as a Soviet hero in 1928, see Kevin Platt and David Brandenberger, *Epic Revisionism: Russian History and Literature as Stalinist Propaganda* (Madison: University of Wisconsin Press, 2006), chaps. 1–2.

trumped when writers linked the "second great defense" of World War II with the Crimean War. The discourse of the two great defenses showed a continuity of behavior that defined the spirit of the city, its citizens, and its sailors.

The Ravages of War

Throughout the period between the two defenses, Sevastopol had built a vibrant and beautiful urban core. In 1940, Sevastopol was, like many Soviet cities, expanding as it developed its industry and incorporated newly arrived workers. Local geography limited the breadth of production to shipbuilding, fishing, viniculture, and some small-scale manufacturing of clothing, spirits, and food processing. The rocky terrain in and around the city posed serious problems for industry, but it created the perfect raw materials for building construction. From the time of the ancient Greeks, Sevastopol had been a stone city. Abundant quarries and a lack of trees dictated the use of the more durable building materials. Because of the abundance of stone, brick construction was minimal. The "pleasant tones" and "monumentality" in the prewar stone construction led to a beautiful city center filled with columns, balconies, and loggias, all of which were restored or reconstructed in the postwar decade.[2] Although many of the Communist Party faithful may have derided the prerevolutionary architecture as eclectic or bourgeois, the interwar and postwar years brought little aesthetic change. The summer of 1941 ushered in several years of destruction that charred the once beautiful urban landscape.

The endless bombardment of the city in 1941 and 1942 and the nearly two-year occupation before the Red Army reclaimed Sevastopol in May 1944 left little evidence of life in the city. All sides in World War II targeted civilian populations in a total war that eclipsed the scale of destruction in the Great War a generation earlier. Because of the 1939 treaty of nonaggression between Stalin and Hitler, the Soviet Union escaped the first two years of the latter conflict. But when Nazi forces invaded, everyday

---

2. Gosudarstvennyi arkhiv goroda Sevastopolia (GAGS), f. P-308, op. 1, d. 23, l. 31. Postwar officials noted the importance of keeping the "practice of prewar, even prerevolutionary construction." Rossiiskii gosudarstvennyi arkhiv ekonomiki (RGAE), f. 9432, op. 1, d. 82, ll. 69–94.

Figure 2. Destruction in the city center. Reprinted with permission of the State Archive of the
City of Sevastopol. Photograph 5222.

life changed immeasurably for Sevastopoltsy and other Soviet citizens.[3]
Thousands of people returning to Sevastopol after the Red Army's 9 May
1944 liberation came face to face with destruction and the three thousand
ragged residents who remained throughout the occupation (figure 2). The
city's annihilation reinforced hatred for the enemy and strengthened the
desire to rebuild the once beautiful city.

Hometowns normally are filled with markers and reminders of the
past—buildings in which one lived, worked, and went to school, as well
as places of entertainment and other fond memories, but everywhere they
looked, Sevastopoltsy saw only a city in ruins. Because the litter of vehicles,
trolleys, and crumbled buildings covered sidewalks and pavement, traffic
ceased along the streets residents once had traveled. Shelled and bombed

---

3. For an overview of World War II on the eastern front, see John Erickson and David Dilks,
Barbarossa: The Axis and the Allies (Edinburgh: Edinburgh University Press, 1994); John Erickson,
The Road to Berlin: Continuing the History of Stalin's War with Germany (Boulder: Westview, 1983);
John Erickson, *The Road to Stalingrad* (London: Weidenfeld and Nicholson, 1974); David Glantz,
When Titans Clashed: How the Red Army Stopped Hitler (Lawrence: University Press of Kansas,
1995); Krivosheev, *Soviet Casualties and Combat Losses in the Twentieth Century.*

streets, trolley lines, bridges, and docks interrupted everything from the movement of goods to the evening strolls so common in the prewar city. Mounds of stone stood in the place of buildings. Tree-lined boulevards were scorched and barely recognizable. The wreckage of planes and tanks, piles of shells, and unexploded mines dotted the landscape. The battles had bombed sites of defense, commerce, and pleasure into oblivion, and only the shells of ships remained in the water.

The Nazi Luftwaffe bombed Sevastopol on the first day of the invasion on 22 June 1941 and started a yearlong destruction of the fortress city that stood in the way of Nazi designs on oil in the Caspian Sea and control of the Black Sea. Since the Crimean War of 1853–56, imperial and Soviet forces had constructed a series of land defenses to protect the city. Three rings of ravines, trenches, and fortified artillery bunkers protected the city by land, while mines, ships, and submarines prevented access by water. Careful German aerial reconnaissance in the months leading up to the first assault led to target planning for hundreds of German bombers that dealt a devastating blow to the fortifications, the city, and the fleet.[4] In late September 1941, the German Eleventh Army under Field Marshal Erich von Manstein started its conquest of the Crimean Peninsula with an eye toward securing the naval base at Sevastopol. Although by mid-November the rest of the peninsula had been taken, Sevastopol remained in Soviet hands. In late December a tireless siege from the air, the Germans' largest artillery pieces, and noxious gas lasted seven months until the German forces claimed the city in early July 1942. Sevastopol crumbled under incessant shelling.

This war against the "subhumans" (*Untermenschen*) could not allow beautiful religious and secular buildings to remain as testimony to Slavic culture. War correspondent and playwright Boris Voitekhov reported in June 1942, when bombing attacks continued for days without interruption, that the Luftwaffe had dive-bombed houses, squares, streets, and wharfs, and showered the city with scrap-metal rails, motors, wheels, and plows in order to destroy both buildings and the residents' will. Planes attacked

---

4. "Sevastopol," National Archive and Records Administration (NARA), Record Group 242 (Collection of Foreign Records Seized), Cartographic and Architectural Branch, College Park, MD. These bombing maps captured from the German military show a conscious targeting of the wharfs and installations throughout the city as well as the center of the city.

anything that moved, and even the dead in the "Fraternal Cemetery" were not left in peace as German planes bombed for "hidden oil reserves."[5] While Voitekhov's recollection may be a bit exaggerated, the scale of the destruction was certain. Nazi forces let fly tens of thousands of bombs and shells in order to leave no trace of the city. German maps showed a conscious attempt to target not only naval assets and fortifications but also the markers of Slavic culture and history in Sevastopol.[6] From ports to naval headquarters to fortified gun batteries, the German Luftwaffe had nearly all the major installations of the city charted well before the war on the eastern front began. Nonmilitary assets also became targets. Maps noted the locations of churches, cinemas, and even cemeteries scheduled for destruction. Sports stadiums, monuments, biology research facilities, and naval command centers all appear on the same maps. With as many as 1,800 sorties per day, the German Luftwaffe achieved most of its goals and destroyed the institutions of life and culture in the city.

The siege had brought fierce fighting and massive destruction to Sevastopol and its surroundings. Even though many Russian troops fought on from their cave hideouts, by mid-1942, most were gassed into the open and shot. The full fury of large-caliber, rail-bound guns, such as the 800-millimeter (31.5 inches) "Big Dora" that shot its 10,500-pound shells over hills and ravines, destroyed all signs of life on the other side. One strike from this massive gun and the others like it completely destroyed buildings and even underground utilities.

The entire city of Sevastopol had moved underground during the long siege. Families and factories found new homes in Sevastopol's many caves. Bomb shelter factories churned out shells, guns, boots, and coats for the front lines. When Soviet forces finally had to abandon the city on 4 July 1942, underground hideaways became a network of partisan dens. The Communist Underground Organization in the German Rear (*Kommunisticheskaia podpol'naia organizatsiia v tylu nemtsev*—KPOVTN) covered the

---

5. Boris Voitekhov, *The Last Days of Sevastopol,* trans. Ralph Parker and V. M. Genne (New York: Knopf, 1943), 105–8.

6. See maps 13613–13613B and DT/TM5 (Dick Tracy/target map 5), NARA, Record Group 373 (Records of the Defense Intelligence Agency). Although most Soviet accounts mention 22 June 1941 as the beginning of the German preparations for attacking Sevastopol, German reconnaissance maps show that planning began at least one month before Operation Barbarossa. Photo 13614 shows reconnaissance from 24 May 1941.

city with posters by night, informed the population by leaflets, sabotaged, and created diversions.[7] But for two years, the Nazis occupied Sevastopol and ruled over the few residents who did not evacuate and had not been killed or imprisoned.

Immediately after Soviet forces reclaimed Sevastopol amid fierce fighting in early May 1944, the three regional committees of the local government quickly gathered representatives of party, government, navy, workers, and religious groups to estimate the scale of damage and prepare reports about the Nazi atrocities.[8] On 14 May 1944, just five days after the Red Army forced the Nazis to abandon Sevastopol, the committees released documents detailing the destruction of nearly every educational, medical, and administrative building in the city and also the damaged and defiled city monuments and memorials. Of 110,000 Sevastopoltsy, only 3,000 remained until liberation. The Nazis sent 24,600 city residents to Germany as captive labor[9] and had also rounded up men and placed them in camps. Soviet reports also noted beatings, starvation, and a lack of water for prisoners. German guards reportedly shot women who brought food and water to their captive husbands, fathers, and sons. One woman was thrown off a twenty-meter-high roof, the enemy reportedly blew up two wagonloads of prisoners of war. Because there was no provisioning of city residents, many starved to death. With all the brutal massacres, a majority of the old and young were left without people to protect them. Orphaned children and the elderly lived in "children's homes" and "invalid homes," but the Nazis

---

7. An abundance of information, heavily weighted toward Communist Party activity, can be found in the works of former municipal party leader Boris Borisov. See Boris Alekseevich Borisov, *Podvig Sevastopolia: Dokumental'naia povest'* (Moscow: Sovetskii pisatel', 1952); Boris Alekseevich Borisov, *Zapiski sekretaria gorkoma* (Moscow: Politizdat, 1964); Boris Alekseevich Borisov, *Shkola zhizni* (Moscow: Politizdat, 1971); Boris Alekseevich Borisov, *Sevastopol'skaia byl* (Simferopol: Krym, 1968). Other helpful works include *Istoriia goroda-geroia Sevastopolia, 1917–1957* (Kyiv: Akademiia nauk ukrainskoi SSR, 1960); *Sevastopoliu 200 let, 1783–1983: Sbornik dokumentov i materialov* (Kyiv: Naukova dumka, 1983).

8. In April 1944 the oblast party and government forwarded instructions created the year before on the proper formation of such committees. The full list consisted of the regional party chairmen; the deputy chairmen of the regional executive committee; a member of the NKVD; and representatives of trade unions, workers, the intelligentsia, and "religious cults if there are such in the region." See GAGS, f. R-79, op. 2, d. 14, l. 22. Reports on atrocities had been common from the first years of the war as a way to convince the Soviet allies to open the much-hoped-for second front against Hitler.

9. GAGS, f. R-79, op. 2, d. 20, ll. 12–14; *Sevastopoliu 200 let, 1783–1983: Sbornik dokumentov i materialov* (Kyiv: Naukova dumka, 1983), 259–66.

soon shipped them off somewhere never to be seen again. As the Nazi forces evacuated by ship, they placed women and children on the decks as "camouflage" to prevent Soviet planes from bombing.[10] Sevastopol's Jews and Communists comprised most of the 27,306 civilians shot or hanged.[11]

As residents began to return from the Crimean countryside, Siberia, and central Asia in the summer of 1944, they found few signs of life. Returning to Sevastopol from Moscow one month after liberation, city party chief Boris Borisov noted that 5,000 buildings had been completely destroyed and only 7 "seriously damaged buildings" remained in the city center.[12] The official numbers from the city committee showed that only 1,023 of 6,402 (16 percent) residential buildings were habitable at all in the entire city.

The long German siege and the Red Army's return to the city two years later took its toll on Sevastopol's infrastructure as well. German forces destroyed the city's water system, shelling wreaked havoc on sewers, retreating forces cut phone and telegraph lines, special battalions destroyed railroad tracks and tunnels, and Nazi railcars hauled industrial equipment, including some of the city's electric generators, back to Germany. All told, Soviet officials claimed a loss of 25 billion rubles.[13]

Although the war ravaged all the city's regions, the obliteration of the city center and its concentration of social services and infrastructure affected residents nearly as much as the loss of their homes and families. War still raged for another year after liberation, and the fight could not pause for mourning. Basic municipal services, many of which had already reached capacity before the war, now had to be reconceived and rebuilt as people streamed back to Sevastopol and strained the city's ability to accommodate even the basic needs of sanitation, food, shelter, health care, and education.[14]

10. *Sevastopoliu 200 let, 1783–1983,* 263.

11. Dmitrii Motorin, *Vozrozhdennyi Sevastopol': Ocherki o vosstanovlenii goroda 1944–1953 gg.* (Moscow: Nauka, 1984), 14.

12. Borisov, *Sevastopol'skaia byl,* 157.

13. *Istoriia goroda-geroia Sevastopolia, 1917–1957* (Kyiv: Akademiia nauk ukrainskoi SSR, 1960), 289–290; GAGS, f. R-359, op. 1, d. 7, l. 23; GAGS, f. R-359, op. 1, d. 10, l. 18.

14. On postwar sanitation see Donald Filtzer, "Standard of Living versus Quality of Life: Struggling with the Urban Environment in Russia during the Early Years of Post-war Reconstruction," in *Late Stalinist Russia: Society between Reconstruction and Reinvention,* ed. Juliane Fürst (New York: Routledge, 2006), 81–102.

Nazi occupation and demographic devastation in Sevastopol mirrored that of many Soviet cities that fell under the thumb of the Nazi military. The brutalization of society made the need for a nurturing state all the more important. The trauma of war and dislocation created a need for stability for residents and for the city's reconstruction. Without the habits of a more comfortable everyday life, the workers charged with rebuilding would be distracted by the new fight to survive in a dead city.

Even though Sevastopol had expanded in the 1930s, the Nazis destroyed all the gains. Whereas Sevastopol's population increased 40 percent from 1897 to 1926, in only the next twelve years it shot up approximately 46 percent (see table 1). But Germany and its allies destroyed nearly all production as they retreated, which left cities without goods. Daily bread was a scarce commodity, and finished goods like clothing were rarer still. In one partially destroyed garment factory, workers had to use their own sewing machines because all others had been destroyed or stolen. The central district lost its pasta, soap, and sausage-making facilities. Bakeries, symbolic and real loci of everyday life, were also destroyed, and what production could be squeezed out of city ovens went to the army. The fish-processing plant survived almost completely, but fishing was limited to the bays because mines still blocked the exit to the sea. Little remained of the water delivery system except for 760 cubic meters per day for personal use and production. A lack of storage matched the scarcity of goods because warehouses, refrigerated units, and icehouses had ceased to exist, which left meat and dairy products to rot in the hot summer sun.

Transportation and communication were destroyed as thoroughly as consumer goods. Most vehicles had been destroyed or pressed into military service. This hardly mattered because the war had devastated auto repair shops and machine tool manufacturing. Vehicles, often war trophies, remained in the city, but they had no spare parts or fuel. They quickly became useless. On their retreat the Nazis destroyed four railroad tunnels and stole rails. Only thirty telephones had service a week after liberation, and these were limited to the party and government.[15] There was no place to get a haircut or watch a movie or play, and there were few places to get medical attention (see table 2).

---

15. *Sevastopoliu 200 let, 1783–1983,* 264–68.

TABLE 1. Population in Sevastopol

Date	Population
February 1897	55,000
December 1926	77,000
January1939	112,000/114,000
January 1941	111,946
4 May 1944	3,000
25 May 1944	10,787
December 1944	47,000
1 January 1945	38,783
May 1945	42,894
January 1946	54,288
May 1946	59,520
January 1947	70,063
March 1948	78,000
September 1949	103,000
November 1950	120,000
January 1956	140,000

Source: RGAE, f. 9432, op. 1, d. 33, l. 151 (1939); GAGS, f. R-79, op. 2, d. 20, ll. 12–14, and GAGS, f. R-79, op. 2, d. 14, ll. 102–4 (1944); GAGS f. R-79, op. 2, d. 22, ll. 37–40 (1945); GAGS, f. R-79, op. 2, d. 64a, l. 1–1ob (1946); GAGS, f. R-359, op. 1, d. 50, l. 29 (1941–47); RGAE, f. 9432, op. 1, d. 241, ll. 26–35, and GAGS, f. R-308, op. 1, d. 68, ll. 1–4 (1948); GAGS, f. R-79, op. 2, d. 157, ll. 56–65 (1949); GAGS, f. R-359, op. 1, d. 88, l. 54 (1950, does not count military). Only the 1950 datum notes specifically that the fleet was not included. It is unclear whether sailors are counted in the other data. From May to December 1944 there was a 435 percent change. Data from 1897, 1926, and 1956 and the larger number for 1939 come from *Narod-noe khoziastvo krymskoi oblasti: Statisticheskii sbornik* (Simferopol: Krymiz-dat, 1957), 18.

TABLE 2. Scale of urban destruction in Sevastopol

Facilities	Prewar number (square meters)	Number able to be restored (square meters)
Municipal residential buildings	980 (272,000)	183 (27,500)
Administrative buildings	22 (36,000)	8 (4,500)
Economic buildings	320 (56,000)	15 (2,600)
Private residences	5,080 (222,000)	820 (28,000)
Barbershops	20	0
Transport cutters	9	2
Ambulatory and polyclinic buildings	13	2
Transformer substations	50	5
Hospital buildings	9	8 (although severely damaged)
Stores	160	2
Theater	1	0
Cinemas	3	0
Local and cooperative enterprises	16	Part of 1

Source: GAGS, f. R-359, op. 1, d. 4, ll. 32–39ob.

Although the Nazis kept many schools open from 1942 to 1944, the advance of Soviet forces led the enemy to destroy all fourteen schools in the city center. Some schools in outlying regions became concentration camps and stables. Windows no longer had glass, and the Nazis destroyed or stole heating and cooking stoves. Before classes could begin again after liberation, the city education department had to organize cleaning campaigns in the schools with particular attention to removing German graffiti from the walls. Chairs, desks, notebooks, pencils, textbooks, globes, and many other items had to be replaced because the fighting had destroyed nearly all educational materials in the city. As the school year began that September, and with a rapidly increasing population returning from evacuation, a shortage of teachers and habitable schools led to three to four shifts of students each day in an attempt to keep the student/teacher ratio close to the prewar average (see table 3). Little had changed since the days when the students had to meet in the city's caves during the siege.[16] Sevastopol stood devastated by wholesale destruction and theft, even "down to children's things."[17]

As children and teachers huddled in cold schools, they also faced the fact that medical care to fight raging disease and infection was virtually nonexistent immediately after the liberation. The war had destroyed all medical facilities in the city, except for a small portion of Hospital No. 1, which, by October 1944, had room for only 175 patients. As dispensaries and clinics began to open during the first postwar months, medical care was theoretically more accessible to the population. But with only one ambulance at Hospital No. 1 in the city center and the public transport network still in shambles, most patients had to walk, hitchhike, or ride livestock to get medical attention. By the end of 1944, there were only one X-ray machine and two microscopes in a city besieged with tuberculosis, typhus, dysentery, malaria, and other diseases. Even if it was possible to get to a medical facility and be diagnosed properly, a patient had to realize that the "assortment and quantity of medications [were] entirely insufficient." Without sufficient housing and food, it was also difficult to entice specialists to come to the city because the "intelligentsiia of [Sevastopol stood] in

---

16. GAGS, f. R-90, op. 1, d. 6, ll. 1–3; ibid., d. 7, ll. 1–2.
17. *Krovavye zlodeianiia nemtsev v Sevastopole* (Sevastopol, 1944), 10–12, cited in *Sevastopoliu 200 let, 1783–1983,* 263.

Table 3. General education data

Year	Schools	Students	Classes	Students/Class
1940	28	15,337	418	36.7
1945	9	3,154	98	32.2
1948	22	10,662	286	37.3
1949	24	11,850	322	36.8
1950 plan	26	12,500	333	37.5

Source: The more accurate numbers above come from the 1949 school year report, GAGS, f. 90, op. 1, d. 91, l. 1.

grave condition."[18] The scale and extent of destruction in Sevastopol and the USSR made a return to the status quo ante impossible as the war continued for another year. Unlike the public pronouncements of hordes of volunteer teachers, physicians, engineers, and other specialists flocking to Sevastopol and other liberated cities, the official and private reports clearly show that the numbers of these personnel were small and that many were sent on temporary assignment from other locations.

The traditional sites of entertainment and relaxation fared no better than the war-ravaged vital services. From beaches to cinemas to theaters to parks full of monuments, Sevastopoltsy had few places to forget about their misery. Libraries, clubs, bathhouses, museums, and churches had all been destroyed. The odor of human waste in Artillery Bay consumed the adjacent Primorskii Boulevard, the traditional place for strolling and summer entertainment. Most of the other major parks and green spaces in the city had been turned into rubble heaps. In addition to destroying houses and factories, the Nazis had "destroyed historical monuments of Russian glory [that were] dear to the hearts of each Russian person." The report's authors noted the particularly savage destruction of "historical monuments to the defense of Sevastopol in 1854–55," including Malakhov Kurgan, the memorial site of a bloody uphill fight.[19] Cinemas and theaters moved into basements, and, during the warmer months, performances for culture-hungry audiences occurred outdoors. Although minimal, these leisure opportunities eclipsed those of the occupation period when German propaganda films

---

18. GAGS, f. R-59 op. 1, d. 10, ll. 1–5.

19. *Krovavye zlodeianiia nemtsev v Sevastopole,* 13–14, cited in *Sevastopoliu 200 let,* 1783–1983, 265.

were the norm.[20] Nazi leaders, keenly aware of the power of entertainment and the importance of the past in creating a sense of self and nation, had set out to destroy all media that the Soviets could use to rally the population. The Nazis consciously attacked and destroyed the means of production and survival in Sevastopol and the USSR, but they also sought to undercut the markers of identification and pride. On the national level this meant the humiliating despoiling of national cultural landmarks such as the homes of author Lev Tolstoy and composers Petr Tchaikovsky and Nikolai Rimsky-Korsakov.[21] In Sevastopol, the assault on the cultural past took the form of defiling churches and decapitating the statue of Eduard Totleben, designer of the Crimean War defenses. World War II was a total war not just on the physical present but also on the mythical past. Reconstruction would require reconceiving and rebuilding each.

Finding Meaning in Sevastopol's Past

Sevastopol's naval past became usable to the city planners seeking to inculcate local identification in a population that as often as not came from outside the region. The hagiographies developed during and after the war located the population in a city that was imperative to the very survival of the country. The past gave meaning and purpose to the future and sought to justify the sacrifices both of the war and of the postwar rebuilding period. In elevating Sevastopol's past, the mythmakers created a sense of place for the newly arrived or disaffected.

Sevastopol's categorical character has always been naval. Although the ancient Greeks established the commercial port of Chersonesus (or Khersones) as the first permanent urban settlement in what is now Sevastopol,

---

20. It should be noted that relatively little is known about daily life during the occupation period. Most of the memoir literature ends in 1942 and begins again in 1944. The relatively few people who lived in the city during the two-year occupation were immediately suspect and therefore less likely to be allowed to publish their recollections. The information presented here is gleaned from a few interviews, most notably with a longtime resident who lived in the occupied city as an adolescent. Mikhail Mironov, interview by author, Sevastopol, Ukraine, 2004.

21. One German officer was reported to have said, "We don't need firewood; we shall burn everything connected with the name of your Tolstoy." *Notes and Statement by the Soviet Government on German Atrocities* (Moscow: Foreign Language Publishing House, 1943), 19–20.

Figure 3. Ruins at Khersones Archaeological Preserve. Photograph by Karl D. Qualls, 2004.

the city's Slavic heritage has been tied to naval warfare (figure 3). Catherine the Great seized the city from the Ottoman Turks in 1774. In 1782, after the construction of three batteries to protect the main bay, the first Russian warships dropped anchor. The following year construction began on a permanent city called Sevastopol, meaning "city of glory." In what would become a recurring problem in the city, construction proceeded slowly because of little government assistance and no comprehensive plan. War broke out again in 1787 as the Turks attempted to take back the city. The two empires forged a temporary alliance in 1798 as Napoleon began to sweep through Europe. War dominated the city's nineteenth century as the Ottoman Turks and western powers fought with Russia for dominance of the Black Sea and access to the Middle East. In both the late 1820s and 1870s, Russia clashed with the Ottoman Turks in the Black Sea and brought Sevastopol's fleet into action.

The twentieth century also started with the city in arms and continued to add to its lore as a naval city fighting for a greater good. Sergei

Eisenstein immortalized the revolt of the battleship *Potemkin* in his film of the same name, but the events of 1905 were among many that ravaged the city in the first two decades of the new century. Like the anti-Nicholaevan revolts of 1830, the uprising in the Black Sea Fleet in 1905 laid bare popular resentment against autocracy. As socialist parties gained strength in the early twentieth century, they drew many sailors into revolutionary circles. The Bolsheviks' November 1917 coup in St. Petersburg quickly spread to Sevastopol, and the navy helped establish "Soviet power" in the city. For the next few years, the entire Crimean Peninsula suffered during the civil war as revolutionary, "white," and foreign forces vied for control. The region's most important city changed hands repeatedly.

Despite all these devastating engagements, Sevastopol is known for the two great defenses of the Crimean War and World War II. Nonresidents know the Crimean War from Lev Tolstoy's *Sevastopol Tales* and Alfred, Lord Tennyson's "The Charge of the Light Brigade." Tolstoy, in particular, captured the desperation and valor of the war. The Russian forces of the 1850s lacked everything from modern munitions and steamships to proper clothing, transportation, and medical care. Yet, for 349 days, the Russian forces held off the combined forces of England, France, and Turkey. Although the enemy never took the city center, shelling destroyed much of it and led to a decades-long process of rebuilding. The Crimean War became known for great sacrifice and suffering and set up the narrative understanding of the second great defense against the Nazis a century later.

Soviet forces faced many of the same problems and fates that the Russian soldiers had a century earlier and further contributed to the city's urban biography. Nazi Germany initially had much better technology and training and the advantage of a surprise aerial attack on the city on the first day of the war. Again, valiant sacrifice and a formidable line of defenses allowed the city to hold out for more than eight months. But the Nazis occupied Sevastopol for the next two years. The brutal campaign to take back the city in May 1944 created another pantheon of heroes. It was literally an uphill battle that led to devastating losses on both sides before the Soviet military recaptured Sevastopol on 9 May 1944. From the brief historical narrative above it is easy to understand why much of the city's identification is tied to warfare.

Although honoring war heroes was nothing new, Tolstoy's reporting from the front during the Crimean War showed the character that would mark his glorious writing career and provide an example for Soviet mythmakers. His attention to the common hero, the man in the trench, and the military leader found resonance a century later as Soviet writers and filmmakers tried to rally the population and allies against Hitler. In Sevastopol and other frontline cities, writers and journalists descended with pen in hand to seek out stories of the extraordinary and to chronicle the plight of individuals and groups. In doing so, they—like Tolstoy before them—humanized the war and brought it closer for their readers. Sevastopol again became a city of heroes, prepared to die, fighting honorably for the Motherland and acting as examples for others. Stalin's telegram to the city quoted in the chapter epigraph sought to reassure people that sacrificial acts were not in vain and that, as Tolstoy had noted a century earlier, their fight for the Motherland would become a major event in history and would inspire future generations.

Although some writers were Sevastopoltsy, many were not; yet they all created hagiographies that postwar local officials used to emphasize the city's uniqueness and a greater attention to residents' needs. The course of the war and reporting often showed that heroism could come from simple tasks, that young residents bore the brunt of the work, that many people went to extraordinary lengths to care for those in need, and that harsh struggles for survival became transformed into normality. Wartime experiences created or recaptured certain images of Russia and Sevastopol and thus served as a conduit with the past for postwar planners, helping strengthen the sense of place that was much needed after dislocation.

Hagiographies certainly were not limited to Sevastopol in the 1940s. War reporters drew on a long tradition of writing exalted stories of individuals. Soviets developed hero stories, much like the saints' lives that were the central texts of a Russian Orthodox education, to educate readers about proper behavior and the ability to overcome obstacles in order to achieve greatness.[22]

Socialist realism had long employed an iconographic model in the quest to create the new Soviet man and woman. Workers were to fashion their behavior after Aleksei Stakhanov, who, the official story stated, through

---

22. Richard Wortman, *Scenarios of Power: Myth and Ceremony in Russian Monarchy,* 2 vols. (Princeton: Princeton University Press, 1995, 2000), shows that Imperial Russian rulers were also familiar with the power of imagery.

determination and planning was able to hew many more tons of coal in a single day than was thought possible.[23] Children were supposed to show loyalty to the state and party as modeled by Pavlik Morozov, who denounced his parents as enemies of the people and thus made himself an orphan. The child's bond to the regime was supposed to be more important than any biological ties.[24] In both these stories, and many more like them that proliferated especially in the 1930s, the individual usually overcame some personal obstacle and, with the help of a mentor from the party, became a hero worthy of emulation. Most of the elements of Soviet hagiographies continued in Sevastopol's war stories; however, the role of the party no longer dominated every transformation to heroism as it had in the 1930s. Of course, articles written by political commissars focused on the Bolsheviks' leading role in inspiring heroic feats, but just as many writers subordinated party influence to the need to act as Sevastopoltsy always had in times of conflict. Sevastopol soon had its own pantheon of heroes to join the well-known examples of the Panfilov men and Zoia Kosmodemianskaia, who martyred themselves in defiance of the Nazi invasion.[25]

In the Soviet Union, World War II was more than just a great conflict—it was, and to some degree remains, a defining moment in Russian history.[26] The Great Patriotic War, as it was known, was a cataclysmic and Manichean event echoing campaigns of the previous seven centuries from St. Aleksandr Nevskii's defense against Swedes, Mongols, and Teutons in the thirteenth century to the heroes of the first Patriotic War against Napoleon's Grande Armée. World War II was not merely a political war; it was a war for survival of the people and their culture. As with all modern wars, the memory of World War II in the Soviet Union was part lived experience and part

---

23. The best research on Stakhanov and Stakhanovism is Lewis Siegelbaum, *Stakhanovism and the Politics of Productivity in the USSR, 1935–1941* (Cambridge, UK: Cambridge University Press, 1988). See especially chap. 6.

24. Catriona Kelly's remarkable re-creation of the myth shows that, in fact, it was quite devoid of ultimate meaning because the story or Pavlik Morozov and the virtues he embodied were infinitely malleable. Catriona Kelly, *Comrade Pavlik: The Rise and Fall of a Soviet Boy Hero* (London: Granta, 2005), 261–63.

25. Rosalinde Sartorti, "On the Making of Heroes, Heroines, and Saints" in *Culture and Entertainment in Wartime Russia,* ed. Richard Stites (Bloomington: Indiana University Press, 1995), 176–93.

26. Amir Weiner, *Making Sense of War: The Second World War and the Fate of the Bolshevik Revolution* (Princeton: Princeton University Press, 2000), 7–9, 18–21.

myth creation. During hostilities, journalists and frontline poets created selective images of warfare and its costs and prospects. Newsreels brought the stark and triumphal visual images of war to mass audiences. After the conclusion of fighting, films and books made heroes and villains out of the participants. Tourism later took the curious to battlefields and sites of mass death to look at plaques, monuments, and museums. All of these forms of retelling aid in the construction of remembrance, help with healing, and perpetuate hatreds. The retelling of the battle of Sevastopol also fulfilled these functions.

Sevastopol's vital naval infrastructure made it an essential target, not only for Nazi forces but also for Soviet propagandists and urban planners. The city's physical destruction and mythical elevation in the Soviet media became the foundation of its postwar urban planning and struggle to rise from its ashes. Wartime film and newspapers and postwar architecture re-created an image of Sevastopol that was based on nineteenth-century precedents and endured into the twenty-first century. Although the devastation of war lasted in the minds of Sevastopol's residents, the Soviet media informed a much larger audience about the dimensions of the battle and the individuals who fought in it. The war's destruction and representations of it by journalists, writers, and filmmakers revived nineteenth-century images of Sevastopol and provided local urban planners with a set of themes on which they could design the postwar city and its biography. Because of Sevastopol's enduring place as national defender, its resurrection after nearly complete destruction was imperative. In return for the collective heroism of the city and the benefits it brought to the state, the state would have to marshal vast resources to accommodate the inhabitants of the city of glory. Preparations for the next war were essential.

Representations of War

With the beginning of the war, the Soviet media quickly began an information campaign designed not only to highlight Nazi atrocities in the Soviet Union but also to create lasting images of the Soviet spirit at work. Morale at home was low, and the USSR needed its allies abroad to open a second front against the Germans. Sevastopol's long siege, like those in Leningrad and Stalingrad, proved great fodder for writers, journalists, and filmmakers. Wartime propaganda reinforced an image of the city familiar to the Russian national biography from the Crimean War that soon found its way into construction plans and memorialization as postwar planners tried to create something from a near tabula rasa.

Throughout this traumatic ordeal, writers-turned-journalists brought the horror and heroes to life in Soviet newspapers and publications around the world and set the foundation for other media. Pain, suffering, and destruction in Sevastopol and other cities were a constant refrain in the party, state, and military newspapers. As the film industry slowly recovered, directors followed suit and brought moving images of the city to Soviet audiences. Architects and city planners ensured that Sevastopol's built space would repeat the messages created in wartime propaganda. Portrayals of individual and collective heroism and suffering left a permanent mark on Sevastopol's urban legacy, its residents, and defenders long after the war had ended.

The near-endless tales of heroes were important for the path of urban reconstruction after the war, but they had precedents in the previous century. Lev Tolstoy, a young soldier-journalist who would later become a great writer had described the Crimean War a century earlier in *Sevastopol Tales* and established the character of the city and its residents:

> The chief thing is the happy conviction that you carry away with you—the conviction that Sevastopol cannot be taken, and not only that it cannot be taken, but that it is impossible to shake the spirit of the Russian people anywhere—and you have seen this impossibility not in the numerous traverses of breastworks, and winding trenches, mines, and guns piled one upon the other without rhyme or reason, as it seemed to you, but in the eyes, the speech, the mannerisms, and in what is termed the spirit of the defenders of Sevastopol.[27]

Tolstoy's subjects were ready to die for their country, and he foresaw the influence their actions could have on future generations. Here Tolstoy established the equation that a battle for Sevastopol was a battle for Russia. He also limited the importance of political and military leaders and instead focused on the everyday heroes who would become examples to future generations. For Tolstoy, heroic examples could be effective in catalyzing

---

27. Lev Tolstoy, *Sevastopol Tales* (Moscow: Progress, 1982), 34.

similar behavior in others. "[A]fter reading in the newspapers and in private letters," he wrote, "about the exploits of the heroes of Sevastopol, his former comrades, [a cowardly officer] suddenly became fired with ambition and to a larger extent with patriotism."[28] The persuasive power of heroism was central to World War II and postwar reportage, too. However, even Tolstoy was derivative because the city's first monument, erected in 1839 to honor Captain A. I. Kazarskii's miraculous defeat of the Turkish fleet ten years earlier, states eloquently and simply on its pedestal that his feats were "An Example for Posterity."

The images of stalwart defense, personal agency, collective effort, and the impossibility of ever taking and holding Sevastopol found resonance a century later as mythmakers tried to rally the city and country during the Soviet Union's darkest hours. From the time the first German bombs fell on Sevastopol, through the 250-day siege and two-year occupation, film, literature, and journalism evoked confidence in an ultimate victory and hope for a better future. Wartime film and reporting prepared viewers not only for victory but also for the nation's resurrection. The themes of heroism, valor, self-sacrifice, and unity against a common enemy all foreshadowed postwar policies of norm busting, "volunteer" labor, and battles against speculation. Building on a prewar tradition of memorializing military events in the city, writers and newsreel producers focused on individual and collective acts of heroism that became examples for the postwar construction workers who had to sacrifice their health and welfare while living in the ruins. Nazi filmmakers reveled in the destruction and pillage of Soviet cities. But their Soviet counterparts saluted heroes and traditions that would become the cornerstone for postwar urban planning. One saw statues of Lenin on the big screen and his name evoked on the printed page, but most depictions of Sevastopol humanized the military forces and implored audiences to remember Sevastopol, the city of glory.

After the lightning-quick and highly destructive Nazi offensive against Sevastopol in November and December 1941, mythmakers in the Soviet press began to link defense against the Nazis to the failure of the Crimean War that Tolstoy had recast as a victory of the local spirit.[29] The connection

---

28. Ibid., 104.

29. The most accessible source of press material in the West on the battles for Sevastopol remains the collection of articles translated for foreign consumption. See *The Heroic Defence of*

between the two defenses heralded a particular urban biography, which often usurped the prominence of the Bolshevik revolution and the establishing of Soviet power. Connections between the second great defense (World War II) and the first (Crimean War) emerged from the pens of journalists, writers, and military and political officers in the days of the siege. As Vice Admiral F. S. Oktiabrskii, commander in charge of Sevastopol's defense, reminded his readers in 1942, "[I]n good time will these deeds of the numberless heroes of the Second defense of Sevastopol be woven into a brilliant fabric of legend, poem, verse and song by the Soviet people and its poets."[30] When Oktiabrskii wrote about the second defense of Sevastopol the Soviet reader (and undoubtedly some of the British and French allies) understood that the first defense had occurred during the Crimean War. Moreover, Oktiabrskii, like Tolstoy earlier, saw into the future and realized that generations to come would erect great myths of the war in order to create a sense of place, belonging, and identification.

Numerous writers linked the war against Hitler's Germany with past valorous campaigns, but no battles were more important to the city's image than the Crimean War. "To the glorious deeds of heroism performed by our fathers in the battles of Chesma, Sinop and Ochakov during the first defense of Sevastopol," Oktiabrskii noted, "we have added the feats of the champions of this heroic epoch, which we call the Second defense of Sevastopol."[31] As commander of the defense, Oktiabrskii had reason to point to a long tradition of resisting invasion.[32] As he was putting pen to paper in 1942, German forces were sweeping Soviet power off the Crimean Peninsula. Oktiabrskii needed to show that his troops had fought hard and that, as during the Crimean War, the invaders would be repelled. The losses in both defenses were extraordinary, and this history soon became ingrained in Sevastopol's urban biography.

Sevastopol (Moscow: Foreign Languages Publishing House, 1942); *Sevastopol: November, 1941– July, 1942: Articles, Stories and Eye-Witness Accounts by Soviet War Correspondents* (London: Hutchinson, 1943). Most of the articles are translations from Soviet newspapers like *Pravda* and *Krasnaia Zvezda*.

30. The *Heroic Defence of Sevastopol,* 14.

31. Ibid., 12.

32. Matthew Gallagher argues that military men in the field rejected many of the theoretical musings of military theorists. This seems to fit well with Oktiabrskii's writings, which are filled with emotion and feeling instead of abstractions. Matthew P. Gallagher, *The Soviet History of World War II: Myths, Memories, and Realities* (New York: Praeger, 1963), 74–78, 179.

Sevastopol's reflection on its past continued long after the Red Army had liberated the city in May 1944. The first issues of the local party/government newspaper, *Slava Sevastopolia* (Glory of Sevastopol), carried an occasional column entitled "From the History of Sevastopol" that presented local history, as well as accounts of past military glory. The underground partisan newspaper *Za Rodinu!* (For the Motherland!) had briefly replaced *Slava* during occupation, but the municipal newspaper never stooped to becoming "Red" anything, as was common in the USSR. Rather, each day after the war residents read about the glory of Sevastopol in the *Glory of Sevastopol* newspaper, thus locating their city and selves in a symbolically honorific place within the larger Soviet Union.[33] Although the title of *Za Rodinu!* suggests a shift from local to national, it is equally clear that it hails local achievements in defending the larger homeland. Most of the earliest postwar columns in both newspapers touched on tales from the Crimean War, linking the present battle against Nazi Germany to the heroic defense a century earlier.[34] On the day before liberation, the newspaper of the Black Sea Fleet, *Krasnyi Chernomorets* (Red Black Sea Sailor), ran an article simply entitled "Sevastopol." It detailed the fierce fighting in and around the city but also retold the city's ancient Greek and Turkic origins and the importance of Prince Potemkin-Tavricheskii in selecting the site for the base of Catherine the Great's Black Sea naval port.[35]

During the war it was necessary to show the domestic audience of soldiers and partisans that they were part of a long tradition and also that they were fighting for more than meaningless buildings and streets. Homes, families, traditions, and a way of life had to be defended. In the days following liberation, as the first sailors and residents made their way back to the city, the naval newspaper described the "glory of the Russian soul" by combining the stories of Crimean War heroes like admirals P. S. Nakhimov and V. A. Kornilov, sailor and quartermaster Petr Koshka, and field nurse Dasha Sevastopolskaia (the Russian equivalent of Florence

33. This is similar to Richard Wortman's understanding of how Russian imperial sovereigns created a higher place for their selves over their subjects. *Scenarios of Power,* 1:3–4.

34. See, for example, "Pamiatnik zatoplennym korabliam," *Slava Sevastopolia,* 27 September 1944, 2; "Chetvertyi Bastion," *Slava Sevastopolia,* 4 October 1944, 2; "Sevastopol'—gorod slavy," *Za Rodinu!* 11 May 1944, 2; "Sevastopol': Istoricheskaia spravka," *Za Rodinu!* 11 May 1944, 3; G. Troitskii, "Lektsiia o pervoi oborone Sevastopolia," *Za Rodinu!* 23 May 1944, 2.

35. "Sevastopol'," *Krasnyi Chernomorets,* 8 May 1944, 1.

Nightingale) with the new heroes of the second defense—Ivan Golubets, the Five Black Sea Men, Ludmilla Pavlichenko (all discussed below), and others.[36] Thus, even if the city's evacuated population had not heard about the heroic defense, which is highly unlikely because of national newspaper and radio coverage, official remembrance marked the residents' return to the city. The effort to educate people about the distant and recent past of the city continued well into 1945 and beyond. For example, the fleet held a lecture entitled "The Historical Past of Sevastopol" for the families of new and returning servicemen. The docudrama film *Battle for Sevastopol,* discussed below, followed the lecture.[37] By devoting so much attention to the past, mythmakers suggested that war valor was a tradition but also that one must defend and preserve that tradition with valor.

Foreign audiences could follow Sevastopol's catastrophic siege in books and newspapers too. Soviet allies also highlighted their heroes, but the USSR needed to show the extent to which its peace-loving population was shouldering the burden against Hitler. The regime made sure to document and publicize incidents of brutality and inhumanity. For the domestic audience, it separated the barbaric "other" from the peace-loving Soviet. The reports also set the stage for the war-crimes trials that followed the end of hostilities. Detailed accounts of female snipers, sailors single-handedly saving shipmates, and outnumbered gunners refusing to abandon their posts all joined the pantheon of heroes from the Crimean War. With death and destruction all around, men and women went to extreme lengths in their battle against German soldiers, and the Soviet populace and hesitant allies abroad needed to know about it. Every author used "heroes and heroines as the official carriers of hope," but cities were also heroized.[38]

Although the numerous struggles to provide for one's family may never be recounted, Soviet officials guaranteed that future generations would have a written record of battlefield heroism. Newspapers hailed feats of the Five Black Sea Men and private Devitiarov, who threw themselves

---

36. Petr Sazhin and G. Pozhenian, "Solntse nad Sevastopolem," *Krasnyi Chernomorets,* 12 May 1944, 1. Their feats are recounted and mythologized in *The Heroic Defence of Sevastopol* and *Sevastopol: November, 1941–July, 1942.*

37. "Segodnia," *Krasnyi Chernomorets,* 21 February 1945, 4. *Battle for Sevastopol* can be viewed at NARA as Russian News (1944), no. 3A, Motion Picture 208-RN-59, Record Group 208 (Records of the Office of War Information).

38. Rosalinde Sartorti, "On the Making of Heroes, Heroines, and Saints," 79.

(armed with grenades and bottles of gasoline) under advancing tanks, and of Ivan Bogatyr and his crew in Pillbox No. 11, who refused to surrender when overwhelmed. Ivan Golubets was one of the most well-known male heroes of Sevastopol. As his crewmates fled their burning ship moored in Sevastopol's harbor, he risked his life to throw bombs overboard before they exploded in the fire and wreaked havoc on the Soviet ships docked nearby.

Women had prominent places in the postwar hagiographies much like that of Dasha Sevastopolskaia in the Crimean War. Maria Baida worked in a village store, and as the war started, she trained as a nurse and became a Red Cross instructor. She eventually took up a rifle and joined in an "unequal skirmish" between a "handful of Soviet men and an entire company of German automatic-riflemen." This theme of fighting to the end against a superior foe was common from Kazarskii through the Crimean War. "Fearless Marusya" had "calm courage" and an "acute hatred for the enemy." Her skill as a nurse led her male comrades whom she bandaged to call her "a brick, a real pal!" Shot in the head and arm, Baida felt no pain, according to her chronicler, and refused to leave the fighting, saying, "I'm going to stick it out to the end!" She even killed one Nazi with her rifle butt when she had run out of ammunition. She took his gun and bullets and returned to the fight. The "brave Soviet girl" fought "like an enraged lioness." She bandaged more men and led them through mine fields because "she was used to putting her own life in danger in order to avert danger from others." This "wonderful girl" was "tender as a sister and brave as a legendary hero." She became a sergeant-major and Hero of the Soviet Union.[39]

Sniper Liudmilla Pavlichenko shot hundreds of Germans and had an existence similar to that of famed Stalingrad sniper Vasilii Zaitsev. Relentless stalking led to important kills as well as the capture of much-needed rifles and bullets. She worked so long and hard that "she felt as if all her bones were breaking." It was at this moment of utter exhaustion that she expressed her wish to be like the Cossack hero Bogdan Khmelnitsky, who her history professor had described as fearless, with a heart "encased in armour, [which] beats quietly and evenly." She wanted to be

---

39. *The Heroic Defence of Sevastopol,* 84–89.

like Khmelnitsky, who was depicted as a "Russian" hero.[40] Pavlichenko had put aside her previous life and training as a historian to volunteer for the Red Army, and she became "the first assistant of the men both in defense and in the offensive. A historian by education, a warrior by inclination, she fights with all the ardour of her young heart."[41]

Absent from both stories was any mention of the Communist Party, Stalin, or the USSR. Khmelnitsky inspired Pavlichenko. Baida transformed herself from nurse to soldier after she saw the suffering of the men to whom she tended. Consistent with many wartime stories, writers abandoned the dictates of socialist-realist party-mindedness in which the party was the primary agent in transforming people and events.[42]

Images of military war heroes were highly gendered in the tales from Sevastopol, but they were inspiring nonetheless. Both Pavlichenko and Baida were heroes in their own right, but writers cast both as secondary to the men who fought. Pavlichenko's biographer described her as the "first assistant" to men, even though she was credited with hundreds of kills as a sniper. Moreover, her link with a male Cossack warrior further confused her gender identity. Baida's story showed her constantly bandaging her male comrades. The author of both tales, L. Ozerov, called the women by their first names and even provided a term of endearment, "Marusya," for Baida. Although the audience came to understand their heroism, sacrifice, and feats, the women were always placed at the service of the men with whom they served. Ozerov addressed their male counterparts by rank and/ or last name, rather than by the more familiar terms reserved for women. This augmented the subjugation of the women by not referring to them with equally respectful terms. Although female heroes displayed feminine traits such as nurturing their comrades, the traits that made them heroes were masculine or gender-neutral. Baida's hagiography defeminized her, despite repeated use of "girl" and "lioness." She was successful because she was calm, fearless, and "a brick and a real pal." According to this account, her comrades saw her as a typical Russian hero for which gender had no

---

40. Serhy Yekelchyk, "Diktat and Dialogue in Stalinist Culture: Staging Patriotic Historical Opera in Soviet Ukraine, 1936–1954," *Slavic Review* 59, no. 3 (Fall 2000): 597–624, shows how central officials in Moscow wanted to brand Khmelnitsky as the uniter of Russia and Ukraine. But viewers of the opera often saw him as a Ukrainian national figure.

41. *The Heroic Defence of Sevastopol,* 89–93.

42. Gallagher, *The Soviet History of World War II,* chap. 5.

place. She followed the example of Dasha Sevastopolskaia, who went onto the Crimean War battlefield, a previously male-only sphere, to minister aid to the soldiers. Baida and other women in World War II also served in what had previously been male-only roles.[43]

Journalists spun tales both to inspire future acts of self-sacrifice and to create a pantheon of heroes and martyrs. In a total war, soldiers and citizens had to do their part, and war correspondents also made sure to highlight the heroes without guns. One war correspondent recalled the story of a woman who picked flowers every morning and walked through the city's rubble to her husband's grave. Despite repeated warnings to abandon the city, she refused. According to the author, when she happened upon Soviet soldiers burying one of their own, she divided her bouquet so that they could properly honor their fallen comrade and played Chopin's "Funeral March" on a nearby piano. To the male soldiers, the "woman with flowers" was a "symbol of the faithfulness of their wives, of the friendship of their sisters, of the solicitude of their mothers."[44] She symbolized the faithfulness and compassion of Russian women, but in her role as comforter, she also again placed women in the service of men.

The individual and everyday citizen also figured prominently in Sevastopol's tales of heroism. Stories such as these showed audiences near and far that everyone had a role to play in defending the Motherland during total war. Journalist and playwright Boris Voitekhov remained adamant about portraying the "extraordinary heroism in everyday routine" that Tolstoy and Oktiabrskii foresaw would "in the future serve as the cornerstone for the new Sevastopol epic."[45] From the unnamed man who jumped overboard from an evacuating ship and swam to Sevastopol because he did not want to leave the port city to a woman who extinguished a fire

---

43. On Soviet women soldiers and images of them, see Kazimiera Janina Cottam and Nikoloai Vissarionovich Masolov, *Defending Leningrad: Women Behind Enemy Lines* (Nepean, Ont.: New Military Publishing, 1998); Kazimiera Janina Cottam, *Women in War and Resistance: Selected Biographies of Soviet Women Soldiers* (Nepean, Ont.: New Military Publishing, 1998); Reina Pennington, "Wings, Women and War: Soviet Women's Military Aviation Regiments in the Great Patriotic War" (master's thesis, University of South Carolina, 1993). The unequal treatment of women in the postwar decade continued unabated. Greta Bucher, *Women, the Bureaucracy and Daily Life in Postwar Moscow, 1945–1953* (Boulder: East European Monographs, 2006).

44. *The Heroic Defence of Sevastopol*, 105–7.

45. Ibid., 104. See also Boris Voitekhov, *The Last Days of Sevastopol*.

that threatened to engulf a municipal food depot, everyday feats of bravery provided inspiration for a worldwide reading audience.

Writer-turned-war correspondent Ilya Ehrenburg claimed that a German officer arrested two girls on Sevastopol Boulevard in Paris after the officer insulted the girls and they struck him. Ehrenburg reported that in court, they stated their desire to "be as brave as the heroes of Sevastopol."[46] The name of Sevastopol, according to Ehrenburg, had "become a symbol of resistance, of the grandeur of human achievement, of proud courage.... The hearts of the entire people will go out to [the heroes of Sevastopol]. Spacious avenues of our cities will be named after Sevastopol."[47] And he was correct. Writers found it necessary to relate stories like the "amusing incident" of a female store manager who tried to save her burning store, caught on fire, and then exclaimed, "Are you crazy! What are you doing?! That water is for emergencies only!" when a group of cart drivers tried to douse her with a barrel of water.[48]

Of the numerous exemplary workers in Sevastopol's underground cave factories, writer S. Klebanov retold the story of "young Stakhanovite Anastasia Chaus" who, despite having her hand severed by bomb shrapnel, returned to her post in the factory and refused to be evacuated because she wanted to continue to "be useful for the front."[49] M. Turovsky suggested that the motivations for such feats of production were the "patriotic women's love for their fatherland, their devotion to the front, to their husbands and brothers."[50] Stalin, the party, and the revolution apparently failed to inspire. But Sevastopol's women, according to the authors, remained subject to men and served with no thought of their own needs and desires. One wonders if the woman with flowers was a symbol to the many thousands of women, like Baida and Pavlichenko, who fought in the war. How was this meant to inspire postwar women who served as the backbone of industry and reconstruction?

These stories and many others created a number of images that would become familiar in Sevastopol's postwar reconstruction. First, whether

46. *Sevastopol: November, 1941–July, 1942,* 9.
47. Ibid.
48. *The Heroic Defence of Sevastopol,* 108.
49. Ibid., 113–14.
50. *Sevastopol: November, 1941–July, 1942,* 52.

male or female, heroism could come from the simplest tasks. One did not have to be a frontline soldier, a political leader, or a great writer to render service to the Soviet Union. Factory workers, teachers, and store clerks all had a role to play. Second, young residents of the city bore the brunt of the work. Nearly all of the heroes, both soldiers and workers, were described as "young," and women were also labeled "girls." This foreshadowed the great reliance on youth labor in the postwar years to make up for the older specialists who often were casualties of war. Third, care for those in need, whether wounded or children, was common throughout journalistic accounts of the battle for Sevastopol and became the foundation for one form of postwar reconstruction discourse—accommodation. In addition to nurses like Baida and Dasha Sevastopolskaia before her, journalists pointed to teachers who, for example, continued preparing the New Year's tree and celebration for their students in the underground shelters throughout the brutal siege at the end of 1941.[51] Last, war stories turned the harsh struggles for survival into normality. M. Turovsky's "The Underground City" related the routines of daily life in factories, nurseries, hospitals, housing, and other arenas that moved into the city's caves and created an alternate wartime normality.[52] When reading the Soviet press of the time, one cannot escape the sense that nearly every story was meant to serve as an example to work harder, sacrifice more, and perform superhuman feats of courage and heroism for country and family so that everyday life could be better than before. With the rising expectations of the postwar years, it was important for the regime to encourage production. Like penal labor or socialist competition, the example of heroes was meant to create order and thereby improve productivity, which could lead to better living conditions. Yet consumer production remained woefully behind heavy industrial outlays.

Celluloid Heroes

Although journalists and writers can quickly and relatively cheaply transmit messages to a geographically dispersed audience, their work often lacks the emotional appeal of visual media. Wartime newsreels continued

---

51. *The Heroic Defence of Sevastopol*, 99–103.
52. Ibid., 109–14; *Sevastopol: November, 1941–July, 1942*, 52–55.

the themes of heroism and sacrifice, but they also showed humans caught in dangerous firefights, some living and some dying. They captured the totality of destruction more vividly and completely than a verbal description could. Moreover, they often intentionally juxtaposed Nazi brutality with the peace-loving Soviet citizen.

Soviet newsreels, unlike the violent and destructive images of Nazi newsreels, showed a peaceful life destroyed by invasion. The German propaganda machine showed Germans and their allies that the battle for Sevastopol was also a battle of civilizations: the power of the Nazi military on one side and the destruction of an "inferior" Slavic culture on the other. German filmmakers captured the massive bombardment from air and land with a particular emphasis on the giant, railbound guns like "Thor" and "Big Dora." Luftwaffe pilots, calm and focused, plunged from the sky toward their targets below. No emotion crossed their faces as they performed their duties and blew buildings and fortifications to rubble.[53] Strong, muscular men, in clearly phallic imagery, loaded shell after shell into enormous guns that raised and belched smoke, fire, and steel over the hills and onto the unseen enemy. Although bombing sorties caused the most widespread destruction, filmmakers preferred the more personalized destruction from shelling. In newsreels like *Giornale di Guerra,* produced for Italian allies, the German planes and an Italian torpedo boat attacked the Black Sea Fleet. German filmmakers, in order to appease their allies, merely spliced in boat attacks and an Italian narrator and inserted scene after scene directly from German-language newsreels of large-caliber guns that better displayed the power of the Axis offensive.[54] Size mattered.

Nazi racial ideology partially explains the choice of footage in Waffen SS newsreels and photographs during the siege of Sevastopol. Poor thatch huts and obliterated gun emplacements instead of the pre-Christian ruins, numerous churches, and the beautiful neoclassical architecture represented the city in Nazi propaganda. Showing the roof of a peasant hut blown toward the sky as walls exploded outward could not have been viewed as a

53. *Combat in Soviet Russia, July 1942,* Motion Picture 242-6005, and *Die deutsche Wochenschau, No. 616,* 242-MID-3128, NARA, Record Group 242 (Collection of Foreign Records Seized).

54. *Giornale di Guerra,* Motion Picture 242 MID 2575, NARA, Record Group 242 (Collection of Foreign Records Seized). Compare this with *German Newsreel Excerpts,* Motion Picture 242.105 and 242 MID 6005, NARA, Record Group 242 (Collection of Foreign Records Seized).

military necessity.[55] Yet this suggests that German propagandists wanted to portray a triumph of one people over another rather than merely a military victory. The residents of Sevastopol were to be viewed as poor peasants living in squalor and not urban residents in modern apartment complexes surrounded by numerous cultural institutions. Concrete bunkers, like Maxim Gorky Fort, encased massive Soviet guns in the area around Sevastopol. Numerous scenes show these military objectives, but German filmmakers depicted the ruins of the guns rather than the clear and present danger of the massive emplacements.[56] After a survey of damage, cameramen turned to the roar of large-caliber guns in order to make clear the reason for the Soviet rubble. In Nazi newsreel footage, Soviet military power never posed a threat to the victorious march of Hitler's men. German soldiers on the screen rarely appeared under fire or in any imminent danger. In fact, in the six newsreels about Sevastopol at the United States National Archives, only one German soldier was wounded and none were found dead. Viewers were to understand that the superior Nazi race was quickly overpowering and destroying its inferior Slavic foe.

For propaganda reasons, the German footage featured only the *destruction* of Sevastopol. The relatively few visual images from the city center showed the power of German destruction, not the remnants of a once powerful civilization. An eight-minute German newsreel, dubbed in Portuguese, showed a delegation of Germans and their allies flying over Sevastopol days after it fell to the Nazis in July 1942.[57] A glimpse of neoclassical architecture appeared as the plane flew from the city center to the outskirts. However, street after street of walls with no roofs created the most lasting impression. The only close-up footage of damage in the city center showed destroyed wharfs and ships, burning residential areas, and the bomb-ravaged Pokrovskii Cathedral; not once did the camera focus on the neoclassical architecture reminiscent of the new monumental buildings of Berlin, Munich, and Nuremberg.[58] By avoiding close-up views of

55. Motion Picture 242 MID 6005, NARA, Record Group 242 (Collection of Foreign Records Seized).

56. Motion Picture 242.105, NARA, Record Group 242 (Collection of Foreign Records Seized).

57. *German Newsreel Excerpts,* Motion Picture 242.230, NARA, Record Group 242 (Collection of Foreign Records Seized.

58. Motion Picture 242 MID 6005. Pokrovskii Cathedral is a turn-of-the-century building best described as eclectic-modern, clearly not neoclassical—the Nazi ideal.

Sevastopol's beautiful architecture and showing exclusively the massive destruction of the city, German filmmakers presented the ruins of a destroyed and vanished civilization to their audiences. The double image of Nazi military power and the absence of life among the ruins helped reinforce the ideology of the superior Aryan race and the helplessness of the weak Slavs.

Although Soviet cultural and political leaders likely never saw most of these images, their familiarity with Nazi ideology helped reinforce the already-present images of the "culturedness" (*kul'turnost'*) of the new Soviet man and woman in juxtaposition with the Nazi "barbarism."[59] The Soviet images in celluloid that spread throughout the USSR followed the lead of wartime journalism and even the century-old journalism of Tolstoy. The serene and beautiful life in Sevastopol had been attacked, but the population's sacrifice and heroism would win in the end.

Soviet newsreels and docudramas, as could be expected from those on the defensive, highlighted the heroism of soldiers, sailors, and citizens during an unprovoked attack. Soviet newsreels lacked sophistication and quality in the first years of the war, but by the time the Red Army liberated Sevastopol in May 1944, the full force of the film industry and other artistic organizations had created powerful and symbolic tales of heroism and victory.[60] The most striking difference between German and Soviet depictions of the June 1942 offensive is that the Soviets took great pains to show the destruction of their territory and soldiers. In the opening scene of the battle for Sevastopol in *The Thirteenth of June, 1942,* the statue of Lenin stood near the wharf, pointing into the distance as smoke wafted behind him.[61] A young, attractive soldier on lookout, with a medal prominently displayed on his chest, peered around the corner of a destroyed wall. Scenes of the city on fire and massive explosions then gave way to Soviet attacks on both land and sea. Likewise, immediately after a marine received a

---

59. The literature on the construction of a new culture in the 1930s is abundant. See, for example, Katerina Clark, *The Soviet Novel: History as Ritual* (Chicago: University of Chicago Press, 1981); Stephen Kotkin, *Magnetic Mountain: Stalinism as a Civilization* (Berkeley: University of California Press, 1995); Karen Petrone, *Life Has Become More Joyous, Comrades: Celebrations in the Time of Stalin* (Bloomington: Indiana University Press, 2000).

60. For a discussion of Soviet film during World War II see Peter Kenez, "Black and White: The War on Film," in Stites, *Culture and Entertainment in Wartime Russia,* 157–75.

61. *The Thirteenth of June, 1942,* Motion Picture-111-M529-46, [National Archives], Record Group 111 (Records of the Office of the Chief Signal Officer).

mortal wound, his compatriots jumped from the trenches and charged the enemy. The Soviets showed their dead in order to create martyrs. Scenes of attacking soldiers helped create the necessary images of vengeance and heroism that popular wartime poems like Konstantin Simonov's "Kill Him" demanded.

Soviet filmmakers also humanized their subjects in order to draw a closer connection with the audience. In the same film, Soviet soldiers in Sevastopol rested in the woods by a tranquil stream, surrounded by birch trees, cooking, eating, sleeping, writing letters home, reading newspapers, and even playing with a puppy. The juxtaposition with the previous scene of destroyed stores and litters full of wounded created a powerful image of the soldiers' humanity, much like newspaper accounts of "hearty laughter of the happy and never despondent Russian[s]" who interrupted their music break to "mow down the enemy."[62] The peaceful and happy life of Soviet citizens, these images suggested, had been interrupted by Nazi barbarians who would now suffer the wrath of heroic fighters defending their homeland.

Narration enhanced the image of sacrifice and heroism in *Battle for Sevastopol* (1944), which chronicled the liberation of the Crimean Peninsula and the city.[63] The popular and powerful narrator, radio personality Iurii Levitan, began the film by describing Sevastopol as a "City of ancient glory; Sevastopol, the legendary city; A city of Russian glory; A hero city." He repeated the same phrases throughout the thirty-five-minute chronicle, interspersed with exhortations of "Our Sevastopol." The most symbolic scenes occurred, of course, at the end of the film. After violent scenes of fighting amid the rubble, a Soviet soldier climbed the Panorama of the Defense of 1854–1855 (dedicated to the Crimean War), where in 1942 the Nazis had raised their flag, and "on the cupola was raised the flag of [Soviet] victory," according to Levitan. Quickly after, the audience saw Soviet military men standing atop the neoclassical gates of Count's Wharf firing guns in celebration. This alone would have been symbolic enough, but the soldiers stood directly above the inscription "1846," the date of the wharf's construction. The scenes atop the Panorama and Count's Wharf linked the heroes of Sevastopol's past, the "ancient glory" of the "legendary city"

---

62. *The Heroic Defence of Sevastopol,* 104.
63. *Russian News* (1944), no. 3A.

mentioned by Levitan, and the great defenders of Sevastopol's present, thereby creating an unbroken chain of heroism.

Soviet filmmakers honored their dead and past heroes in order to emphasize the struggle and sacrifice needed for victory in war. Scenes of mile-long columns of German POWs preceded Soviet women weeping over their dead sons, husbands, and brothers, but larger groups of dead Nazi soldiers left no doubt in the viewers' minds as to who the victor was. Filmmakers also paid homage to the Black Sea and fleet. In one of the final scenes of *Battle for Sevastopol,* sailors and soldiers, standing near dead Germans and a Nazi flag floating offshore, removed their hats as the waters of the Black Sea lapped the coast and the ships of the fleet once again dropped anchor in Sevastopol's bays. The headless statue of General Eduard Ivanovich Totleben, the designer of the city's defenses during the Crimean War, once again guarded the city as the camera panned down to the inscription at its base, which read, "Defense of Sevastopol." The visual connection of Sevastopol's liberation with the heroic past of the city, symbolized in Totleben, continued in the vision of postwar architects.

Tolstoy had defined Sevastopol in a time of great national struggle, and Soviet writers and filmmakers revived the same themes with the same intent: to create a lasting image of the city and to inspire patriotism and sacrifice by publicizing heroic acts. Fear of impending doom, anger toward incompetent leadership, and dejection caused by loss spread eastward with the march of German tanks and artillery; it gave way to relief, joy, and hope for the future as the Soviet forces marched toward Berlin. The years immediately following the liberation of Sevastopol brought great hardship to an already beleaguered city, but with the worst of times over, residents returned to their city expecting short-term sacrifices for long-term comfort. As if the horrific destruction of homes and factories were not enough, Sevastopoltsy faced the back-breaking task of rebuilding their city. Individual and group initiative distinguished the 362 days between liberation and the end of the war in Europe from the years that followed.

Despite all the despair and hardships, the wartime propaganda blitz created momentum, hope, and a sense of collective suffering and solidarity for the task ahead. Newspapers and films prepared readers for the immediate task of defeating the enemy, as well as for what lay beyond. Heroism was not limited to soldiers giving their lives in battle. Whatever the feat, if it was done in the service of others, it could be valorized. The simplest daily tasks of teachers, workers, clerks, and others could become heroic. Newspaper stories and docudramas also highlighted young men and women who normalized harsh struggles. Yes, wartime life was difficult, but true heroes went about their work without complaint. This was instructive to the young men and women who came to rebuild Sevastopol only to find housing, food, and sanitation all in short supply. They would have to learn how to carry on as normal, despite the harsh realities of daily life.

Paternal orders to fulfill one's "task" (*zadacha*) and "assignment" (*zadanie*) helped mobilize citizens for the front, but it also trained them for the sacrifices necessary after victory.[64] During the war, the military and "the people" replaced the party's primary role. The call to arms had little or nothing to do with Marxism-Leninism-Stalinism. Defending one's homeland and people mattered most. No figures could have been more important for creating a sense of moral retribution than Ilya Ehrenburg and Konstantin Simonov. Their often hate-filled and vindictive poems and articles urged readers to kill Germans on sight because they had raped and pillaged Mother Russia.[65] Ehrenburg wrote, "If you haven't killed at least one German today, your day has been wasted."[66] The binary "we-they" paradigm served well to unite a multinational country for war, and it also reminded citizens to search for "enemies of the people" and to think of the world as divided into two camps in the years after the war. But could portrayals of heroes, martyrs, and a defeated enemy sustain the population in the face of daily burdens? The misery of the following decade would test this sense of unity, faith in Moscow's willingness and ability to live up to its promises of social welfare, and residents' abilities to endure squalor and hardship.

Visual images of heroic struggle, self-sacrifice, and the long history of Sevastopol moved from the screen and found a new face in the city's

---

64. For an analysis of wartime news coverage see Jeffrey Brooks, "*Pravda* Goes to War," and Louise McReynolds, "Dateline Stalingrad: Newspaper Correspondents at the Front" in Stites, *Culture and Entertainment in Wartime Russia,* 9–27, 28–43.

65. Forty years after the war, English-speaking audiences gained access to the power and emotion of wartime journalism through the words of Ehrenburg and Konstantin Simonov's articles in *Krasnaia Zvezda*. See Ilya Ehrenburg and Konstantin Simonov, *In One Newspaper: A Chronicle of Unforgettable Years* (New York: Sphinx, 1985).

66. Ilya Ehrenburg, "Ubei [Kill]," *Krasnaia Zvezda,* 24 July 1942.

monuments, buildings, streets, parks, and squares. An article in *Problems of Modern City Building,* the theoretical journal of the Academy of Architecture, reminded architects that *"Memorial architecture* acquires enormous significance in restored cities. Arches, obelisks, monumental memorials will have here not only agitational and memorial significance, but also will play a large role in the creation of an expressive city silhouette."[67] Planners realized it was "impossible to ignore the historical appearance of a city when planning restoration" or "to ignore our [Russian] national heritage."[68] During the war, mythmakers had conjured up the heroes and institutions of Russia's past to rebuild national unity. Postwar plans in Sevastopol reflected this process as architects designed squares and monuments to fallen heroes and planned for the restoration of other memorials. But planning was contentious as center and periphery battled for their visions of the future. The struggles of local officials in the early days after liberation prepared them for recurring problems in the decade to come.

---

67. V. N. Semenov, "Osnovy planirovki vosstanovlivaemykh gorodov," *Problemy sovremennogo gradostroitel'stva* 1 (1947): 8 (emphasis in original).

68. Ibid., 5–6.

2

LOCAL VICTORY OVER MOSCOW

Planning for the Future

> The great city was lying in front of me in the noble silence of heroic war
> death. It was destroyed by the Germans, but it didn't surrender.... And here
> is what was left of it: rocks, the sea and the sun...and valorous glory which
> will revive these heaps of stones.
>
> LEONID SOBOLEV, quoted in ALEKSANDR DOBRY and IRINA BORISOVA,
> *Welcome to Sevastopol*

Despite Sobolev's optimism, valorous glory cannot build on its own. The resurrection of a dead city needs a plan, people, and materials from which to rise from its ashes. In a way, however, Sobolev was correct. The wartime recitation of heroes continued into the postwar reconstruction period as an attempt to incite yet more sacrifice for the Motherland. The new sacrifice was not for defense but for rebirth. The new city would be born of two parents, one in Moscow and one in the city itself. From Moscow the city gained the initial plans and the materials necessary to rebuild. From local leaders it gained a clarification and reworking of the central plans to fit the character and traditions of the city so as to make it unique as a hometown and not just another mass-produced urban landscape. The Crimea had once been the location of Potemkin villages; local residents and leaders fought to ensure that the postwar city had more substance than facades and rhetoric. The tension in center-periphery relations consumed much of the postwar decade.

Local leaders in Sevastopol realized that challenging central authority would be difficult. It was also dangerous. How and why did the men and women sent to administer the city become "local" and advocate for local concerns against their superiors in Moscow? Municipal architects and party and government leaders seized on Stalin's recent promotion of building according to local conditions to remove Moscow-based architects and to develop a reconstruction plan themselves, a plan that championed an image of the city that was more in harmony with its traditions and history.[1] Although Moscow planning teams wanted to create a museum city dedicated to World War II exploits by using monumental arches, obelisks, and a massive Stalin statue, localization created a more local seaside aesthetic for buildings, preserved monuments, and restored popular parks and even Primorskii Boulevard's well-known chestnut trees. Sevastopol's architects transformed Moscow's vision into a city focused on its prerevolutionary heritage and not just the most recent conflict. The Crimean War again took center stage as local planners followed wartime propagandists in equating the first great defense of the mid-nineteenth century with the second great defense of World War II. Sevastopol's naval and local officials carved out a "little corner of freedom" from which they could create their own understanding of the city's importance.[2] The "saints and martyrs, places of worship, and a heritage to emulate" were as essential to postwar Sevastopol as they were to Western war memorials.[3]

Although only a handful of cities like Stalingrad suffered damage as extensive as Sevastopol's, Operation Barbarossa had decimated whole swathes of territory west of the Ural Mountains. Thousands of towns and villages were sacked, and 25 million people wandered homeless and jobless.[4] The scope of destruction reached far into the Soviet interior, where no bombs had fallen. With the Nazis and their allies controlling the Soviet breadbasket, food became scarcer in the interior. The western reaches of the Soviet Union also had dominated industrial production prior to World War II. The Nazi invasion destroyed nearly every element that affected

---

1. GARF, f. A-150, op. 2, d. 20, ll. 1–1ob.

2. "Little corner of freedom" is taken from the discussion of nature preservation groups in Douglas Weiner, *A Little Corner of Freedom: Russian Nature Protection from Stalin to Gorbachev* (Berkeley: University of California Press, 1999).

3. George Mosse, *Fallen Soldiers: Reshaping the Memory of the World Wars* (New York: Oxford University Press, 1990), 7.

4. R. W. Pethybridge, *A History of Postwar Russia* (New York: New American Library, 1966), 18–20; Alec Nove, *An Economic History of the USSR* (New York: Penguin, 1976), 287.

daily life and industrial production. Fortunately, the Soviets had disman-
tled and shipped eastward hundreds of factories that began to supply the
war effort in 1942 and turned the war toward Berlin.[5]

After the victory at Stalingrad and the retreat of Nazi forces westward,
planning started on how to rebuild war-devastated cities. The regime
sought to meet the population's needs by centralizing urban planning, this
time in the Committee on Architectural Affairs (*Komitet po delam arkhitektury,* or KA). However, the much-hoped-for speed and efficiency failed
in the face of destruction too vast for the rapid rebuilding that was envisioned. The KA allocated space for the reconstruction, but finding the
materials to make the plans real was the responsibility of the state planning
agency, Gosplan. Scarce resources and vague directives bred competition
among ministries rather than the intended cooperation and coordination.
As in the industrial boom of the 1930s, obsessive central planning and statistical production targets placed little weight on advice from the periphery
and insisted instead on dictates from Moscow. For postwar planning this
meant that the KA often ignored local architects and provided few clear directives regarding scale, aesthetics, and implementation. The Soviet Union,
in short, was left in a precarious position for postwar reconstruction.

Two policies—accommodation and agitation—were central to the con-
ception of postwar planning and reconstruction. Accommodation encom-
passed a set of policies designed to meet everyday consumer needs in an
effort to keep the population content and to maintain the illusion of socialism's superior humanity. The cradle-to-grave system of social welfare and
services provided benefits to single mothers and their children, down-on-
their-luck workers, quota-busting Stakhanovites and shockworkers, wid-
ows, and orphans. Agitation was a popularized propagation of political,
social, and cultural messages that sought not just to convince but also to
motivate further action. In architectural terms, agitation usually came in
the form of memorials, toponymy, and symbolic aesthetics. While these

---

5. For data see John Barber and Mark Harrison, *The Soviet Home Front, 1941–1945: A Social
and Economic History of the USSR in World War II* (New York: Longman, 1991), 127, 138; Mark
Harrison, *Accounting for War: Soviet Production, Employment, and the Defence Burden, 1940–1945*
(Cambridge: Cambridge University Press, 1996), chap. 7. For a comparison see *The Impact of
World War II on the Soviet Union,* ed. Susan Linz (Totowa, NJ: Rowman and Littlefield, 1985),
66, 89.

themes will be the focus of the next two chapters, it is important to trace their prewar roots and the effect on postwar planning.

Development of Urban Planning and Architecture in the Soviet Union

Postwar urban reconstruction did not appear out of a vacuum; rather, the chief foci of postwar planning and construction—the transformative power of built space and the rationality of designing cities to meet the needs of the population—developed out of a complicated search for a modern Soviet style. The chaos of revolution and civil war in Russia and the emerging Soviet Union had actually allowed architects to be their most creative. Revolutionary ideas affected architecture as well. The rhetoric of social justice, leveling, creating a new society, propagandizing new values, and establishing a rational and scientifically based system found young champions in the architectural community. Realistic plans were unnecessary in the 1920s. The state had no money to commission projects, and former noble and merchant patrons had either fled the country or been stripped of their wealth. Architects put their fancies on paper and debated the future face of their new country.[6] Commissions had all but ceased, so the architectural community stayed in its studios and dreamed. The outgrowth of this period of financial poverty was artistic wealth. The fertile minds of young architects in particular sought to design a new urban space, one that even before the revolution was called "socialism without politics."[7]

Modern architects wanted to break away from the old forms of neoclassical, neorenaissance, and eclectic architecture and create a new form that would be representative of, and contributing to, their new world. Many of their ideas fell into a broadly modernist camp equivalent to many trends in

6. S. Frederick Starr, "The Revival and Schism of Urban Planning in Twentieth-Century Russia," in *The City in Russian History,* ed. Michael Hamm (Lexington: University of Kentucky Press, 1976), 222–42; S. Frederick Starr, "Visionary Town Planning during the Cultural Revolution," in *Cultural Revolution in Russia, 1928–1931,* ed. Sheila Fitzpatrick (Bloomington: Indiana University Press, 1978), 207–40; Richard Stites, *Revolutionary Dreams: Utopian Vision and Experimental Life in the Russian Revolution* (Oxford: Oxford University Press, 1989), 190–204.

7. William Craft Brumfield, ed., *Reshaping Russian Architecture: Western Technology, Utopian Dreams* (Washington, DC: Woodrow Wilson International Center for Scholars, 1990), 295.

the West that emphasized air, sun, and greenery in cities. Constructivists urged less attention to facades and more to functional buildings.[8] Functionalism also found expression in the deep concern of these architects for improving everyday life. Architects in revolutionary Russia began taking their cues from prerevolutionary trends like Ebenezer Howard's "Garden City" movement in England. The health and happiness of residents were to be improved by decreasing population densities, increasing the amount of green space (e.g., parks, tree-lined boulevards, and other open spaces), and zoning industry away from residential areas.

These architects thought of their work as a way to radically transform society.[9] The "creation of SOCIAL CONDENSERS for our times," according to Moisei Ginzburg (a constructivist leader and later one of the architects competing to design postwar Sevastopol), "is the essential objective of Constructivism in architecture."[10] By "social condensers," Ginzburg meant a structure that would be transformative in improving people's everyday lives. For example, constructivist housing units had dining facilities, public laundries, day cares, and other services that freed women from domestic duties and ensured that all received equal access to services and also benefited from the comradeship of neighbors. This was an attempt to end the perceived isolation of the many newly arrived peasants in major cities throughout Russia and the USSR and to "engineer" the newly arrived into Soviet citizens.[11]

Modernists, however, were starkly divided about how to achieve a modern world. Rationalists in the Association of New Architects (ASNOVA)

---

8. For a primer on the voluminous literature on constructivism, see Catherine Cooke, ed., *Russian Avant-Garde Art and Architecture* (London: Architectural Design, 1983); Selim Omarovich Khan-Magomedov, *Pioneers of Soviet Architecture: The Search for New Solutions in the 1920s and 1930s,* trans. Alexander Lieven (New York: Rizzoli, 1987); Anatole Kopp, *Constructivist Architecture in the USSR* (London: St. Martin's, 1985); O.A. Shvidkovskii, *Building in the USSR, 1917–1932* (New York: Praeger, 1971).

9. Ebenezer Howard, *Garden Cities of Tomorrow* (London: Swan Sonnenschein, 1902).

10. "Report on the First Congress of the Union of Contemporary Architects," *Sovremennaia Arkhitektura* 5 (1928), quoted in Anatole Kopp, *Constructivist Architecture in the USSR* (London: St. Martin's, 1985), 70.

11. For a comparison of the imperial and Soviet urbanization of Moscow, see Joseph Bradley, *Muzhik to Muscovite: Urbanization in Late Imperial Russia* (Berkeley: University of California Press, 1985); David L. Hoffmann, *Peasant Metropolis: Social Identities in Moscow, 1929–1941* (Ithaca, NY: Cornell University Press, 1994). Both authors stress the influence of urbanization on changed behaviors.

opposed Ginzburg and his cohort in the Union of Contemporary Architects (OSA). The OSA argued that form followed function. But the rationalists believed that form itself had a transformative psychological quality and should therefore be stressed over the function of the building. Rationalists, who were themselves divided, looked for objective answers to the perception of architectural forms. These men hoped to be able to create an architectural form, derived from the cult of science, that would produce on all viewers the exact impression intended by the designer. Because of the close collaboration between these architects and other artists, it should not surprise us that many architectural ideas were similar to Vasilii Kandinsky's manifesto for painting and his assertion that colors and shapes had the power to transform human emotions.[12] Architects argued for "rationalized labor in unity with science and highly developed technology." In combining architecture and politics, they hoped to create a "powerful productive-economic and cultural-ideological factor in building socialism," and to "arouse a feeling of cheerfulness, clarity, assurance, strength and joy" through architecture. ASNOVA, in short, argued for a transformative aesthetic, while OSA urged a transformative form.[13] Thus, while constructivists sought to meet the needs of the population in new housing projects or urban planning, rationalists wanted to make an artistic and psychological statement. Thus, one group primarily looked toward accommodation while the other promised agitation in architecture. Both accommodation and agitation were direct outgrowths of the modernist revolutionary zeal to transform society and people for the better, and both groups realized that built space was a powerful medium that could have a direct and profound influence on the way people lived their lives and related to the state and its ideology.

Traditionalists (those who favored the neoarchitectural styles of the pre-revolutionary period) and the new All-Union Society of Proletarian Architects (VOPRA), although they differed with each other, both viewed modernists with equal disdain.[14] Although VOPRA condemned OSA and

12. Wassily Kandinsky, *Concerning the Spiritual in Art* (New York: Wittenborn, Schultz, 1947).

13. *Izvestiia Asnova* 1 (1926): 1; *Sovetskaia arkhitektura* 1–2 (1931–1932): 46, 47, cited in Khan-Magomedov, *Pioneers of Soviet Architecture,* 593–94.

14. For details on VOPRA's rise to power, see Hugh Hudson, *Blueprints and Blood: The Stalinization of Soviet Architecture, 1917–1937* (Princeton: Princeton University Press, 1994), chap. 6. One

ASNOVA as well as the traditionalists, the "new" proletarian style that emerged in the 1930s took from OSA a concern for efficiency, standardization, and utilization of local materials. From ASNOVA it took a desire for architecture to "reflect the power and greatness of the constructors of socialism, and, strengthening the faith of the working class in victory, organize its will and consciousness for struggle and labor," or, as Hugh Hudson pessimistically summarized: "to awe the peasants and workers into submission before their new god Stalin and his autocratic state."[15] Many modernists, after all, had helped the proletarian architects diminish the influence of the bourgeois traditional architects. The new Stalinist architecture thus continued modernist concerns with the power of form and function in transforming life.

Whether as members of OSA or ASNOVA, modernists in the new revolutionary state saw town planning as the ultimate expression of architecture's ability to transform. Modernism was divided between the constructivist OSA and rationalist ASNOVA but also further subdivided between urbanists and disurbanists. Urbanists, led by Leonid Sabsovich, wanted a decentralization of cities but not the total elimination of urban centers, as was favored by the disurbanists, who were led by Mikhail Okhitovich. Debates between urbanists and disurbanists, however, created an architectural community more attuned to the transformative nature of built space. Urbanists had wanted to maximize building densities and thereby extend social services to the most people in the most efficient and rational manner. Their opponents, the disurbanists, wanted to minimize density and surround people with nature. Both groups placed accommodation of people's needs at the center of their planning.

Architectural activity in the 1920s and the 1930s created a collage of ideas that dominated Soviet architecture and city planning during postwar reconstruction. Plans for Moscow, Leningrad, and other cities had attempted to ameliorate the conditions of urban living by combining urbanist and disurbanist trends. Decades of urban theory debates had culminated in the

---

should note, however, that my conclusions argue directly against Hudson's supposition that creativity and concern for the population among architects died in the 1930s.

15. "Rezoliutsiia sektsii IZO istituta LIIa komakademii po doklady t. Mordvinova o 'Melkoburzhuaznom napravlenii v arkhitekture' (Leonidovshchina), priniataia 20/XII 1930g.," *Sovetskaia arkhitektura* 1–2 (1931): 18, quoted in Hudson, *Blueprints and Blood,* 133. Hudson's pessimistic summary also from this, p. 133.

Moscow Plan of 1935.[16] Modernist architects may have been out of favor, but they had left their imprint on Soviet urban planning theory. Both urbanists and disurbanists shared a desire to improve the standard of living for all inhabitants by building socialism through increasing the amount of living space per person, improving transportation, providing better access to social services, and living life amid nature. VOPRA condemned both groups, especially the disurbanists, who would have spread the Soviet population throughout the USSR, thus making it more difficult to control, educate, and employ in industry. So the proletarian architects used modernist ideas and plans to create the model for all Soviet urban planning and construction: the Moscow Plan of 1935.

The Moscow Plan, although much of it remained on paper, sought to provide a livable environment in the new socialist cities. But socialist architecture meant different things to different people. For political figures like L. M. Kaganovich, Soviet cities were socialist because private property had been eliminated.[17] For architects, a socialist city was one in which the built environment aided the "construction of a new life, a new way of life."[18] "Nonsocialist" prerevolutionary construction (i.e., not collective or communal but rather isolated, individual, single-family housing) was to be eliminated by building community kitchens, laundries, nurseries, and more. Rezoning was the most important element of the Moscow Plan. Planners limited the number of industries in close proximity to residential areas, cleared shorelines for recreational areas and open spaces, and concentrated construction in the city center and especially along main streets. Zoning the city for industry, public buildings, and residences created order and reduced sources of noise and air pollution. For the first stage of construction, new buildings were to have grand facades on the street front, like modern Potemkin villages. The Moscow Plan set a precedent of rational planning that would account for production, administration, and

---

16. *General'nyi plan rekonstruktsii goroda Moskvy* (Moscow: Moskovskii rabochii, 1936).

17. L. M. Kaganovich, *Za sotsialistichskuiu rekonstruktsiiu Moskvy i gorodov SSSR* (Moscow: Moskovskii rabochii, 1931). This is from his 1931 speech that effectively ended the antiurbanist movement. For more, see Blair A. Ruble, "Moscow's Revolutionary Architecture and Its Aftermath: A Critical Guide," in *Reshaping Russian Architecture: Western Technology, Utopian Dreams,* ed. William Craft Brumfield (Washington, DC: Woodrow Wilson International Center for Scholars, 1990), 111–44.

18. *Sovremennaia Arkhitektura 3* (1928), quoted in Kopp, *Constructivist Architecture in the USSR,* 156.

leisure (each in its respective zone) in order to enhance the efficiency of the city and improve the quality of life.

Whereas the Moscow Plan envisioned an accommodating urban environment, ongoing competitions for the design of the Palace of Soviets began to create the official style of Stalinist construction. After seeing many preliminary plans, the Council for the Construction of the Palace of Soviets issued guidelines for the next competition that urged "monumental quality, simplicity, integrity and elegance." The best design was to consist "both of the new methods and the best employed in Classical architecture."[19] Modernist trends were now to have a pseudoclassical appearance. The proportions and ratios of classical architecture conveyed a clear message of power, and rationalists had been searching for an objective, nonclassical language for architecture on the eve of the competition. Although the Palace of Soviets was never erected, it created the "Stalinist aesthetic" of monumental, neoclassical-inspired architecture at precisely the same time that proletarian architects were condemning traditional architecture.[20]

On the eve of World War II, Soviet planners had worked to rationalize cities, solve urban deficiencies, and promote the image of Soviet strength, wealth, and authority in facades. Postwar planners often merely adjusted prewar plans to postwar conditions. The ravages of war, however, created a tabula rasa in many razed cities and made planning easier because buildings did not have to be destroyed before rebuilding began. For many cities, like Sevastopol, the damage had been so complete that prewar plans no longer accommodated current conditions. But the lack of resources and coordination that marred the Moscow Plan and others like it in the late 1930s also limited postwar reconstruction. However, when life was so bleak in the rubble, architects and urban planners returned to these fundamental principles. Despite the demagoguery of the proletarian architects that all previous styles were prerevolutionary bourgeois remnants and imitations of capitalist imperialist architecture, the Stalinist aesthetic adopted a form of neoclassicism from traditionalists, and urban planning borrowed concepts

---

19. Quoted in Khan-Magomedov, *Pioneers of Soviet Architecture,* 402.

20. The location for the Palace of Soviets much later became the largest swimming pool in the world. After the collapse of the Soviet Union, the city of Moscow and the patriarchate demolished the swimming pool and constructed a replica of the original Christ the Savior Cathedral, which had been demolished to prepare the ground for the Palace of Soviets.

of rational planning for the needs of the population from modernists. The "modernist traditionalism" that resulted created a built space designed to transform individual behaviors and attitudes and to overwhelm through monumental, quasi-neoclassical forms.

Postwar planners borrowed heavily from earlier models, but with the country's infrastructure destroyed, its consumer and construction industries retooled, and much of its labor pool in uniform (dead, alive, or imprisoned), reconstruction required as much sacrifice as the war itself.[21] Local residents and officials realized that the government's renewed emphasis on heavy industry limited the possibility of rapid municipal reconstruction, and therefore they wanted more control over reconstruction plans. Sevastopol's leaders provided central planners with data and anecdotes on local misery. But they also "spoke Bolshevik"—they appropriated the regime's rhetorical strategies to get from the Soviet system what they wanted.[22] Eventually, Soviet officials in Moscow came to see postwar reconstruction as the new touchstone of progress, just like the grand construction projects of industrialization in the 1930s. They realized that rapid reconstruction that *accommodated* local concerns could create a sense of community, which could then be redirected toward a larger, united Soviet identification created through agitation. The heroic stories of wartime could now be transformed into monuments, new place names, and grand feats of labor.

Moscow's Competing Visions for Sevastopol

The Council of People's Commissars (Sovnarkom) created the KA on 8 April 1943 and invested the new organization with the "architectural and planning work for the restoration of cities and other populated areas of the urban type destroyed by the German invaders."[23] The Sovnarkom decree elaborated

---

21. The precise number of dead, approximately 27 million, is debated. See Glantz, *When Titans Clashed,* 292–300; Krivosheev, *Soviet Casualties,* chap. 3; John Erickson and David Dilks, eds., *Barbarossa: The Axis and the Allies* (Edinburgh: Edinburgh University Press, 1994). In the latter, see especially John Erickson, "Soviet War Losses: Calculations and Controversies," 255–77, for a thorough discussion of the problems of quantifying losses.

22. Kotkin, *Magnetic Mountain,* chap. 5, describes "speaking Bolshevik" as a way to learn and use rhetorical tools both to survive in the Soviet system and to get from it what is desired.

23. RGAE, f. 9432, op. 1, d. 3, l. 54.

only on the rubric of architectural structures: "triumphal arches, obelisks, columns and others." Sovnarkom apparently understood that urban designers might not have recognized that symbolic architecture was to be held to the same standard as housing and basic infrastructure in the rebuilding period. Sovnarkom's emphasis on memorial and monumental architecture underscored the regime's desire to re-create a mythology for reconstructed cities, in addition to strengthening political, civic, and economic structures. For older cities like Novgorod, Pskov, and Smolensk, this meant preserving the architectural heritage in monuments, churches, and kremlins.[24] But even in relatively younger cities like Sevastopol and Stalingrad, symbolic architecture was to be a key component to the rebuilding plans.

Because of its relationship to the navy, Sevastopol was seen as one of the most important cities in all of the Soviet Union. Even before the end of the war, architects in Moscow began designing the new Sevastopol and fourteen other priority cities of the Russian Soviet Federated Socialist Republic (RSFSR).[25] Sevastopol, which the Red Army liberated thirteen months after the watershed Sovnarkom resolution that began urban reconstruction planning, received its first indication that it would be reborn on 9 August 1944. Boris Rubanenko, deputy chair of the KA, sent a brief note to one Sud'bin of the navy's Central Planning Bureau informing him that a closed competition to redesign postwar Sevastopol had to be completed by 15 November. But the KA consistently postponed that deadline.[26] From the start, naval and architectural officials worked on the reconstruction of the city, although not always for the same goals.[27] In August 1944, the

---

24. G. Gol'ts, "Smolensk: K proekty vosstanovleniia goroda," *Arkhitektura SSSR* 10 (1945): 3–6; V. A. Lavrov, "Istoricheskie pamiatniki v plane vosstanavlivaemykh gorodov," *Problemy sovremennogo gradostroitel'stva* 1 (1947): 10–17; V. A. Lavrov, "Puti vosstanovleniia Pskova," *Arkhitektura SSSR* 13 (1946): 3–7; V. A. Lavrov, "Vosstanovlenie velikogo Novgoroda," *Arkhitektura SSSR* 9 (1945): 9–15; N. Voronin, "The Destruction of Old Russian Cities," *VOKS Bulletin* 4 (1943): 14–21.

25. The priority cities were Rostov-on-Don, Novgorod, Pskov, Smolensk, Voronezh, Kalinin, Novorossiisk, Sevastopol, Kursk, Orël, Velikie Luki, Murmansk, Viazma, Briansk, and Krasnodar. Cited in L. Irin, "Restoration Plans for Fifteen Cities," *USSR Information Bulletin,* 2 April 1946, 277. Priority cities were designated as such according to their importance as industrial or transportation centers required for military preparedness.

26. RGAE, f. 9432, op. 1, d. 243, l. 1.

27. While the biography of the first postwar chief municipal architect, Georgii Lomagin, is murky, we know that his successor, Iurii Trautman, had served in the military during the war before he became Barkhin's chief opponent and eventually wrested control of city planning from him in 1946. With Trautman, we see a combination of civilian and military goals.

KA directed prominent Moscow architects Moisei Ginzburg and Grigorii Barkhin to submit competing proposals for Sevastopol's reconstruction.[28] Moisei Ginzburg, once the leading theorist of constructivism and designer of Crimea's southern shore in the 1920s, represented the Academy of Architecture. Grigorii Barkhin, professor of architectural planning and adviser to graduate students at the Moscow Architecture Institute, spoke for the navy. Absent from the competition, however, was Georgii Lomagin, Sevastopol's prewar municipal architect who had resumed his post after the war. This signaled a trend in the early years of the postwar design competitions. Only the best Moscow architects could be trusted—and guided—to design monuments to Soviet power.

The architectural community suffered shakeups in the 1930s, but they were relatively bloodless compared with those of other artistic unions and institutions. Barkhin, Ginzburg, and other architects in charge of postwar urban redesign had survived the political crackdown. Despite their previous sins (Ginzburg and Barkhin had both designed constructivist buildings), their loyalty to the official line was now more certain.[29] The scale of damage in the Soviet Union made well-trained architects indispensable, regardless of their past shortcomings. However, professional review boards eventually realized that both plans lacked the specialized knowledge that only local officials could bring. States may make things legible, but locals make things intelligible by providing the local knowledge necessary for *effective* planning.[30]

---

28. RGAE, f. 9432, op. 1, d. 243, l. 1.

29. Some of the major architects included Georgii Gol'ts (Smolensk), Boris Iofan (Novorossiisk), Lev Rudnev (Voronezh), V. N. Semenov (Rostov-on-Don), and Aleksei Shchusev (Istra). Architects, like other artists, suffered a milder purge in 1948 in connection with the reimposition of stricter controls on artistic creativity. For architecture see K. Alabian, "Arkhitekturnaia praktika v svete reshenii TsK VKP(b) o literature i iskusstve," *Arkhitektura i stroitel'stvo* 14 (1947): 1–4; G. A. Simonov, "Vazhneishie zadachi sovetskikh arkhitektorov," *Arkhitektura i stroitel'stvo* 3 (March 1948): 1–4; "Na sobranii aktiva moskovskikh arkhitektorov," *Arkhitektura i stroitel'stvo* 4 (April 1948): 13–16; "O lozhnoi kontseptsii knigi 'Gradostroitel'stvo,'" *Arkhitektura i stroitel'stvo* 4 (April 1948): back cover; "Za marksistskuiu nauku ob arkhitekture," *Arkhitektura i stroitel'stvo* 9 (September 1948): 1–3. Peter Blake, "The Soviet Architectural Purge," *Architectural Record* 106 (September 1949): 127–29, provides a limited evaluation of this bloodless purge.

30. James Scott defined "legibility" as the state's destruction and regulation of the complexities in society. The hypercentralization, however, diverged dramatically from reality. In Sevastopol, officials had to provide local knowledge and then translate central directives, making them intelligible to constituents. See James C. Scott, *Seeing Like a State: How Certain Schemes to Improve the Human Condition Have Failed* (New Haven: Yale University Press, 1998), chap. 6.

Moisei Ginzburg's plan for Sevastopol promoted the new architectural policy of memorial and monumental architecture. Ginzburg's variant for the relatively young Sevastopol created a city of monuments to war and revolutionary heroes. He proposed a four-point program:

1. Maximal utilization and opening of Sevastopol's landscape peculiarities (e.g., bays and ravines)
2. Maximal utilization of material valuables preserved in Sevastopol
3. Rational solution for all vital functions of the city as an organism
4. Opening of the city's artistic form as a hero-city, a city of Russian glory.[31]

Ginzburg essentially ignored the first three points of his comprehensive plan and elaborated primarily on the architectural symbolism of point 4. This talented architect likely believed, in absence of clear instruction, that this was what the KA expected from his initial draft plan because it was the only point on which Sovnarkom elaborated when it created the KA. Thus, his project provided ensemble sketches but did not show zoning of housing, recreation, and municipal services—the "vital functions" of point 3. Moreover, without a budget, no one knew how expensive his vision might become, especially considering the city's "landscape peculiarities" of hills, ravines, and bays.

Ginzburg's plan for Sevastopol, perhaps as a response to the vicious attacks against him in the architectural purges of the previous decade, memorialized the war, highlighted naval interests, and glorified Stalin. He planned an ensemble for the naval command, party, and government on the central hill near a proposed statue to Stalin. In doing so, he connected the political leaders and institutions in one complex and gave a center to the political geography of the city. Ginzburg also planned a symbolic center for Sevastopol. But he scattered memorialization throughout the city. Near the Crimean War Panorama on Historical Boulevard Ginzburg proposed a new World War II museum and an 80-meter-high "Obelisk of Victory," thus creating a square of the two defenses. A line of monuments was to run from one of the oldest structures in the city, Count's Wharf, up the central

---

31. RGAE, f. 9432, op. 1, d. 243, ll. 9–11ob.

hill to a "monumental sculpture of Stalin dominating this part of the city," and on to the Square of the Two Defenses.[32] Ginsburg ensured that Stalin's statue and the Obelisk of Victory could be seen from the shore and nearly every part of the city. He visually conflated Stalin's power with the victory over Nazi Germany. Ginsburg conducted extensive research on monuments around the world and incorporated many of these ideas with an eye toward creating important symbols of socialism and heroism. Rather than accommodating local physical needs, he highlighted Moscow's need to project its power. Despite linking the two midcentury defenses, as had been done in wartime reporting, Ginzburg ignored the wartime emphasis on the heroic deeds of average citizens. He promoted glorification of victory and leaders instead of placing the recent battle in the larger context of Sevastopol's history. He further ignored local accommodation and agitation based on local tradition.

Grigorii Barkhin's much more detailed proposal differed greatly, both from Ginzburg's emphasis on the "outdoor museum" approach and from the city's prewar past. Honoring his patrons in the naval command, Barkhin formed a new centerpiece for the city. On the high central hill, he created a massive ensemble for the navy. Large government and party buildings found new homes at important intersections in the center. He marginalized large memorial complexes to the periphery, except for a grand new Square of Parades that would have consumed the existing square and much of two adjacent boulevards that had served as recreational and leisure areas for more than a century. New monuments to war victory and Stalin found center stage in what was to become the rallying point for demonstrations, celebrations, and parades. With the stroke of his pen, Barkhin had placed the latest war and its leaders at the symbolic center of the city and its history and marginalized all previous events. His understanding of the vague KA and Sovnarkom instructions and his desire to win the competition led him to play it safe and curry favor with the institutions of power instead of trying to meet the population's needs. Elaborate administrative buildings for the local organs of both government and party encouraged additional official support in Moscow.[33] Barkhin's calculation worked, and

---

32. Ibid., l. 11.
33. GAGS, f. R-79, op. 2, d. 30-a, l. 9, 9ob. For more on the agitational significance of Barkhin's plans, see chapter 4.

the KA awarded him the commission. Nonetheless, it soon became clear to many residents that neither Ginzburg nor Barkhin had devoted much attention to the daily struggle for survival of the people living in the rubble.

Prompted by Sevastopol's chief architect, Georgii Lomagin, review panels in Moscow began to condemn Barkhin for planning on a scale unsuited to Sevastopol and its topography. In March 1945, a review board in Moscow noted that Barkhin's proposed museum on the Square of Parades dwarfed neighboring buildings.[34] The "Glory" (*Slava*) monument, originally designed at more than 100 meters high, towered over the Square of Parades at the ancient seaside entrance to the city. The square stretched along the sea, incorporating part of the city's oldest wharf and street. Barkhin followed the vague signals from Moscow on the importance of war memorialization and designed Glory to overpower all other structures and command the attention of passersby. In doing so, he destroyed the tradition of two historical areas of the city. The footprint of the massive tower also would have hindered the flow of traffic and marchers on the square designed for parades and demonstrations.

Three prominent architects stated in a joint opinion that "even if one [took] into account [Sevastopol's] significance as a hero-city, a city of two defenses," the scale of Barkhin's plan for the city center was much too large.[35] Comparisons abounded to Leningrad and Moscow. The dissenting opinions clearly showed that both the size of a city and its place and rank among other cities should determine the scale of its agitational space. But scale was not the only problem. The review panel also condemned Barkhin's square as a hideous eyesore in one of the most important and beautiful regions of the city.[36] Catalyzed by Sevastopol's own municipal architect, critiques of Barkhin's plan indicated that future proposals needed to pay greater attention to local conditions rather than assume an empty wasteland on which the new Sevastopol could be built.

---

34. RGAE, f. 9432, op. 1, d. 241, ll. 11–12.

35. "Hero-city" was a designation given to cities that had survived long sieges or that had been the location of heroic battles. Their place in the pantheon of heroes afforded them high status in the press and special consideration in postwar rebuilding; hero-cities were to become monumental sites of remembrance.

36. RGAE, f. 9432, op. 1, d. 243, ll. 42–43ob.

Sevastopol slowly came back to life during the year between liberation and Germany's capitulation. Naval construction brigades furiously started rebuilding the ports and docks of the fleet, but the rest of the city carried on without direction. Officials in Moscow watched Barkhin's laborious and protracted attempts to redesign the city while negotiating vague instructions from the center. The need to survive led residents and local leaders to begin rebuilding without waiting for Moscow's blessing. Food production and distribution, housing, health care, education, and other services could not wait for Moscow officials to organize the general reconstruction. Most residents likely cared little for Moscow's grandiose blueprints as they gathered their rubble and raided nearby ruins for anything to help raise a roof over their heads. Uninterested in what Barkhin might envision, people rebuilt their homes where they had once stood, not knowing or caring that the plot was now reserved for an apartment, hospital, school, or factory.

Local Mediation of Central Plans

Neither Ginzburg nor Barkhin had adequately provided for the preservation of local traditions or for accommodating a population struggling for survival. Local officials in Sevastopol remained stunned and frustrated by a prolonged planning process that continued to ignore short- and long-term needs for sanitation, food production, health care, transportation, and other services. Moscow had been granting piecemeal concessions to local authorities in all these areas in the months following liberation. But a systematic solution still awaited the city's new general plan for reconstruction, which seemed more concerned with glorifying the regime and war feats in general rather than with Sevastopol's particular place within Russian and Soviet history.

Local architects and officials combined the renewed emphasis on Russia and its past that had arisen in the 1930s and during the war in order to transform the definition of politically correct aesthetics. Socialist realism, the official cultural policy since the 1930s that is often defined as "national in form, socialist in content," presented challenges and opportunities for postwar planners. The war created fluid populations and ravaged many markers of local space. Architects therefore began to focus on crafting a local form rather than something that was inherently national. If new residents could gain a stronger tie to a hometown (*rodnoi gorod*),[37] they could develop an emotional attachment to the city and might be willing to work harder (and sacrifice more) to see it rebuilt. Sevastopol's leaders—particularly Iurii Trautman, Lomagin's successor as postwar chief architect—used this to their advantage.

Moscow's architectural establishment signaled the shift to local over national when it urged planners to consider conditions of geography, topography, construction materials, style, and even history. The urge toward uniformity that had arisen in the mid-1930s with the Moscow Plan gave way under the extraordinary demands of rebuilding the populated areas of the western USSR. Although standardization plans for building types became the norm, most cities adapted central dictates to local tastes. One writer on Stalingrad seized on the new official line and stated that postwar plans should "develop a series of architectural-planning tasks in connection with [the city's] *historical* and *social* significance."[38] Thus, the city's place in history (urban biography), its dimensions, function (e.g., administrative, industrial, resort), natural environment, resources, local building materials, and the condition of the "housing stock"—the number and size of residences—all influenced draft plans and the final design of the city.[39]

Architects often consulted with historians so that cities would have unique characteristics that set them apart. Initially, they tried to create cities that were "individual" in form, rather than simply to reproduce a rational prototype based on standardized plans drafted in Moscow. For Novgorod, preservation of the kremlin and churches was paramount. Yalta had to restrict vehicle traffic so as not to interfere with tourists. Novorossiisk needed to plan with the vistas of and access to the sea in mind.[40] The content still had to be socialist, which forbade any nods to modernism that would be hard for the average citizen to understand. Attention to the local also yielded plans for more livable environments: "[I]t is not the comfort

---

37. This call to the hometown was one of the most prevalent propaganda techniques. A banner near a construction site read, "SEVASTOPOLTSY! What did you [ty] do for the restoration of your hometown?" *Slava Sevastopolia,* 28 May 1949, 1. The word *rodnoi,* not accidentally, is the only one written in script on the banner. Using the familiar, singular form of "you" also stressed the need for individual contributions.

38. N. Poliakov, "Planirovka Stalingrada," *Arkhitektura SSSR* 6 (1944): 2 (emphasis added).

39. Ia. P. Levchenko, "Opyt proektirovaniia gorodov," *Problemy sovetskogo gradostroitel'stva* 2 (1949): 43. Elena Iarskaia-Smirnova suggested "urban biography."

40. RGALI, f. 674, op. 1, d. 186, ll. 16–17.

of the machine," noted one prominent architect, "but the comfort of the person that interests us...[to] give maximal comfort."[41] Rostov-on-Don's plan simply stated that planning created a "more comfortable, healthy, and beautiful" city.[42] "The beauty of a city is not the sum of beautiful facades," announced the official journal of the Union of Architects, "but first and foremost the proportionality of all elements of the city organism, of its 'humanity,' of its harmonious connection with nature."[43] However, the emphasis on local individuality over formalist methods potentially undermined the very base of the Soviet system, which was modern, rational, planned, and centralized. This tension continued to be a problem throughout the postwar decade.

During a planning review in Moscow in late 1945, Sevastopol's new chief architect, Iurii Trautman, provided a local alternative to centralized design teams as he continued Lomagin's critiques and openly opposed many key elements of Barkhin's plan.[44] A few months later, Trautman issued an alternative plan, "A Short Consideration for the Experts on the Draft of the Plan of Sevastopol's Center," in which he highlighted the city's history and unique qualities.[45] To some, it may have appeared that Trautman was creating a local fiefdom in Sevastopol at precisely the same time Moscow was attacking others who chose to challenge its authority. Trautman, however, carefully managed the discourse by repeating earlier official pronouncements on considering local conditions. In doing so, he differentiated himself from Barkhin the outsider. Trautman decried the fact that Barkhin neither knew nor incorporated "local conditions and traditions" in his plan.[46] He condemned Barkhin for planning as if Sevastopol were a completely de-

41. V. N. Semenov, "Osnovy planirovki vosstanovlivaemykh gorodov."

42. V. N. Semenov, "O general'nom plane goroda Rostova na Donu," *Problemy sovremennogo gradostroitel'stva* 2 (1949): 22.

43. "Iskusstvo gradostroitel'stva," *Arkhitektura SSSR* 8 (1944): 2.

44. Georgii Aleksandrovich Lomagin, the prewar architectural leader, had been reappointed chief architect in January 1945 by the Directorate of Architecture (GARF, f. A-150, op. 2, d. 26, l. 11). On 9 October 1945 the directorate demoted Lomagin and placed Trautman in his place. Trautman's friend from his school days in Leningrad, Valentin Mikhailovich Artiukhov, became the head of the building inspectorate (GARF, f. A-150, op. 2, d. 30, l. 17). This was an attempt to replace a local official with two outsiders from Leningrad, but Artiukhov became chief architect during the Khrushchev and Brezhnev years and proved to be as local as Trautman became during his tenure.

45. RGAE, f. 9432, op. 1, d. 243a, ll. 52–58; GAGS, f. R-308, op. 1, d. 21, ll. 9–14.

46. RGAE, f. 9432, op. 1, d. 243a, l. 52.

stroyed space on which he could create without consideration for existing buildings, streets, and landmarks. Barkhin's grand plan to redesign the "traditional places of rest for the citizens of Sevastopol and sailors" (Primorskii and Michmanskii boulevards) was proof that he cared little for the traditions of the hero-city Sevastopol that had defended the Motherland for more than a century.[47] Trautman rejected Barkhin's unnecessary reconceptualization. The local architect argued for reconstruction rather than a project that destroyed the city's history in favor of accommodating new, grandiose party and government buildings. Such a project, Trautman argued, would be both an aesthetic mistake and a waste of precious resources. By contrast, restoration would create additional housing more quickly to serve local needs and place fewer strains on scarce resources and labor.

At some point in Trautman's education, he had learned how to use the regime's discourse against itself in order to fight homogenization. He condemned Barkhin's "abstract academism" that failed to accommodate the "real needs of the city."[48] Trautman skillfully used the language of a November 1945 Sovnarkom directive ("On Measures for the Restoration of RSFSR Cities Destroyed by German Invaders") that finally began to provide some clarification for urban planners. The decree demanded rapid reconstruction of city centers, housing, and even valuable architecture. Perhaps most important for Trautman and other local officials interested in wresting control from Moscow-based planners, the decree called for the "improvement of the everyday conditions of cities' population."[49] Trautman opposed Barkhin's ideas and proposed to take over the design process by suggesting that he and his staff "rework the draft of the center on the basis of the *new general directives* and more favorable *initial qualities.*"[50] His "new general directives" referred to the November decree, and "initial qualities" suggested that planners should start by understanding Sevastopol, its traditions, and its remaining built environment. Trautman had carefully parsed Moscow's directives on tradition and local conditions and added an economic justification for repairing rather than building completely anew because he understood that Moscow was also concerned about budget savings.

---

47. Ibid., l. 55.
48. Ibid., l. 57.
49. GARF, f. A-150, op. 2, d. 20, l. 1.
50. RGAE f. 9432, op. 1, d. 243a, l. 52 (emphasis added).

Review panels soon agreed with Trautman and followed his lead in denouncing Barkhin in much the same language. In April 1946, architect A. Velikanov noted the "academic and abstract" characteristics of the plan and lamented the destruction of Sevastopol's tradition and history. In criticizing the Square of Parades, he noted that it would destroy the "distinctive, customary and most memorable places of Sevastopol.... These places entered literature, all the history of the city is connected with these places, even the city's heroic defenses are connected with them. To change the city's appearance means to fully destroy it, to make a new city, a different city, a city not having a continuous connection with the old Sevastopol."[51] Velikanov's attempt to return Sevastopol to its historical roots buttressed Trautman's arguments and reinforced the foundation for reworking Barkhin's schemes to meet local demands. Velikanov also noted the importance, as did wartime writers, of keeping the city connected with its past. His last sentence clearly shows his understanding of the importance of markers in creating a sense of place and identification. To "change the city's appearance" would mean that the historic Sevastopol and its sacrifice for the Motherland so important to Russian history would cease to exist.

Fellow architect A. M. Zaslavskii faulted Barkhin for working "in the name of an abstract idea" and a "formalistic, out-of-scale, impractical approach."[52] Both architects I. N. Sobolev and Zaslavskii criticized the scale of the Square of Parades and the congestion of symbols on and around it. Sobolev called for removing the 100-meter tower from the square, restoring the former dimensions of Primorskii and Michmanskii boulevards, and reducing the size of some naval buildings so as not to dominate the proposed theater and the Crimean War Panorama complex.[53] In questioning scale, the architects were concerned not only with size but with priorities. Barkhin's scale prioritized World War II and the navy over leisure (e.g., the boulevard and theaters) and the memory of the Crimean War. Like Velikanov and Trautman, Sobolev and Zaslavskii sought greater attention to traditional forms of life and remembrance in Sevastopol.

---

51. Ibid., ll. 5–8; GAGS, f. R-308, op. 1, d. 21, ll. 28–31. Quotes from RGAE, f. 9432, op. 1, d. 243a, ll. 8, 7. Note his use of the plural "defenses" to link World War II with the Crimean War.

52. RGAE, f. 9432, op. 1, d. 243a, ll. 21–22; GAGS, f. R-308, op. 1, d. 21, ll. 16–17.

53. RGAE, f. 9432, op. 1, d. 243a, ll. 40–47; GAGS, f. R-308, op. 1, d. 21, ll. 40–47.

A review panel of the KA demanded that the "elements of giganto-mania" be eliminated.[54] The 1935 Moscow Plan and the ongoing Palace of Soviets at 415 meters tall suggested that size mattered. Barkhin, like many other architects, had taken his cue from these formative projects. He did not realize, however, that new policies to consider local conditions would sometimes trump the gigantomania that continued in Moscow and other cities. V. V. Baburov (head of the Main Directorate for Planning and Constructing Cities) praised Barkhin for his work on the aesthetics of the city but then brandished the sword of cultural criticism by noting that Barkhin's work was "connected with neither the traditions nor the scale and character of Sevastopol's ensemble." Barkhin also had "deviated to the point of abstraction," and his proposal carried the "imprint of abstract academism."[55] The cacophony of opposition, started by Lomagin and then Trautman, led the KA to reject Barkhin's proposal.[56] The battle initiated by local architects and taken up by prominent colleagues in Moscow brought Sevastopol's demands to the fore. Trautman used the official rhetoric of local individuality and antiformalism to eviscerate Barkhin's ill-informed planning. Speaking in the name of the population, if not always directly on its behalf, Trautman secured a place for himself in history as the architect of a hero-city.[57]

Someone had to champion local conditions, and seeing that Sevastopol had been languishing for two years, Trautman began his transformation to becoming a local official by mediating between rigid central planning and chaotic individual construction. The 1944 law that created the position of chief municipal architect in Soviet cities gave these men control over all con-struction, restoration, greening, and *blagoustroistvo* (the improvement of public services from utilities to transportation to street lights) and the power to approve to all projects for the city.[58] After Trautman won jurisdiction for designing the new Sevastopol, the city entered a period of relative au-tonomy in planning and rebuilding. Reconstruction now trumped razing

---

54. RGAE, f. 9432, op. 1, d. 243a, ll. 1–4. Quote at l. 3.

55. RGAE, f. 9432, op. 1, d. 243, ll. 106–10; GAGS, f. R-308, op. 1, d. 21, ll. 55–59; RGAE, f. 9432, op. 1, d. 154, ll. 159–63.

56. RGAE, f. 9432, op. 1, d. 243, ll. 111–15; RGAE, f. 9432, op. 1, d. 154, ll. 155–58.

57. Barkhin's daughter continued to argue into the 1980s that her father was the true architect of Sevastopol. A. G. Barkhina, *G. B. Barkhin* (Moscow: Stroizdat, 1981), 115–18, 164.

58. RGAE, f. 9432, op. 1, d. 6, l. 3.

and building anew as Barkhin had proposed. Trautman realized that a city needed a sense of tradition and that the faltering economies and industries of Sevastopol and the USSR could not supply money, labor, or materials for a complete redesign. He and his local team created a plan that preserved the essence of the city center while eliminating, adding, and redesigning buildings to fit the needs of the population and fleet. The new locals worked to protect Sevastopol's unique heritage from the grandiose plans of outsiders who would have destroyed local tradition and history.

Becoming local did not mean being born in the city because many of the prominent municipal leaders after the war were, in fact, appointed to the city administration from such diverse places as Leningrad, Moscow, Bashkiriia, and Simferopol. Becoming local meant that a person collected and used knowledge of the city's condition and the concerns of its residents to influence policy. Outsiders (*inogorodtsy*) were not native Sevastopoltsy. More important, outsiders supported Moscow against local officials who were trying to preserve tradition. Moscow's unfulfilled promises and lax oversight over ministry distributions to Sevastopol inadvertently made many outsiders into locals. Newly appointed officials to Sevastopol generally arrived in the city as outsiders, but sympathy for the population quickly transformed their view of Moscow's planning process. Even high officials in Sevastopol lived in the rubble alongside laborers. A year after starting in Sevastopol, the office of the chief architect had been allotted only one apartment, rather than the two apartments and one barrack that had been promised. This failure forced the staff to live like the rest of the homeless residents.[59] The local population, however, did not always view Sevastopol's leaders as local even if Moscow did. Opposition to central dictates was enough for the municipal and national elite to consider the deviations local, but residents demanded unyielding attention to their daily needs.

A City for Sevastopoltsy

In dealing with the physical needs of the population, Trautman had a strong ally in Tamara Alëshina, who arrived from Bashkiriia soon after liberation

---

59. GAGS, f. R-79, op. 2, d. 31, ll. 40–40ob.

to lead the City Planning Commission (Gorplan). From September to December 1946, Trautman and Alëshina developed a plan to counter what they viewed as unrealistic proposals created in faraway Moscow. Gosplan, Alëshina's central institution in Moscow, was planning for a population of 80,000 by 1950, but with a population already at 60,000 in late 1946 (an increase of 50,000 people in just thirty months), Sevastopol's planners countered with a more likely target of 112,000. This was more than merely an argument about future population. Because so much planning centered on a service-to-population ratio, a higher number meant greater resources for the city. Nearly all allocations from the center depended on existing or projected population numbers. By arguing for a larger population target, Alëshina was trying to ensure that Sevastopol would get enough food, clothing, heating fuel, construction materials, labor, and all the other goods that were distributed based on the size of the local population.

Trautman and Alëshina were furious with Moscow's inattention to housing. Central ministries failed to deliver materials and labor. Barkhin's proposal for a naval complex on the central hill would have razed twenty-seven buildings, including ten that had suffered little damage.[60] They argued that Barkhin's penchant for symbolism and aesthetics ignored the dire need for housing in the ruined city. He was completely out of touch with the city that he had been charged with rebuilding. The local plan, realizing that designs and building materials would be slow to arrive, urged that "in the first period of construction stone from destroyed buildings will be utilized."[61] Throughout the city, residents adopted a do-it-yourself attitude as they rebuilt homes, wholly unconcerned with central planning.

Although much of the first order of construction remained the same, the local group redesigned the plan to meet Sevastopol's needs better. Trautman's revised construction agenda sought to accommodate transportation, medical, educational, and other needs. Without adequate roads and public transportation, urban development would remain slow. A shortage of trucks and paved roads slowed the movement of raw materials to and finished products from factories. Shopping for even the most basic necessities often required a trip to the city center, outside of which little commercial activity existed immediately after liberation. Unlike Barkhin, Trautman

---

60. GAGS, f. R-308, op. 1, d. 41, l. 40.
61. RGAE, f. 9432, op. 1, d. 241, l. 43; GAGS, f. R-308, op. 1, d. 26, l. 4.

developed plans for bus, trolley, and cutter traffic to cross the bays in order to reduce the difficulty of travel. Bus routes connected the center with worker settlements and the cities of Yalta, Balaklava, and Simferopol. Trolley lines, although long in developing, eventually connected the two largest settlements at Matiushenko Hill and Ship Side (Korabel'naia storona) and around the central ring road with its complex of commercial, government, party, and naval buildings.

The devastation to previous roadbeds made rapid repair improbable; thus, Trautman considered cutter traffic the best short-term solution to connect the city's regions with the center. After sweeping the bays for mines, cutters could quickly begin to shuttle residents throughout the city's far-flung regions and bring commuters to the beaches. However, despite the vast ship-building capabilities of the city, civilian cutter service remained woefully undeveloped throughout the first postwar decade as the docks devoted nearly all attention to military construction and repair.[62] This highlights one of the key problems in reconstruction. Even with good plans, unless ministries could be forced to comply, little positive was accomplished.

The USSR's social welfare program also promised medical care and education, and Sevastopol's planners sought to meet these needs. Trautman and Alëshina planned for 1,200 beds in clinics, hospitals, and maternity homes. In order to prevent undue pressure on the medical institutions, disease prevention was also paramount. Four bathhouses were to augment facilities at large factories. Epidemic centers and a malaria prevention complex were to have oversight for preventing outbreaks that could ravage the city.[63] Education also followed the "rational planning" model of statistical calculation. Having determined that in four years the city's population would reach 112,000, the planning commission assumed that 20 percent would be school-age children. With a target of 22,400 children in school by 1950, Alëshina and Gorplan designed eighteen schools with a capacity of 8,720 students.[64] This planned deficit was really an extension of the trend toward multiple shifts during each school day in order to maximize the scarce resources of teachers and building space. The plan for three shifts

62. RGAE, f. 9432, op. 1, d. 241, l. 45.
63. Ibid., ll. 62–62ob.
64. Ibid., l. 44.

was in fact an improvement over the immediate postwar years, during which many schools served four sets of students each day.[65]

Food remained one of the chief problems in Sevastopol and most other cities after the war. Collectivization had devastated Soviet food production in the 1930s. War reduced village labor, littered fields with corpses and ordnance, and ravaged the network of goods distribution. Because Sevastopol had little arable land near the major population centers, it relied on fishing and nearby collective and state farms to feed the city. Planners hoped to attract farmers to the city by erecting a new House of Collective Farm Workers as temporary living and storage for people bringing agricultural goods to market. Hotel rooms for five hundred people and one hundred rooms for collective farm workers in particular were planned for the first order of construction. Farmers could then sell their goods at newly planned regional markets. The proposal also included a new enclosed central market to replace chaotic, open-air stalls. Newly built fish- and meat-processing plants and beverage distilleries for the "service of the population of all regions" were promised to fill an expanded network of stores.[66]

The key turning point in Sevastopol's resurrection came in October 1948 when Stalin and the Council of Ministers decreed that the city would be rebuilt in "three to four years," which both recentralized the rebuilding process and provided resources to carry out Trautman's vision for the new city.[67] Just weeks before the decree Stalin visited Sevastopol and telegrammed Georgii Malenkov about the "depressing impression" of slow rebuilding in the city. He suggested that the population would judge the regime harshly for its mismanagement. Why had the regime intervened after the recent earthquake in Ashkhabad, he asked Malenkov, but not in a "first-class naval stronghold"? Stalin then suggested both a special commission to plan rebuilding and a three- to four-year timetable with the appropriate "monetary

65. GAGS, f. R-359, op. 1, d. 38, ll. 1–4. Shift schooling was the norm throughout the Soviet Union, before and after the war. John Dunstan, *Soviet Schooling in the Second World War* (New York: St. Martin's, 1997); E. Thomas Ewing, *The Teachers of Stalinism: Policy, Practice, and Power in Soviet Schools of the 1930s* (New York: P. Lang, 2002); Larry Holmes, *The Kremlin and the Schoolhouse: Reforming Education in Soviet Russia, 1917–1931* (Bloomington: Indiana University Press, 1991); Larry Holmes, *Stalin's School: Moscow's Model School No. 25, 1931–1937* (Pittsburgh: University of Pittsburgh Press, 1999).

66. RGAE, f. 9432, op. 1, d. 241, l. 44.

67. RGAE, f. 9432, op. 1, d. 154, ll. 348–353ob.

resources and construction materials with machinery for this task."[68] Stalin clearly recognized that the Berlin crisis had raised the stakes with his former World War II allies. Restoring the base of Sevastopol's Black Sea Fleet was now imperative.

The chief rationale for rapid reconstruction, however, was at least as much about accommodating the population as it was rebuilding a naval stronghold for the Cold War. Of course, this concern was not merely humanitarian; Stalin feared that the population would "assess" the regime's "weakness" in the ability to organize the reconstruction task. While the generalissimo did not elaborate on the consequences of this failure, it seems certain that he feared possible civil unrest if a weak government could not meet the basic needs of its citizens. Earlier in the year, railway workers had engaged in isolated but public strikes because of declining standards of living. Only when the Ministry of Railways finally distributed more funds did the strikes abate.[69] Did Stalin fear another munity of the Black Sea Fleet as in 1905? Probably not, but as the Cold War heated up, even the slightest opposition in a city of Sevastopol's importance could not be allowed. It also seems that Stalin realized the validity of the complaints against slow reconstruction. In calling the effort weak, he showed that the criticism had merit. Thus, accommodation, he believed, would pacify the residents and sailors in this vital city. In short, he was hinting at the social contract he had extended in the 1930s: in return for the population's passivity, he would provide for material needs.[70] Despite four years of reports from local leaders noting the city's squalor, it took Stalin's personal observations to speed Sevastopol's transformation.

The October 1948 resolution planned a radical increase in the tempo and scale of construction, but in many ways this also accentuated housing problems. Stalin's suggestion of a special commission prompted the Council of

---

68. Archive of the President of the Russian Federation (ARPF), f. 45, op. 1, d. 109, l. 106. I am indebted to Per Brodersen for alerting me to the presence of this document, which is copied in the United States Library of Congress Manuscript Division, c/o Volkogonov Holdings, box 23, wheel 16.

69. Donald Filtzer, *Soviet Workers and Late Stalinism: Labour and the Restoration of the Stalinist System after World War II* (Cambridge: Cambridge University Press, 2002), 85–88.

70. This seems to support Vera Dunham's "Big Deal" thesis that material goods were used as a weapon of compliance, although she limits her "deal" to the middle class. Vera Dunham, *In Stalin's Time: Middleclass Values in Soviet Fiction* (Durham, NC: Duke University Press, 1990).

Ministers to create the Directorate for the Restoration of Sevastopol (*Uprav-lenie po vosstanovleniiu Sevastopolia,* or UVS), which the council charged with coordinating all ministries and building trusts with interests in the city. The reorganization brought new administrators, long-awaited resources and labor, and an increased budget directly from Moscow. Although the UVS eliminated local autonomy, it also increased the probability that Sevastopol would be raised from ruins. Before the decree, little major construction had been completed, and instead of the massive architectural symbols of Soviet power, rubble dominated the city streets. The UVS sought to bring ministries together and reduce the amount of competition for resources. Each ministry would now be held accountable for fulfilling its plan. Sevastopol now had greater resources and attention than any other destroyed city.

For two years, speaking for local concerns had given architects in Sevastopol a degree of autonomy, but the quicken-the-pace decree stressed the need for efficiency and teamwork. Moscow's centralized collective replaced the individual or localized work of Trautman's office as Sevastopol rebuilt. Once Trautman's team had identified the needs of new construction, architects and engineers in Leningrad and Moscow workshops adapted standardized blueprints to Sevastopol's seismic needs, thereby limiting the role of local officials. With the recentralization of 1948, Trautman received the first indication that his position was tenuous. Although his ouster was over a year away, he knew that he had lost overall authority for the city's new face. But Trautman's team had clearly established the overall vision between 1946 and 1948 as one that accommodated local everyday needs and agitated through the use of Sevastopol's history, with a strong focus on the nineteenth century. We will further investigate these trends in the next two chapters.

Between 1948 and 1950, the UVS created the organizational and material base necessary for rapid reconstruction of the beautiful and imposing buildings in the city center. Although Moscow and Leningrad workshops designed many of the projects, local architects had enough input to create Corinthian facades that mirrored the ruins of the ancient Greek city of Khersones just to the west of the city center. The UVS guided ministerial coordination over grandiose neoclassical hospitals, banks, theaters, and hotels, and Sevastopol was able to preserve its heritage and tradition in architectural styles, monuments, and street names through the intercession of local officials.

Redefining Local Leaders

Planning continued well past the elaboration of Trautman's local plan in 1947, and tensions between center and periphery remained in a state of flux. As Moscow took control and finally insisted on rapid reconstruction in three to four years, the stakes got higher and interministry fighting reached a crescendo. Sevastopol was but one of many cities devastated by war, and it was desperate for labor and building materials that were in short supply. Most of the 27 million war dead were of working age, and the majority of factories had been located in the occupied zones. Of those factories transferred by rail beyond the Urals, nearly all were retooled for the war effort. Making brick, cement, glass, and lumber was not as high a priority as making weapons. Thus, with high production targets to meet, the local divisions of national organs began to shift blame, trying to prove that they were not at fault for inadequate reconstruction. The parent organs in Moscow shifted the blame for noncompliance to local officials.[71] Conversely, the men and women in Sevastopol saw Moscow and its ministries trying to enforce rules on paper without a clear understanding of local conditions. Scapegoating increased in proportion with Moscow's urge to rebuild rapidly.

Having removed Barkhin from the planning process and created a local variation, Trautman became a target for criticism. Citizens' complaints about housing, food, sanitation, and a lack of everyday services since the first months after liberation had provided Trautman with the examples he needed to oust Barkhin. With the recentralization of construction in October 1948, the local media began to print articles that not only condemned poor-quality construction but also criticized Trautman and his plan. The attacks on Trautman used his own strategy of confrontation by claiming that he had ignored local concerns. Most public criticism appeared in the newspaper column "We Will Rebuild Our Native Sevastopol in 3–4 Years." Anonymous and signed articles in the city's party and government newspaper criticized Sevastopol's architects for not working hard enough, not receiving and providing enough political instruction, and not preparing living space for arriving workers. One critic wrote that concentrating on

---

71. James R. Harris, *The Great Urals: Regionalism and the Evolution of the Soviet System* (Ithaca, NY: Cornell University Press, 1999), chap. 6.

main roads, to the detriment of well-traveled pedestrian stairways and inclines over and around the city's hills and ravines, threatened "to break the legs" of residents.[72] The press attacks against Trautman—which may have been staged, as suggested by their presence in a government and party newspaper—were merely the prelude for what was to come. In the next two years, the chief municipal architect would be demoted and eventually removed from the city, all with the population's best interests in mind, according to his critics.

Most interested parties in Sevastopol were judged by the *quantity* of buildings they constructed, but chief municipal building inspector Mikhail Amelchenko and his superiors in the State Architectural-Construction Inspectorate (*Glavnoe upravlenie gosudarstvennogo arkhitekturno-stroitel'nogo kontrolia,* Gosarkhstroikontrol, or GASK) became Trautman's chief critics and the leading proponents of renewed collectivism. GASK was responsible for *quality* construction, which was rare in the city. Inspectors found fault with Trautman and others who approved construction that was outside the norms of the general plan or that failed to comply with building codes. Responsibility for any accidents, such as collapsed roofs or workers falling from scaffolding, could be blamed on inspectors. Therefore, GASK had the most to lose by allowing Trautman and his successor, A. V. Aref'ev (a Stalin prize–winning architect), to continue ignoring unplanned or willful construction. The architects, on the other hand, viewed GASK officials as outsiders with plans but little understanding of Sevastopol's needs.

This disagreement encapsulates the essence of local–outsider battles in Sevastopol. Central officials with power who were often well intentioned were generally ignorant of local conditions and thus could not properly accommodate residents. Local officials, who had less power, lived in the rubble with their fellow residents and saw the uninformed dictates as roadblocks to a more thoughtful reconstruction task.[73] Trautman, Aref'ev, and others generally wanted to accommodate the health and welfare needs

---

72. See in the column "Vosstanovym rodnoi Sevastopol v 3–4 goda!" the following articles: "Vpered, k novym trudovym pobedam!" *Slava Sevastopolia,* 6 November 1948, 1; "V plenum Sevastopol'skogo gorodskogo komiteta VKP(b)," *Slava Sevastopolia,* 17 November 1948, 1; "Vse vnimanie stroitel'ei blagoustroistvu shkol FZO," *Slava Sevastopolia,* 19 November 1948, 1.

73. Compare the workings of Sevastopol's local politics to Timothy Colton's reflections on Moscow's administration. *Moscow: Governing the Socialist Metropolis* (Cambridge, MA: Harvard University Press, 1995), 356.

of the local population. Proper housing sometime in the distant future was an unsatisfactory substitute for even immediate housing, even if it was ramshackle. Moscow bureaucrats saw only numbers and disembodied reports from their local plenipotentiaries who feared blame for poor-quality or ill-organized construction and felt that their professionalism was being ignored. With so few trips into the devastated city, and therefore no good sense of the scale of devastation, Moscow officials really could have acted in no other way.

Sevastopol, like most other cities, could not meet the building goals set in faraway Moscow, and the new decade brought renewed attention to these failures. On 14 February 1950, the heads of GASK from Kyiv, Leningrad, Moscow, Sevastopol, and seven Soviet republics submitted reports on planning and building during 1949 to the Ministry of City Building (*Mingorstroi*). Amelchenko presented a scathing analysis that focused on how and why, at least in his eyes, Sevastopol had failed so miserably. His personal attacks and tirades generally compensated for the fact that he could not lay blame at the feet of the Council of Ministers and its hasty and imprecise resolution to complete rebuilding in Sevastopol in three to four years. Sevastopol was far from unique in its failures. A 1951 meeting showed that Murmansk still did not have a complete plan, geological data, or the basic information needed to design a sanitation system. Even in Stalingrad, the jewel of Stalin's victory, housing along the Alley of Heroes, one of the main streets of the city, had not yet been planned. It is clear, however, that Russian Federation officials did not want the full truth revealed and that they tried to soften criticisms. In the draft resolution from this meeting, for example, someone carefully edited out criticisms of the "low architectural quality" and "unsystematic" construction in Gorky, which had not even been occupied during the war. The redactor also removed condemnation of irresponsible code enforcement and the high percentage of one-story construction.[74] A year later, residents in Smolensk were still "living in banyas and lavatories," and Viazma, "despite the great attention of the party and government," still did not have a plan.[75] Like Sevastopol, these cities were among the fifteen priority cities for reconstruction in the RSFSR. One can only imagine the prolonged devastation in ignored cities.

---

74. GARF, f. A-150, op. 2, d. 478, ll. 24–31.
75. On Smolensk, see GARF, f. A-150, op. 2, d. 644, ll. 69–94, and on Viazma, see ll. 95–111.

With their workers regularly fleeing the city in search of better work and living conditions, many local construction trusts flouted formal approval and built illegal residential and recreational facilities in the city's outskirts. A factory boss in Sevastopol's Inkerman district not only built a club for her workers without consent but also used expensive stone from the nearby quarry that had been reserved strictly for the ensembles of the city center.[76] Many other factory managers and even municipal agencies, realizing that housing was scarce and knowing that labor flight would make them miss production targets, erected barrack housing for their workers who lived in tents and mud huts. Managers responsible for meeting construction deadlines and output targets realized that a worker without a roof would produce less than one with adequate, if not optimal, shelter and food. Factory officials realized that superiors would judge them on output, not conformity to construction laws.

Amelchenko charged Trautman and city executive committee chairman V. I. Filippov with "violating construction legislation."[77] He accused the two men of repeatedly ignoring building codes, approving illegal construction, lacking control over building, and making independent decisions without consultation with others, meaning GASK. Amelchenko claimed that when Trautman issued permits, they were delayed so long that residents started building illegally, hoping for ex post facto approval. Most egregious, according to the report, Trautman's "delay in the formation of necessary documents" frequently prevented the resettlement of workers from tent cities.[78]

The inspector's appeal to Moscow in the name of the health and welfare of workers was precisely the same formulation that Trautman had used in 1946 to secure the commission over Barkhin. The rhetorical device for redirecting the course of rebuilding remained the same even though Trautman had argued for individual and local initiative and Amelchenko urged a return to collective and centralized construction. Accommodating the needs of the population remained central to the rhetoric of postwar rebuilding because the regime had placed social welfare at the center of the social contract. Although any student of the USSR knows that the

---

76. RGAE, f. 9510, op. 4, d. 328, ll. 511ob.
77. Ibid., ll. 513, 514ob.
78. Ibid., ll. 517ob-518.

population suffered from abuse and neglect much more than it thrived in the loving embrace of the regime, reference to accommodating the population remained a key tool in educating residents about the regime's intent, despite setbacks. Rivals also used charges of a lack of attention to accommodation, most often using the term *zabota* (care or concern), as a way to condemn each other.

Local officials, when called to defend themselves, responded with the only language they thought might be useful. Admitting the problems in city administration and the performance of planning and construction units, although in line with the demands of self-criticism, would have been counterproductive.[79] Ministries and state agencies failed to provide labor, capital, and materials, but finding fault with central planning as a whole was still taboo. Criticism of individuals and lower divisions of ministries was expected, but there was still an unwritten code forbidding underlings' public accusations against the elite. Trautman and others realized that staffing increases consistently fell behind the rapid increase in work. However, they defended themselves by saying that their faults had the best interests of the workers at heart. Approval of willful construction was a humanitarian act, not lax leadership.

Amelchenko's scathing report to Mingorstroi in February 1950 seems bitter, vindictive, and unwilling to address the real problem of overzealous dictates from Moscow, which also failed to provide the necessary resources for him to accomplish his task. He disparaged nearly all public officials in the city, in particular the head of construction trusts, for shoddy construction and violation of building norms. With only Amelchenko and three senior inspectors, GASK could review each site only once every eight months as the number of buildings under construction increased from 193 in 1948 to 595 in 1949. The city needed better worker training, material supply, and supervision, none of which was forthcoming or under the authority of GASK. Had Amelchenko been provided with a full complement of trained inspectors, had construction workers been given more than a rudimentary six-month training course, and had local planning officials been given enough workers, materials, and clear direction, much of the illegal and poor-quality construction could have been avoided. However, in order

---

79. Alexei Kojevnikov, "Rituals of Stalinist Culture at Work: Science and the Games of Intraparty Democracy Circa 1948," *Russian Review* 57 (January 1998): 25–52.

to avoid blaming Moscow, yet realizing that he could be judged guilty of permitting low-quality construction, Amelchenko did what he needed to survive: he found a scapegoat in the equally culpable foes in Sevastopol. Through the party machinery Amelchenko had Trautman removed from his post and replaced by Aref'ev on 8 February 1950.

Just two weeks later, the Directorate of Deputy Ministers of the Russian Federation and the Interdepartmental Commission for the Examination of Projects for Construction in Sevastopol met in the city twice a day for one week. Most of the Moscow officials had their first look at the postwar city and met with local leaders to discuss the pace and quality of construction. Some officials showed their ignorance by suggesting further wooden construction although there was no local timber and numerous decrees had mandated only stone construction in the center.[80] The Moscow officials' ignorance of local conditions went well beyond construction materials and right to the heart of the city's traditions and identification. Monuments, memorials, and traditional leisure spaces formed the tangible markers of place.

When central authorities suggested changes to the city's premier park, which Barkhin had earlier planned to shrink to allow more space for monuments, the new head of Sevastopol's government, Sergei Sosnitskii, submitted a modest request that planning for Primorskii Boulevard, one of the oldest places in the city, not be changed because the "citizens of Sevastopol are very accustomed to the present layout, they love [it] and will be thankful if it remains in its present condition."[81] When V. A. Shkvarikov, head of the Directorate of Architecture, suggested that more advisers from Moscow take part, Alëshina argued that the "boulevard must preserve its historically complex arrangement."[82] That included replanting chestnut trees destroyed during the war. If plans changed again, she reminded them, Sevastopol would lose one million rubles in funding. Without saying it in so many words, Alëshina was telling Shkvarikov that more interference from Moscow was the last thing Sevastopol needed.

Both Alëshina and Sosnitskii defended their work as benefiting local residents, often against the wishes of the regime. Moreover, they presented

---

80. GARF, f. A-150, op. 2, d. 254, ll. 14–25.
81. Ibid., ll. 30–48. Quote at ll. 35–36.
82. Ibid., ll. 38–39.

their defense of Sevastopol's interests as the word and will of the people. Sosnitskii invoked the "citizens of Sevastopol" and suggested that accommodating their desire to retain elements of the prewar city's familiar layout would make them "thankful." He signaled the quid pro quo of accommodation and quiescence but also showed that he was ultimately powerless by noting that residents would be thankful. It appears that he understood that a whim from Moscow could change everything. But he was also determined to note that accommodating local desires could have a mollifying effect.

In April 1951, in response to what he viewed as interference, Aref'ev, who until the previous year had been a prominent architect in Moscow, launched a heated campaign against all outsiders. At a meeting in Moscow he lambasted that "odious figure" Amelchenko and questioned not only his ability to perform his duties but even his qualifications as chief inspector. Relying on his prominence as a Stalin Prize recipient, Aref'ev chided nearly all the top officials of the Russian Federation's (although not the USSR's) architectural administration for failing to support Sevastopol's construction and planning brigades. Aref'ev boldly demanded that the government remove outsider architects from Leningrad and Moscow from Sevastopol's planning teams. As Aref'ev must have anticipated, V. Tsingalenok (chairman of GASK) rose to the defense of Amelchenko and the local GASK organ and in return attacked Aref'ev's administrative abilities, character, and principles.[83]

Other Moscow officials joined in the retaliatory attacks. Architect Aleksandr Kuznetsov called Aref'ev's planning agency a "completely undisciplined organization" and demanded reform.[84] Architect Valentin Golli condemned Aref'ev for doing little better than his predecessors and for trying to rebuild the city on his own rather than "work[ing] with the collective."[85] The individual approach to planning touted by Trautman could no longer be tolerated, especially as the Leningrad Affair, which resulted in the purge of numerous figures connected to powerful Leningrad-based political figures, made it quite well known that all decisions ran through Moscow and that no major decisions were to be made without

---

83. GARF, f. A-150, op. 2, d. 478, l. 60ob.
84. Ibid.
85. GARF, f. A-150, op. 2, d. 644, l. 405.

consent from the proper authorities. The speed of reconstruction demanded at least some division of labor and use of standardized plans despite the local demands and seismic needs. As the Cold War heated up following the Berlin crisis and during the Korean War, Sevastopol's importance also increased and could not be entrusted to local officials. Despite attacks on local leaders, Kuznetsov, unlike his colleagues, also realized the real locus of the problem: "After the resolution of the Council of Ministers about the economics of construction" it became clear that all the general plans and drafts of city centers throughout the USSR had "serious mistakes."[86] In other words, much of what had already been approved once and considered correct had to be changed to conform to the ex post facto norms from the Council of Ministers.

The transformation of newly arrived officials into local leaders was one of the most intriguing processes during Sevastopol's postwar decade. Many of the specialists who came from Moscow, Leningrad, and even Bashkiriia quickly took up the fight of the local community. Rather than blindly following Moscow's dictates, they envisioned and tried to construct a more livable environment with proper housing, health care, food distribution, and education. These locals were so successful in speaking for, if not from, Sevastopol's residents that central officials actually changed their plans. But opponents in the capital learned from the humbling experience of being outmaneuvered and turned the language of localism against the very people who wielded it so successfully in the early years of reconstruction. By the end of the 1940s, Trautman, one of the clear leaders of the local movement, found himself removed from his post after GASK charged that his delays in drawing up required paperwork condemned residents to live longer in tents and other temporary structures. Accommodating the local community now became a way to argue for central control and more standardization for greater efficiency. But even after Trautman was ousted, his replacement, an award-winning architect from Moscow, called for the removal of all outsider interference in Moscow. Clearly, then, focus on the unique characteristics of place and the needs of the population became central in winning the contest between center and periphery.

---

86. GARF, f. A-150, op. 2, d. 644, l. 431.

While Cold War historians often viewed "high" Stalinism as a period of stultifying centralization, more recent research has corrected that perspective. In Sevastopol, there was a great deal of negotiation. With the country's infrastructure destroyed, its consumer and construction industries retooled for war, and much of its labor depleted, postwar rebuilding required coordinated effort to maximize the speed of reconstruction and the amelioration of horrible conditions in destroyed cities. With a paucity of resources and information, central planners had to hope for postwar sacrifice equal to that of wartime defense. But even the wartime defense had to be stimulated by a retreat to Russian history and nationalism. In a similar way, the center gave in to many of the periphery's demands for historical preservation and restoration of the city's architectural landmarks. Accommodation, then, became a principal form of agitation.

Even officials assigned to the city from Moscow, Leningrad, and other places soon realized that a phoenix could not rise by itself from the ashes of Sevastopol. Enforcing strict building codes meant little to the newly local officials who saw their construction workers sleeping in tents, underground dugouts, mud huts, and crowded wooden barracks during cold and windy winters. Sevastopol's party-state elite and urban planners believed that it would be healthier for workers and better in the long run to the health of Sevastopol if a factory manager built stone housing without permission and all the proper documents rather than erecting more temporary barracks and tents. In the decade following the liberation of Sevastopol, central planning gave way to local autonomy that in turn reverted to central authority once the new agenda had been established. For Sevastopol it was the best of both options. The earlier period of relative autonomy allowed local officials to develop a local plan, and then when centralization returned, it came with the resources necessary to fulfill the local vision.

As the KA's initial attempts to centralize planning failed under the burden of so many destroyed cities, Trautman and others seized on the prevailing rhetoric of recognizing local conditions. Only local officials, they argued, had the information at hand to preserve tradition, utilize local resources properly, and plan the appropriate facilities for an ever-increasing population. In an era that was punctuated with father Stalin's care and concern for his children and decrees urging the use of local resources, arguing for accommodating the local population was an effective weapon. In fact, outsiders like Amelchenko eventually turned the rhetoric of accommodation against locals in an effort to reassert central control. Thus, whether arguing for local autonomy or centralized control, local accommodation was paramount. Much of this concern was genuine, as in the case of factory managers who ignored construction laws to house their workers. In other cases, like the bureaucratic squabble between Amelchenko and Aref'ev, it was likely feigned to gain power, control, or prestige. In either situation, "local" meant something in postwar Sevastopol, and anyone who failed to recognize this fact was soon out of favor.

In one sense, the two competing visions of centralization and localism both had the best interests of the population in mind. Party-state elites in Moscow, for example, wanted centralization for efficiency's sake. Financial and administrative efficiency would improve the economy and national power and prestige. Local spokespeople, however, sought to defend the urban biography. Within the parameters of the city, both geographic and historical, a unique identification had developed that provided residents with their own center—a place where they could define themselves as "us." These two visions for the future face of Sevastopol were not mutually exclusive. Even before the 1917 revolutions, Marxist groups had based their claims for legitimacy in the future on their desire for accommodating the masses working under the yoke of bourgeois capitalists. Likewise, the way to disenfranchise the latter group was to bring order to a chaotic system in which profit and capital were the driving forces. But the quest for centralization did not mean a complete abandonment of variation within the system, at least when it came to some cultural issues, even during high Stalinism. Even Lenin realized, in the months immediately following the revolution, that cultural symbols and the historic past were essential elements that needed to be preserved against the iconoclasts.[87] The combination of historical remembrance and centralized order remained after World War II, and rapid reconstruction came only after a negotiated settlement between Sevastopol and Moscow.

To make matters worse, officials tried to implement directives in an atmosphere of unclear divisions of responsibility and authority. When authority was clear, institutions often had no mechanisms of enforcement

---

87. See Richard Stites, "Iconoclastic Currents in the Russian Revolution: Destroying and Preserving the Past," in *Bolshevik Culture: Experiment and Order in the Russian Revolution,* ed. Abbott Gleason, Peter Kenez, and Richard Stites (Bloomington: Indiana University Press, 1985), 1–24.

except to appeal to higher authorities. The outcome of this structure of authority was predictable: confusion, a lack of efficiency, and scapegoating. The examples of confusion are too numerous to mention, but a few examples should suffice. Two months after the war, the Committee on Architectural Affairs asked Voznessenskii if it could create an arbitration bureau because there was too much chaos in decision making.[88] Quarrels were breaking out among the local architectural officials and all the organs that the committee was supposed to coordinate. Although the committee's plan was killed, there was no end to the confusion over who had authority and what should be done when conflicts arose. Things only got worse when four years later a reorganization of the architectural and planning apparatus led to the liquidation of the committee. One of the soon-to-be-sacked officials complained that the local organs would be "deprived of the unifying guidance of the center" to overcome difficulties and create a single policy.[89] The confused and confusing Soviet system thwarted all efforts at efficiency as plans had to have multiple layers of approval from the local, oblast, and federation authorities all the way up to the all-Union level in many cases.

The multilayered system in itself prolonged the planning task, but when different agencies in the approval process contradicted one another, lower officials were often in a quandary about whom they should listen to. Obviously, approval from the Council of Ministers had to be heeded, but this did not mean that it was free from errors or further interference from other organizations. The fact that some inspection agencies were subsets of the organs they were inspecting often impaired quality construction. For example, in the rebuilding years the chief municipal architect had authority over the local division of GASK just as the organ in charge of architectural affairs did at the oblast, republic, and all-Union levels. The contradiction was as obvious to most contemporaries as it is to us today: the ability to objectively inspect the work of one's superior is quite limited. Granted, the culture of criticism and self-criticism allowed for an underling to criticize a superior often without repercussion, but many still realized that to control effectively the quality of construction, these two had to be separated.

---

88. GARF, f. 5446, op. 7, d. 2250, l. 179.
89. GARF f. 5446, op. 51, d. 3108, l. 1.

The example of postwar urban replanning for Sevastopol directly challenges notions of top-down rule in the USSR. Various new local officials from Leningrad, Bashkiriia, and other places advocated for their new neighbors against Moscow. Residents complained and offered suggestions on matters from architecture to public safety and health. Pulled by their professional ethos, their own experience of living in the rubble, or even a desire to get ahead, newly arrived officials living in Sevastopol questioned and undermined the plans of the central authorities in a period generally seen as one of the most repressive in the Stalin era.

3

ACCOMMODATION

Bringing Life to the Rubble

After distorting the history of Soviet architecture for 30 years, after giving a formalistic analysis of the creation of the Soviet masters of architecture, Arkin in this [encyclopedia] article disorients the readers' understanding of the basic problems of Soviet architecture. He does not reveal its ideological and artistic content, its basic idea—the Stalinist concern for the individual.

A. Peremyslov, "Ideolog' kosmopolitizma v arkhitekture D. Arkina."

In 1949, at the height of the anticosmopolitan campaign, the prominent historian, architect, and professor David Arkin endured scathing attacks in closed meetings and official publications for not correctly noting that the main idea of three decades of Soviet architecture was the "Stalinist concern for the individual." More than just another attack on an intellectual, it also was a reaffirmation of one of the key symbols of postwar reconstruction: building for people. The term *zabota* (care or concern), often joined with a reference to Stalin, was ubiquitous in the Soviet press after World War II, no less so than in discussions of the massive urban reconstruction projects made necessary by the devastating Nazi invasion in 1941. While it is specious to argue that Soviet architecture was driven purely by concern for the individual, it is also inaccurate to deny the central role of accommodation in Soviet urban planning. The previous chapter detailed the debates over Sevastopol's postwar development. But how were people living in the rubble while waiting for the new city to arise? Were they being accommodated, and if so, how and by whom?

The Soviet socialist experiment shared many traits with the modern democratic welfare state. Massive dislocations from war and economic destruction necessitated programs to improve standards of living but also to provide legitimacy and allegiance to the state.[1] The Soviet state's promises, set forth most explicitly in the 1936 Stalin Constitution, provided members of society with their needs and wants—from employment, education, and health care to pensions and leisure opportunities. The unspoken quid pro quo was quiescence from society. Those who followed the rules of the game would be rewarded; those perceived as violating the rules would be punished and forbidden access to the state's gifts. But the constitution was not the only form of zabota.[2] Bureaucrats and specialists had to turn dictates into practice. Accommodating the population's material needs, even when implementation was flawed, was essential in maintaining a focus on social ideals and the promised, but always elusive, glorious future. Failure to at least attempt to accommodate the population could have led to a backlash by various segments of society that felt emboldened by or angry about wartime sacrifices. As Stalin made clear in his 1948 telegram to Malenkov, he feared Sevastopol's residents might be angered by poor state provisioning.

The rebuilding process became essential to maintaining the image of a paternal state. Cities, groups, and individual members of society all benefited, although unequally, from the state's largesse. The abandonment of equality in the 1930s continued after World War II as the regime ranked cities and people based on their usefulness to the state. Equal pay had long since disappeared, rations varied by category of labor, and the cultural,

---

1. The literature on welfare states is vast, but for primers on a broad array of approaches and definitions see Gosta Esping-Andersen, *The Three Worlds of Welfare Capitalism* (Princeton: Princeton University Press, 1990); Amy Gutman, ed., *Democracy and the Welfare State* (Princeton: Princeton University Press, 1988); George Steinmetz, *Regulating the Social: The Welfare State and Local Politics in Imperial Germany* (Princeton: Princeton University Press, 1993); Richard Titmuss, *Essays on the Welfare State* (New Haven: Yale University Press, 1959). For Russia more specifically, see Chris Burton, "Medical Welfare during Late Stalinism: A Study of Doctors and the Soviet Health System, 1945–1953" (PhD diss., University of Chicago, 2000); Stephen Kotkin, "1991 and the Russian Revolution," *Journal of Modern History* 70 (June 1998): 384–425.

2. Numerous studies have looked at the various ways in which the Soviet regime sought to mollify the population and accommodate at least some of their consumer and leisure needs. See Dunham, *In Stalin's Time,* 15–19; Kotkin, *Magnetic Mountain,* 238–79; Nicholas Timasheff, *The Great Retreat: The Growth and Decline of Communism in Russia* (New York: Cambridge University Press, 1946), chap. 12; Zubkova, *Russia after the War,* 68–73; E. Iu. Zubkova, *Poslevoennoe sovetskoe obshchestvo: Politika i povsednevnost', 1945–1953* (Moscow: ROSSPEN, 1999).

technical, and political elite had far better housing and access to goods. Soviet planners treated cities much like people, putting the needs of important industrial and military cities like Sevastopol at the top. Moscow, of course, received most of the state's attention and resources. If something was available in the Soviet Union, one could find it in Moscow. Republic capitals were also high on the priority list. Cities at the epicenter of the USSR's state security, like Sevastopol or the scientific city of Akademgorodok, took on greater importance as the Cold War developed. As in non-authoritarian states, lobbying could persuade the regime to place greater relative value on a particular locale.

Just as local architects and planners wrested control of the general plan for reconstruction from the grip of Moscow functionaries in an effort to meet local needs, local bureaucrats and specialists remained the backbone of planning and provisioning work in Sevastopol. Members of Sevastopol's local government and bureaucracy were torn between their duties to the state and those to friends and neighbors living in squalor. Urban planners, architects, physicians, teachers, union leaders, and economists experienced a conflict between their professional ethics and the demands of the party and state. These groups became what historian Lynne Viola calls "hybrids" who were "caught between state and society" and who "became translators of policy, language, and needs" as they balanced their professional, political, and local selves.[3] Moreover, many of these groups had competing interests, which led to scapegoating as an "adaptive strategy" or "strategy of self-protection."[4]

In the postwar world in which entire cities remained leveled, local officials had to prioritize in order to maximize scarce resources for greatest benefit. Housing was the top priority in many cities where residents lived in whatever they could find or build for themselves. Most evacuees returned to find their homes destroyed; others fought to evict squatters from

---

3. Lynne Viola, introduction to *Contending with Stalinism: Soviet Power and Popular Resistance in the 1930s,* ed. Lynne Viola (Ithaca, NY: Cornell University Press, 2002), 12.

4. These terms come from Harris, "Resisting the Plan in the Urals, 1928–1956," in Viola, *Contending with Stalinism,* 202. He suggests that "resistance" may not be the correct term for officials who were blatantly insubordinate but were also committed Bolsheviks. Harris elaborates on these ideas in *The Great Urals,* 4–6, passim. Greta Bucher has also highlighted bureaucratic scapegoating and passing of responsibility in the provisioning of women. Bucher, *Women, the Bureaucracy and Daily Life in Postwar Moscow, 1945–1953,* 6–9.

their property.[5] Pressing also was the need for sanitation and epidemic prevention absent running water and sewage disposal. Public health required sanitation, medical care, and adequate food—the minimum to ensure a healthy working population. Beautification was a lower, but still important, priority. This showcased the achievements of the state in reconstruction but also provided at least the illusion—as many people apparently saw it—of a return to normalcy and even progress.[6] But housing, public health, and beautification were not mutually exclusive. A new park with its paths, benches, trees, and flowers served both as beautification and as a green space for exercise, relaxation, and recuperation. Ample and adequate housing, likewise, could present an appealing facade to passersby and provide the necessary size and facilities to prevent the spread of infections too common in overcrowded and poorly cleaned residences. The health, behavior, and education of the city's children became a more pressing problem as reconstruction commenced because a new city demanded a new generation of citizens willing and able to sacrifice for the Motherland.

Although repeated claims of improving residents' living standards often conflicted with reality, one must also note a conscious and repeated attempt to fulfill expectations at the local level. In the rubble of the Second World War, successful fulfillment of the plans left much to be desired as other pressing concerns diverted money, labor, and materials, all of which were in short supply. Many urban planners continued to pursue accommodation, and local residents and officials demanded the services the regime had promised. Municipal leaders attempted many forms of accommodation, with some successes and some failures, but the primary causes of failure were the lack of resources and focus combined with the unavoidable consequences of massive urban and industrial devastation during the war and the inefficiency of Soviet central planning.

---

5. On postwar problems of recovering property after returning from evacuation, see Rebecca Manley, "'Where Should We Resettle the Comrades Next?': The Adjudication of Housing Claims and the Construction of the Post-war Order," in Fürst, *Late Stalinist Russia,* 233–247.

6. Rather than the normalcy of a society in crisis, it appears that many if not most people expected less repression, an extension of the wartime relaxations, and some attention to material needs. See Mark Edele, "A 'Generation of Victors'? Soviet Second World War Veterans from Demobilization to Organization, 1941–1956" (PhD diss., University of Chicago, 2004), especially chap. 7; Christine Varga-Harris, "Constructing the Soviet Hearth: Home, Citizenship and Socialism in Russia, 1956–1964" (PhD diss., University of Illinois, 2005), 8–9; Zubkova, *Russia after the War,* chaps. 1 and 3.

Housing and Construction

As we have seen, Sevastopol's housing stock had been decimated and only seven half-destroyed buildings remained in the city center.[7] The question of a structure's habitability was debatable, but journalist Harrison Salisbury noted that the head of the city executive committee considered any building with three walls and a ceiling salvageable.[8] Only five hundred of fifteen thousand dwellings in Sevastopol met this definition, according to Soviet journalist and playwright Boris Voitekhov.[9] Thus, a small girl and what remained of her family had to find shelter in the vault of Gosbank, the only part of the building left standing (figure 4).[10] In a photograph outside the makeshift home, the girl's vacant stare with the rubble and laundry line as a backdrop illustrates well the hardships of the city's residents. Tamara Alëshina spoke of a "housing crisis [that] from year to year is aggravated," and she continued to lament Sevastopol's housing crisis in her correspondence for at least four years after liberation.[11] It was aggravated primarily because construction could not keep pace with the inflow of new workers. Alëshina became one of the most important specialists and local officials in advocating for more people-centered rebuilding.

Despite the obvious residential destruction, early Moscow-based planners of postwar Sevastopol cared little for housing issues and left most residents to rebuild on their own outside the city center. The housing phase of development started roughly five years later. For some, like a teenage Mikhail Mironov, it meant living in a cave with no water, sewer, or heat until 1956.[12] Lilia Korchinskaia, although living in the city center off of Lenin Street, suffered in the stale putrid air of a bombed-out house's subbasement with rodents and massive flies a constant reminder of her lack of sanitation.[13] While there was a sense of camaraderie in the workers' barracks

---

7. *Istoriia goroda-geroia Sevastopolia, 1917–1957,* 289–90; GAGS, f. R-359, op. 1, d. 10, l. 18.

8. Harrison Salisbury, *Russia on the Way* (New York: Macmillan, 1946), 317. A Union-wide definition of "habitable" remains elusive.

9. Voitekhov, *The Last Days of Sevastopol,* 105–6.

10. GARF, f. A-259, op. 7, d. 212, l. 14.

11. RGAE, f. 9432, op. 1, d. 241, l. 27; GAGS, f. R-308, op. 1, d. 68, l. 2; GAGS, f. R-359, op. 1, d. 7, l. 23.

12. Mikhail Mironov, interview by author, Sevastopol, Ukraine, 2004.

13. Lilia Korchinskaia, interview by author, Sevastopol, Ukraine, 2004.

Figure 4. Girl at Gosbank vault. GARF, f. A-259, op. 7, d. 212, l. 14. Reproduced with permission of Gosudarstvennyi arkhiv Rossiiskoi Federatsii, Moscow.

in the suburbs, Zoia Il'inichna remembers most the cold winter winds that ripped through the hastily constructed wooden barracks with tar-paper windows and wide gaps between the planks.[14] Shacks began to pop up in ravines throughout the city, drawing residents closer to stagnant pools of water and the epidemics that came from them. As late as 1951, seventy-five people on Soviet Street on the main central hill crowded into 150 square meters of damp, dark, and cold staircases and bathrooms in a destroyed building with water flowing from the walls.[15] Wherever one could find an unoccupied plot and a sufficient quantity of rough building materials, houses emerged.

A lack of adequate housing remained one of the few constants in the city, yet more and more people either came voluntarily or were "mobilized" to rebuild the hero-city. The war had devastated the labor force. Most new workers in Sevastopol found an unbearable life. Many of the mobilized

---

14. Zoia Il'inichna, interview by author, Sevastopol, Ukraine, 1997.
15. RGAE, f. 1562, op. 33, d. 404, ll. 3–10.

workers from Moldova and Ukraine were usually in such poor health that they constituted a liability. A commission of physicians suggested that it was better to return them rather than allow them to infect the population and compete for scarce resources. These young men and women had come from regions where food was scarce even before the 1946–47 famine. Their malnourished and undersized bodies were more susceptible to disease and not fit for hard labor, especially after several days' journey in cattle cars. Understaffed and overworked construction units simply refused to accommodate more of these recruits because the cost was greater than the benefit.[16]

Young laborers rarely stayed past their six-month training period, which led to a dearth of skilled construction workers and the need to continually mobilize and train new workers. These reinforcing problems of poor labor discipline and housing further delayed the city's recovery. With their new skills in hand and labor in short supply everywhere, few seemed to have worried a great deal that they were breaking the law by "willful quitting" without permission. Even as late as November 1953, after living conditions had improved greatly in the city center, a bank official reviewing high construction costs noted that in one construction trust 1,457 new workers arrived while 834 fled. Nearly twenty thousand work days had been lost in the first ten months of 1953. The official blamed low discipline, the great distance between housing and work, and low pay as the chief reasons for illegal flight. With scattered data from the various construction units in the city, it is difficult to be certain of the motivations for flight. Moreover, a willful departure was not necessarily a criminal one. That said, many were choosing to move elsewhere. The time and money put into training new workers often led to little production. Whether the labor flight was criminal or not, there was something of a revolving door on Sevastopol's work sites that surely made efficient and quality construction difficult. But little of this was unique to Sevastopol. As historian Donald Filtzer has shown, labor turnover and desertion remained high among young workers in high-priority sectors of the economy like mining, construction, and iron and steel production after World War II. Moreover, the judicial

---

16. GAGS, f. R-107, op. 1, d. 10, ll. 14–22a.

system often failed to prosecute labor violations and desertion, which likely emboldened other would-be deserters.[17]

With the repeated loss of labor and their workers housed in tents and underground shelters, many factory bosses, without permission, began building their own barracks, not waiting for Moscow to fulfill its promises. The city building inspector, who had to answer for any dangerous construction that was not up to code, began to level charges against construction that had not been planned and approved.[18] The chief city architect, realizing that workers' housing was essential, petitioned the procurator to ignore the building codes and not punish or prosecute illegal construction.[19] As late as 1950 city architects approved illegal wooden barracks over procurator objections because several factories needed living space.[20] The procurator ruled against or ignored the building inspectorate's complaints of illegal administrative buildings, cafeterias, and more. The judiciary also failed to punish construction trusts that stole stone from archaeological sites to use as building material.[21] Building inspectors had the obligation to report violations, but architects and factory bosses, keenly aware of conditions in Sevastopol, flouted the law in order to house workers and thus reduce their flight and the expense of training new workers. How much of the motivation was humanitarian and how much was a self-serving need to meet production targets is impossible to know with certainty. But the results were unmistakable. For a section of the population, life was made a bit easier because of local initiative, despite legal constraints. Caught between state demands and a society in need, each official had to negotiate a way through often competing interests.

With such a fluid labor pool, prisoners of war were the only constant in the early postwar years. Because they could not flee, construction trusts trained German, Romanian, and Japanese POWs. Prison labor was a better investment than the fluid domestic labor force. Although it is impossible

17. GAGS, f. R-359, op. 1, d. 201, ll. 78–88; Filtzer, *Soviet Workers and Late Stalinism,* chap. 5.

18. GARF, f. A-150, op. 2, d. 987, ll. 139–89; GAGS, f. R-308, op. 1, d. 71, l. 58.

19. GAGS, f. R-308, op. 1, d. 112, l. 58.

20. Ibid.

21. GAGS, f. R-308, op. 1, d. 25, l. 90; GAGS, f. R-308, op. 1, d. 64, ll. 1–20; GAGS, f. R-308, op. 1, d. 71, ll. 3–11. A deputy of the city council also charged the procurator for not acting against violations in food distribution. GAGS, f. R-79, op. 2, d. 111, ll. 38–42.

at this point to determine the precise number of POWs in Sevastopol from the available data, a 1945 report from one of the city's largest construction trusts, Sevastopolstroi, hinted at the prevalence of German labor. Nearly 2,900 workers in one department learned basic building skills, and 2,045 of them were POWs. Over one-third of those who received specialized training were also German soldiers.[22] In July 1945, Sevastopolstroi reported that POWs accounted for 87.6 percent of the work, and the next month it drafted a plan to add 20,000 more POWs from the sixteen camps in the city and its outskirts and throughout Crimea.[23] As Soviet demobilization and the repatriation of POWs changed labor dynamics, officials in Moscow finally began to realize that many citizens resented the presence of the enemy.[24] POWs consumed food and other goods and services that were diverted from Soviet citizens. In a future without a POW labor force, new domestic workers were essential. But domestic labor stability demanded adequate living conditions that need not be afforded to prisoners. This may have been a major factor in the massive reinvestment in the city's reconstruction in late 1948.

War veterans, who carried new clout after their victory and who often demanded what the constitution promised, had started some of the discussion about improved housing. However, it was not until the Council of Ministers and Stalin decided that the reconstruction of Sevastopol had to be completed quickly that real change began.[25] Much more money, resources, and labor poured into the city starting in late 1948. The increased tempo and scale of construction only further highlighted housing problems. Although the UVS had the authority to coordinate all ministries and building trusts with interests in the city, the Potemkin village of success

---

22. GAGS, f. R-182, op. 1, d. 78, l. 7.

23. GAGS, f. R-182, op. 1, d. 77, ll. 1–8. In five units, POWs fulfilled 139,099 "person-days" of a total 158,735. GAGS, f. R-182, op. 1, d. 79.

24. Numerous residents reported in interviews that they saw the POWs, the very people they were taught to hate during the war, working in relatively good conditions in the city center and could smell the food that was delivered to the camps in large trucks while residents were scrabbling meals together.

25. The resolution that sped up the reconstruction is still secret, but many documents make reference to it, including the notes to a draft resolution in RGAE, f. 9432, op. 1, d. 154, ll. 348–53ob.

continued to outpace reality despite new administration, long-awaited resources and labor, and an increased budget from Moscow.[26] The local media often tried to provide the best picture of worker housing, but complaints were too common to ignore.[27] Newspaper photos showed a factory training school (FZO) dorm with drapes, beds, pillows, blankets, nightstands with cloth covers, and large bouquets of flowers greeting some of the new workers. The reality behind the photo, however, was much different.[28] Just two months after the inviting photographs, workers in the same dorm complained in the main city newspaper about their inaccessible library without a librarian. The absence of nurses in the clinic made it equally useless. Moreover, in what was a consistent complaint in the postwar decade, they called the cafeteria food terrible and monotonous.[29] Other workers complained of not having a place to wash themselves, wash linens, or cook food.[30] The latter complaints also hint at reasons that epidemics appeared repeatedly in worker housing.

Two of the largest construction organizations also failed to build adequate housing. One investigation showed a need for major repairs to roofs, stoves, and more. The same barrack needed mattresses, hot water, and a good cleaning. The dorm of another construction organization saw "daily fights break out" in the women's dorms. "[F]ights, drunks, and others" were the norm.[31] Photographs were an attempt to convince the wider population that the regime was fulfilling claims of accommodation, but it could not convince the worker-students living in disorder who petitioned for actual attention to their needs.

Early in 1949 several residents from the Malakhov and Kulikovo settlements complained in newspapers and magazines that their housing still

---

26. It is important to realize that the decision for a new administration in Sevastopol occurred at the same time that many ministries were being reorganized. This could have been an attempt to bring greater efficiencies by taking decision making from various architectural organizations and placing power in the hands of an RSFSR administration with the authority to demand resources from ministries.

27. For an analysis of complaints to a Moscow newspaper regarding poor construction, see Christine Varga-Harris, "Green Is the Color of Hope? The Crumbling Facade of Postwar Byt through the Public Eyes of *Vechernaia Moskva*," *Canadian Journal of History* 34, no. 2 (1999): 193–219.

28. See *Slava Sevastopolia*, 7 December 1948, 1.

29. "Pis'ma trudiashchikhsia," *Slava Sevastopolia*, 11 February 1949, 1.

30. "Nam pishut: Ne sozdany elementarnye bytovye usloviia," *Slava Sevastopolia*, 10 December 1948, 2.

31. GAGS, f. R-79, op. 1, d. 63, ll. 62–63.

lacked electricity, regular water supply, radio service, mail delivery, and telephone connections and that laundry services poorly washed their linens.[32] In response, the city government created street committees to clean and repair new dorms in the absence of further assistance from the state.[33] Yet in 1951 a worker-student again noted that a dorm for new FZO graduates was "dirty and uncomfortable," not prepared for winter, and had no glass in the windows.[34] Because of the inefficiencies of the system, one also could not guarantee that construction would not be destroyed quickly after completion. In one case workers ripped up a new sidewalk in order to lay underground utilities. The workers simply left a gaping hole and the surrounding area littered with construction debris.[35]

Winter posed particular problems for residents because the state could not guarantee an adequate supply of heating fuel. Repeatedly, city officials had to organize collection campaigns, and they pleaded to higher officials and ministers for delivery of promised coal and wood. Most workers lived in shabby wooden barracks with large, uninsulated gaps between planks. With strong sea winds and no natural heating sources of its own, the city was completely at the mercy of the Soviet distribution network. City officials realized that they had insufficient transportation to gather the wood necessary to make it through the winter.[36] Because in some cases only 1 percent of expected deliveries arrived, heating in the city remained in a "catastrophic condition."[37] Two city leaders wrote that "hospitals, children's institutions, schools, communal enterprises, and the population" suffered from the state's neglect.[38] Providing examples of the state's failure to help the most helpless was an attempt to use shame to change behavior. The city government and party pleaded with the oblast for a mere two trucks and four horses.[39] Officials also contacted their counterparts in the city of Briansk directly with a plea from the "laborers of Sevastopol [who]

32. Report No. 11 from the city executive committee on a *Krokodil* article, "Pis'ma trudiashchikhsia," GAGS, f. R-79, op. 2, d. 156, ll. 114–28.

33. GAGS f. R-79, op. 2, d. 161, ll. 1–3.

34. "Pis'ma v redaktsiiu: Zabytoe obshchezhitie," *Slava Sevastopolia,* 31 January 1951, 3.

35. E. Krylova, "Na gorodskie temy: Navesti poriadok na ulitsakh goroda," *Slava Sevastopolia,* 30 January 1951, 3.

36. GAGS, f. R-359, op. 1, d. 4, l. 12.

37. GAGS, f. R-79, op. 2, d. 25, l. 32.

38. GAGS, f. R-359, op. 1, d. 45, l. 94.

39. GAGS, f. R-359, op. 1, d. 3, l. 8; GAGS, f. R-359, op. 1, d. 4, l. 22.

will be sincerely thankful" for timber.[40] Central planning and distribution had failed, so local officials had to beg for what the state had promised. Deficiencies in local resources forced dependence on a flawed distribution and transportation network stretched thin by the vast scale of destruction and rebuilding.

The decision to flee was likely easy for some workers. Local officials caught between the state's empty directives to provide scarce resources took matters into their own hands in an effort to heat the city and provide adequate worker housing. People knew that their lives were hard and also knew that the Soviet utopia had promised better. Local officials, living in the city's horrid conditions, intervened on residents' behalf for housing and heating because the city's continuing growth demanded that better living conditions be provided in order to retain a skilled workforce. Once central officials created expectations, residents from students to workers began to demand suitable living conditions. Local officials tried to accommodate some demands. Some local officials no doubt simply wanted to provide for their fellow residents. Others may have insisted that the promises of the past be fulfilled. Still others might have felt emboldened by the relative decentralization and relaxation of authority in the war years and sought to fill a perceived power vacuum. For their part, many specialists, local officials, and factory bosses, knowing that their personal and professional success depended on the well-being of the population, violated the law to provide for their constituents. But for some of their constituents the efforts were not enough to keep them in the war-ravaged city.

Although the postwar strategies of identification led to a remarkably re-silient urban biography into the twenty-first century, physical reconstruction was far from a perfect process. Why were there so many failures in the early years of planning and rebuilding? Repeated calls for more attention to the population's needs punctuated the postwar period, which, if nothing else, shows that plans did not ensure realization of them. As Peter Holquist has noted, "utopian planning and messy dysfunctional realization" were reinforcing.[41] Although it would be unfair to characterize Sevastopol's postwar planning as "utopian," it certainly was foolhardy and unrealistic

---

40. GAGS, f. R-359, op. 1, d. 27, l. 1.
41. Peter Holquist, "New Terrains and New Chronologies: The Interwar Period through the Lens of Population Politics," *Kritika* 4, no. 1 (Winter 2003): 171.

given the amount of damage and the state's industrial priorities. When overly ambitious plans could not be realized, they merely begot more planning. The idealism behind the postwar plans was inconsistent with the industrial potential of a nation ravaged by war. Central planning and the culture of directives actually did little to create efficient production. Beginning in the early 1930s, bosses employed theft, bribery, creative accounting, storming, and other measures to meet absurd production targets.[42] Plan fulfillment was little different in postwar Sevastopol.

War had ruined what little construction industry existed on the peninsula, and Sevastopol's location far from timber stands provided few inexpensive alternatives. Eventually, nearby stone quarries became a major source of materials, but extracting the stone involved a great expenditure of labor, time, and money. Only in the late 1940s with the advent of new methods of quarrying and shaping stone did solid and relatively high-quality construction begin on a large scale (figure 5). Until these breakthroughs Sevastopol was reliant on the vagaries of Soviet production and distribution and therefore had little control over production targets. The war had simply created too much destruction. In Germany and Japan, where urban destruction was also extensive, reconstruction took decades. Moreover, the Soviet Union's rejection of Marshall Plan aid forced planners to make do with the limited resources produced by a destroyed industrial sector. No other country lost as many laborers as the Soviet Union, and after repatriation of war prisoners back to Germany the USSR faced a crisis in trained building specialists. While training schools churned out young men and women for construction brigades, their skills were nearly as bad as the materials with which they worked. Therefore, it is amazing that within a decade Sevastopol's central regions were more or less restored, leaving only the outskirts in perilous conditions.

Individual initiative both benefited and hindered rebuilding. Sevastopol's position at the end of the rail line led to theft of building materials as they passed through other destroyed and desperate cities.[43] Residents also raided construction sites in order to procure scarce building materials for their homes when it appeared that Moscow had little intention of

---

42. This is brilliantly illustrated in the memoirs of Gennady Andreev-Khomiakov, *Bitter Waters: Life and Work in Stalin's Russia,* trans. Ann E. Healy (Boulder: Westview, 1997).

43. GAGS, f. R-79, op. 1, d. 63, ll. 107–13; GAGS, f. R-79, op. 2, d. 63, l. 84.

Figure 5. Reconstruction on Nakhimov Prospect. Reprinted with permission of the State Archive of the City of Sevastopol. Photograph 3258.

rebuilding housing before industry.[44] Willful rebuilding clearly disrupted planned construction elsewhere and created unintended ripple effects. Most residents outside the city center were left to build or rebuild their residences on their own. But they had little access to new brick, stone, and mortar. In the periphery, people resorted to the rubble of their homes or the ruins of ancient architectural sites to rebuild their lives. Building materials regularly disappeared from work sites and storehouses. Despite repeated attempts by local and central officials to halt the ravaging of historical treasures, like the ruins of ancient fortresses and churches, the need for building materials trumped the preservation of national landmarks.[45] The relationship between preservation and progress generated tensions as different segments of society attempted to fulfill their needs. As in much of

44. GAGS, f. R-79, op. 2, d. 339, ll. 92–93.
45. Theft was common from Khersones and Inkerman Monastery. GARF, A-150, op. 2, d. 186, l. 45; GAGS, f. R-308, op. 1, d. 57, ll. 4–5; GAGS, f. R-308, op. 1, d. 108, ll. 4–5; GAGS, f. R-308, op. 1, d. 64, ll. 1–20; "Pis'ma v redaktsiiu: Zabytoe obshchezhitie," *Slava Sevastopolia,* 31 January 1951, 3.

the 1930s, competition for scarce resources trumped the alleged efficiencies of central planning.

Carelessness in maintenance and a lack of well-informed planning threatened fulfillment of grand plans to restore and improve living standards. Reality simply did not match planning, mostly because central planners were ignorant of local conditions. As noted above, some central officials still wanted wooden construction in a city that had no wood. If those in charge of approving and overseeing plans had no idea what Sevastopol was up against, then how could reconstruction proceed smoothly? Repeated reports by the city construction inspectorate showed that insufficient staffing in design and inspection organizations, little supervision on the work sites, workers trained too hastily, and poor-quality construction materials thwarted an earnest desire to aid the population.[46]

Public Health: Disease, Medical Care, and the Food Supply

With such an appalling housing crisis and a destroyed sanitation network, the explosion in infectious diseases could have been surprising to few in a city that grew more crowded by the day. For years after liberation, human feces floated in Artillery Bay by the city's premier park.[47] The city sanitation inspector declared in 1946 that "Sevastopol Bay is one of the best in Europe...[but] fecal water continues to flow into it." Much of this, he claimed, came from the outdated sewer system built in 1912 and "special enterprises" throwing their waste on beaches to the tune of 7,000 cubic meters per day. Citing "special enterprises" was an indirect way to blame the navy for polluting. The inspector blamed the wholly unsanitary condition of the "places of mass swimming for the population and Red Fleet" for gastrointestinal illnesses.[48]

Overcrowding became a serious problem as the rapidly increasing postwar population overloaded meager municipal services. Statistical planners had estimated that a person needed an average of 9 square meters of living

---

46. For examples see GAGS, f. R-308, op. 1, d. 107, ll. 16–18; GAGS, f. R-79, op. 2, d. 221, l. 26; GARF, f. A-259, op. 6, d. 6563, l. 4.

47. GAGS, f. R-359, op. 1, d. 4, ll. 32–39ob.

48. GAGS, f. R-59, op. 1, d. 65, ll. 10–12.

space to prevent excess residential density and the accumulation of waste and spread of disease.[49] Still, by March 1948, the sanitation norm in Sevastopol stood at 3 square meters below what was considered healthy, and people continued to live in makeshift housing that counted toward quantitative measures but provided far from a good quality of life.[50] With no city services in these areas, the inevitable result was recurring and devastating public health problems. Even senior naval officers had to live with their families in basements with no running water or toilets.[51]

In early July 1944 the city's chief sanitation inspector noted multiple causes of the high infection rates and issued temporary measures to curb further outbreaks. An antiepidemic commission organized cleaning campaigns on a weekly or monthly basis, but with a lack of waste receptacles and vehicles to haul away trash and sewage, it was difficult to make headway. The absence of a functioning bathhouse by early July forced residents to shower at the distant Polyclinic No. 2 or the disinfecting station (*dezostantsiia*). Dormitories lacked showers; barbers needed disinfectants and a place to work; and potable water averaged only 7–8 liters per person per day. Food service, the sanitation inspector noted, was little better. Servers lacked proper clothing and worked in completely unsanitary serving areas with dirt floors and unfinished walls. Because the chief inspector had only four assistants instead of the nine he considered the absolute minimum for effective control of outbreaks, the problems indeed may have been much worse than the report stated. Too few coworkers meant that sanitation inspectors failed to identify violations and effectively enforce sanitation codes.[52] These conditions were especially frustrating for health specialists because their professional culture demanded attention to the public's

---

49. The so-called sanitation norm varied between 6 and 9 square meters of living space per person. See Alfred John Dimaio, Jr., *Soviet Urban Housing: Problems and Policies* (New York: Praeger, 1974) for the best study of housing policy in the three decades after the war. See also the most important technical planner, Ia. P. Levchenko, "Gorodskaia cherta i general'nyi plan," *Problemy sovetskogo gradostroitel'stva* 2 (1949): 53–56; "Zonirovanie gorodov po kharakteru zastroiki," *Problemy sovetskogo gradostroitel'stva* 1 (1947): 18–23; and two of his chief planning guides, *Planirovka gorodov: Tekhniko-ekonomicheskie pokazateli i rascheti* (Moscow: Gosudarstvennoe izdatel'stvo literatury po stroitel'stvu i arkhitekture, 1952); and *Tekhniko-ekonomicheskie osnovy planirovki poselkov* (Moscow: Izdatel'stvo Akademii Arkhitektury SSSR, 1944).

50. RGAE, f. 9432, op. 1, d. 241, ll. 26–35; GAGS, f. R-308, op. 1, d. 68, ll. 1–4.

51. Korchinskaia, interview.

52. GAGS, f. R-359, op. 1, d. 7, ll. 3–5ob.

needs, even when the state failed to provide resources adequate for even minimal health standards.

With all these shortcomings in a city ravaged by war, the list of maladies was initially surprisingly small: one case of typhus, fifty-seven of dysentery, sixty of influenza, one of whooping cough, fifty-three of malaria, and one of erysipelas.[53] Not surprisingly, most cases of dysentery and typhus (common ailments of overcrowding) were found in workers' dorms—yet another factor in labor turnover.[54] A year later, in 1945, living conditions were little better, and local officials began to point to substandard housing as the cause of many outbreaks. At least one of the dormitories of the municipal construction trust had mildewed mattresses and few linens, trash piled high, and a cafeteria in the basement with earthen floors and unplastered walls.[55] The problems were clear: not enough doctors, hospital beds, trash trucks, linens, soap, and more; but since most of the European part of the USSR remained in shambles, the regime simply could not meet these goals in the short term, even if it wanted to.[56]

With the end of the war and the beginning of demobilization, the population rose rapidly (see table 1 in chapter 1) and the health crisis became more acute despite improvements in the health care infrastructure by the end of 1946. With more hospital beds, a new birthing center and nurseries, and more specialization in tuberculosis, trauma, and cancer, Sevastopol appeared to be on the verge of recovery. The rate of natural population growth rose in one year from 1.8 percent to 2.8 percent.[57] Although these data could indicate improvement, it is clear that many problems had not yet been overcome. Hospitals remained filthy with no soap for either hands or linens. In the winter, Hospital No. 1 often lacked heat and food other

53. Ibid. We do not have clear statistics on population for this time in July 1944. We know that 10,787 people had registered in the city by 20 May 1944 and that by year's end the population reached 38,783. GAGS, f. R-59, op. 1, d. 65, l. 12. This means that cases of typhus, whooping cough, and erysipelas were between 0.93 and 0.26 per ten thousand. Instances of dysentery were between 53/10,000 and 15/10,000; influenza between 56/10,000 and 15/10,000; and malaria between 49/10,000 and 14/10,000.

54. GAGS, f. R-79, op. 2, d. 17, ll. 10–12.

55. Ibid., ll. 14–14ob.

56. On the problems identified in 1944–45 see GAGS, f. R-79, op. 2, d. 17, ll. 1–10ob; GAGS, f. R-79, op. 2, d. 35, l. 10; GAGS, f. R-79, op. 2, d. 26, ll. 44–51ob; GAGS, f. R-359, op. 1, d. 4, l. 26.

57. Considering that new arrivals in the city were mostly in their teens or early twenties, these data hardly seem to say much about health care, but they do indicate a demographic shift to the young, who were less likely to die and were still able to have children.

than abundant fish. The poor quality and quantity of dairy products also threatened the health of small children, who were desperate for calcium, fat, and calories to fuel proper development.[58]

Local medical professionals remained publicly active in fighting the spread of communicable diseases, just as architects, planners, and factory bosses tried to solve the housing shortage.[59] Even though there were just under one hundred physicians in the city, during one year they provided more than 2,300 lectures, 5,800 mass discussions, seven radio lectures, and eight newspaper articles. Factory workers, city employees, schoolchildren, collective farm workers, and training school students comprised the main audiences. Whether this public outreach was the catalyst or not, the spread of many diseases fell dramatically. All forms of typhus decreased between 1945 and 1946. Meningitis and whooping cough also became less frequent. The most dramatic drop, however, came in the number of new malaria cases (85.1/10,000 to 19.8/10,000) (table 4). Inoculations against typhus, increased use of quarantines, and the development of a malaria station all likely helped to slow the spread of certain infections.

Despite these respectable gains, other epidemics that were more difficult to combat continued. Tuberculosis remained out of control with over 2,500 infected residents, of whom 52 died in 1946 alone (including 3 children). Dysentery, scarlet fever, and measles raged. Cases of dysentery increased by nearly ten times in 1946 (about seven times as a percentage of the population) and cases of both scarlet fever and measles doubled.[60] Crowded living spaces, vast amounts of untreated water, filthy linens, and waste (human and other) littering the streets and bays made these epidemics unavoidable. The crush of a postwar population boom dramatically affected the city's health. Each additional person led to more overcrowding and waste and consumed more of the limited food and health care. Unfortunately, the increases in population and waste were not immediately met

---

58. GAGS, f. R-79, op. 2, d. 37, ll. 113–34.

59. For more on the structure and changes of the postwar medical community in the USSR, see Burton, "Medical Welfare during Late Stalinism," especially chap. 2.

60. GAGS, f. R-79, op. 2, d. 37, ll. 113–34. Measles and scarlet fever likely increased with the return and birth of children, who were the victims and vectors of these diseases. Statistics for dysentery are likely inaccurate given the possibility of misdiagnosing a host of gastrointestinal illnesses that present similarly. With trained personnel and good equipment lacking in the earlier years, we cannot guarantee the accuracy of diagnoses.

TABLE 4. Disease data for Sevastopol, 1944–47

Disease	1944		1945		1946		1947	
	Cases	Cases/10,000 population	Cases	Cases/10,000 population	Cases	Cases/10,000 population	Cases	Cases/10,000 population
Typhus	81		26	4.8	3	0.43	42	5.4
Relapsing fever			25	4.6	0	0	16	2.1
Typhoid fever			138	25.4	136	19.4	101	12.9
Paratyphoid	15	3.9	1	0.2	21	3.0	12	1.5
Dysentery	146	37.6	36	6.6	322	46.0	353	45.3
Scarlet fever	4	1.0	61	11.2	135	19.3	108	13.8
Diphtheria	32	8.3	65	12.0	63	9.0	93	12.0
Meningitis			19	3.5	11	1.6	8	1.0
Measles	215	55.4	138	25.4	359	51.2	29	3.7
Chicken pox			28	5.2	47	6.7	148	19.0
Whooping cough			23	4.2	3	0.4	332	42.6
Mumps			168	30.9	144	20.6	44	5.6
Malaria	3,227	832.1			2,530	361.1		
Influenza			462	85.1	139	19.8		
Toxic dyspepsia	235	60.6					74	9.5
Tuberculosis								

Sources: GAGS, f. R-59, op. 1, d. 12, ll. 1–17 (1944). In the data for 1944, the 81 cases of typhus actually includes relapsing fever and typhoid fever. Malaria data for 1944 include all cases. Data from the other years count only new cases of malaria contracted in a given year. GAGS, f. R-79, op. 2, c. 37, ll. 113–34 (1945–46); GAGS, f. R-59, op. 1, d. 97, l. 4 (1947).

with an increase in the number of trash cans and sanitation vehicles. Municipal authorities repeatedly complained that construction, consumer, and human waste remained on the streets because there were too few vehicles and horse carts to manage it all.[61]

For local officials and specialists, the need to fight these problems was obvious if not quickly attainable. The state's demands for more workers and faster rebuilding dramatically affected society. It fell to local officials to figure out how to ameliorate the worst problems. Because short-term housing improvement was impossible and a shortage of machinery left trash and sewage on the streets for long periods of time, city administrators imposed drastic measures in order to combat persistent maladies. In addition to the citywide cleaning campaigns in the spring and throughout the year, four new Pioneer camps opened with the goal of giving children time out of the unsanitary city. At the upriver camps water was cleaner and more abundant. Each child had a weekly shower plus many swimming opportunities. Clean linens every week and adequate quantities and quality of food were the norm in all but the fleet's camp.[62] What was common practice throughout the USSR in the summer months meant survival for Sevastopol's children.

Although all children were subject to Pioneer activities, the focus on strengthening the health of the children was paramount.[63] A 1949 outbreak of scarlet fever closed the city's schools and led to the disinfection of all books at the children's library.[64] Inoculations against typhus and dysentery for all residents over eight years old started in earnest in 1947, but it must have failed because in 1949 the city government issued new measures for cleaning dorms and linen in order to prevent the further spread of typhus.[65] Moreover, the regime invested resources in a dysentery vaccine that was

61. See GAGS, f. R-359, op. 1, d. 7, ll. 3–5ob; GAGS, f. R-359, op. 1, d. 4, ll. 32–39ob; GAGS, f. R-79, op. 2, d. 156, ll. 135–40; GAGS, f. R-308, op. 1, d. 128, l. 62.

62. GAGS, f. R-79, op. 2, d. 13, l. 103.

63. GAGS, f. R-79, op. 2, d. 63, ll. 64–65ob.

64. GAGS, f. R-79, op. 2, d. 158, l. 107. The exact dimensions of this outbreak are unclear. The same report shows 256 of the city's 12,010 students had scarlet fever and 456 people were hospitalized with it. This means that at least 200 non-school-age people (most likely young children) had been hospitalized. With the 1949 population at almost 10,000, the number of hospitalized cases was over four times higher than the total number of cases in 1947. GAGS, f. R-59, op. 1, d. 154, ll. 40, 49.

65. GAGS, f. R-79, op. 2, d. 77, ll. 72–76; GAGS, f. R-79, op. 2, d. 157, ll. 67–71.

completely ineffective. As populations shifted during the 1946–47 famine and more workers migrated to Sevastopol, many likely carried lice with them. One report noted that the notoriously ill Moldovan workers were selling their linens, thus likely spreading infection further. The same year, 1947, the city's only functioning banya temporarily closed because it lacked fuel and electricity.[66] A rabies outbreak led the city government to demand again a registration of all dogs and a quarantine for all service dogs that might have been infected.[67] As rabies continued, the city organized hunting parties to shoot stray dogs and cats and offered a bounty for each hide.[68] Plague in the nearby Kacha region in 1949–50 led to two-month quarantines, disinfections, and the distribution of special clothes and gloves to swine husbandmen.[69] Despite the efforts of municipal and medical personnel, they could not fully overcome the disease created by the near complete destruction.

Even normal medical care remained difficult because the quality and quantity of hospitals and clinics remained poor, and some regions of the city remained without medical facilities for many years. Except for the two horses of Hospital No. 2, there was still no ambulance service for several years, despite three ambulance centers.[70] This deficiency was not lost on city residents. One naval senior lieutenant complained of the numerous cars that had passed a pregnant woman, a man on crutches, and a sick woman walking along the side of the road. The commander of the Black Sea Fleet later issued an order that demanded the creation of fixed-route transportation (*marshrutki*) and that obligated citizens and sailors to pick up passengers.[71]

In addition to the scarcity of transportation, a lack of the most basic equipment, like X-ray machines, made diagnoses of some ailments impossible.[72] The physical condition of many hospitals and clinics was so poor that one's health could actually deteriorate during treatment. The surgical wing of the main city hospital had a leaky roof and exposed wiring, which

---

66. GAGS, f. R-59, op. 1, d. 97, ll. 1–20.
67. GAGS, f. R-79, op. 2, d. 220, l. 206.
68. GAGS, f. R-79, op. 2, d. 339, ll. 311–13.
69. GAGS, f. R-79, op. 2, d. 220, l. 39.
70. GAGS, f. R-79, op. 2, d. 37, l. 122.
71. GAGS, f. R-79, op. 2, d. 31, l. 54.
72. GAGS, f. R-359, op. 1, d. 49, l. 11. The X-ray machine likely arrived soon after the report was issued because a new directive in the city required food handlers and barbers to have a chest X-ray to detect tuberculosis. GAGS, f. R-79, op. 2, d. 112, ll. 11–18.

the chief surgeon feared would lead to electrocutions.[73] Also, because of a lack of habitable buildings in the first years after the war, the Sechenov Institute of Physical Therapy, which had sustained heavy damage, served simultaneously as an infectious disease clinic, squatters' camp, and home to a motorcycle club. The tubercular patients were free to roam the beach outside the institute side by side with the healthy population.[74] When repairs began in the early 1950s, workers found unexploded ordnance throughout the building.[75] Without adequate state resources, local officials had to improvise and utilize even the most dangerous structures for housing and health care. The inability to treat and properly quarantine the highly contagious remained a constant worry and surely spread epidemics further.

Poor nutrition was likely a key factor in the susceptibility to infection and the inability to fight it. As was common throughout the Soviet period, food (or more specifically the lack thereof) generated a great deal of attention from the regime and the population. Access to a variety of foods with adequate vitamins and minerals was paramount to survival in the rubble. As was common throughout the Soviet period, the regime and population continuously discussed problems of food scarcity.[76] In the postwar period the vagaries of Soviet collective farming, which gave way during the war, combined a dearth of rural labor and draught animals, fields littered with war wreckage, and a hoarding mentality as peasants feared another war.[77] Although war casualties greatly reduced the number of consumers, the devastation to much of the food-growing and manufacturing sectors of the economy meant continued pressure on per capita consumption. For Sevastopol, which lacked many of its own food resources, providing adequate nutrition for labor and health remained difficult. Longtime residents returned to the city and were more likely to endure the suffering, although

73. GAGS, f. R-79, op. 2, d. 341, l. 81.

74. GAGS, f. R-79, op. 2, d. 219, ll. 46–54.

75. S. D. Almazova, "Etazh i liudi," in *Vozrozhdenie Sevastopolia: Sbornik,* comp. Vera Kuzmina (Simferopol: Tavriia, 1982), 93–105.

76. See, for example, N. Pogodin, "Planirovka Stalingrada," *Arkhitektura i stroitel'stvo* 6 (1944): 2; Vladimir Semenov, interview by author, Sevastopol, Ukraine, 2004; "Segodnia."

77. Timothy Johnston discusses the rumors of war and subsequent hoarding in his unpublished paper "Oral News: Wars and Rumours of Wars in the Soviet Union, 1945–1947." A version of this paper appeared as "Subversive Tales? War Rumours in the Soviet Union 1945–1947," in Fürst, *Late Stalinist Russia,* 62–78.

grudgingly. But young laborers who were so vital to rebuilding Sevastopol moved fluidly in and out of the city. Therefore, food supply, like housing, was imperative not only to meet the promises of the regime's social contract but also as an agitational tool to retain much-needed labor for the city's resurrection.

As with construction materials and heating supplies, Sevastopol also lacked its own food resources, and what it could provide was often substandard. Complaints about the accessibility, quality, and assortment of foodstuffs in local shops and markets remained consistent throughout Sevastopol's first postwar decade.[78] The city sanitation inspection report for 1946 shows that 2.5 years after liberation, problems persisted. The inspector did not mince words when he reported that "morbidity is connected with the violations in feeding of the population."[79] Much of the blame fell on the military, which he said needed greater regulation because the food it judged as waste and therefore unfit for sailors and soldiers was passed on to the central market, where it was then "sold from hand to hand." In addition to the rotten salt beef and fish, the inspector noted the high rate of gastrointestinal problems originating from spoiled sausage, "Bulgarian" vodka, vodka "chacha," and denatured alcohol. The city's fly problem, especially in restaurants and markets, spread diseases farther.

From production to distribution, quality control was lax. The inspector cited numerous problems in the central bread factory that turned out adulterated bread. Pollution from traffic on adjacent Gogol Street and the open mixing process that continued while the factory was under reconstruction both contributed to unhealthy production. Earlier, blowing sand had been a problem until the factory planted trees as a windbreak. Rodents and cockroaches were everywhere, and "military organizations serve[d] as a bad example for civilian organizations" by transporting bread in open trucks (which quite possibly also conveyed waste) down filthy roads and by passing it from person to person without gloves.

Other food production facilities fared little better. At the main meat-processing plant, flies overran the facility during the hot summer months. Workers threw carcasses and other animal waste in the city sewer system without any treatment and thus perpetuated the already dangerous

78. GAGS, f. R-79, op. 2, d. 111, ll. 219–25.
79. GAGS, f. R-59, op. 1, d. 65, l. 33.

manifestations of waterborne diseases. Many of these same workers became disease carriers because they lacked proper clothing from gloves and smocks to hats and boots. The location of the processing plant in the city center made its wretched conditions even worse and likely contributed to mass infections of the surrounding population. Of all the sausage samples inspected in 1946, inspectors deemed 80 percent to be rotten. Eggs, caviar, fish, cheese, ice cream, flour, and even chocolate candy were inspected and destroyed. He suggested that about 13,000 kilograms of bread and fish, 100 kilograms of fresh meat, seven hundred tins of meat, and two tons of curds were contaminated. When edible food arrived in one of the city's sixty-nine cafeterias, it quickly spoiled because only eighteen of them had refrigeration. Throughout these facilities the inspectors found a lack of ventilation, natural lighting, showers, and other hygiene areas and an overabundance of trash and production waste littering the grounds.[80]

Despite quarterly reports and numerous resolutions, it seems that little improved over the next six years. Over 3,400 people were hospitalized with "severe gastrointestinal" problems in 1951.[81] In 1952 the sanitation inspectorate forwarded to the procurator charges against the meatpacking plant for not completing its new slaughterhouse and smoking room. Walls and floors went uncleaned, and the meat hooks were rusted. Most alarming, workers continued to dispose of raw sewage in the bay and threw bones in the courtyard for wandering cats and dogs that could then spread disease to the human population.[82]

Even with a horrid food supply, as major holidays approached, the city administration used special food distribution to improve temporary living standards "for Sevastopol's laborers."[83] Ice cream, beer, kvass, cider, bread, sausage, pirozhki, fruit, and more flooded distribution points throughout the city.[84] Although the practice was not unique to Sevastopol or the postwar period, local officials made sure to provide well at key times of celebration. During holidays that celebrated the regime, its leaders, and its past, people were able to procure at least some common food luxuries. This policy

---

80. GAGS, f. R-59, op. 1, d. 65, ll. 1–44.

81. GAGS, f. R-59, op. 1, d. 238, ll. 2–41.

82. GAGS, f. R-59, op. 1, d. 264, ll. 1–12.

83. GAGS, f. R-79, op. 2, d. 112, ll. 179–92; GAGS, f. R-79, op. 2, d. 157, ll. 73–80. Quote at GAGS, f. R-79, op. 2, d. 112, ll. 58–66.

84. GAGS, f. R-79, op. 2, d. 60, ll. 37–38.

presented the USSR as a land of prosperity and plenty. But the swings of plenty and hunger, not too unfamiliar from the feast and fasting of Orthodoxy, did little to promote good health. Rather, it appears that food distribution was often merely another tool wielded to gain support from a beleaguered population. Most residents likely saw through this ploy but accepted the temporary improvements anyway. One has to wonder, however, whether the staccato approach to food distribution did more harm than good by showing what was possible and then withholding the treats for most of the year.

Although the 1946–47 famine was exceptional in the postwar period, people had become accustomed to harsh living conditions and a lack of food.[85] As some long-term residents remembered, access to fish and Black Sea dolphin made the famine period more tolerable in Sevastopol than in other regions where people suffered so terribly.[86] Although the 1947 famine caused urban birth rates to fall in 1948 and then recover in 1949, births per capita actually increased in Sevastopol in 1948. The access to fish and dolphin may have lessened the famine and therefore allowed couples to continue adding to their families. However, significantly elevated infant mortality during the famine years suggests that even if dolphin helped, vulnerable infants still lacked necessary nourishment (table 5). Rural infant mortality in Crimea was roughly half as high as in cities, which suggests that there was a relatively better diet in the countryside.

City administrators took the initiative in drawing agricultural goods to Sevastopol to improve food distribution. Some of the measures included cleaning the marketplace, improving its security, adding a new warehouse, providing transportation and hotel space, and eventually building a new central market with refrigeration, running water, and more.[87] Local leaders sought to improve not only food procurement but also its distribution throughout the city and thereby to accommodate the needs of more of the population.

---

85. On the famine elsewhere, see Michael Ellman, "The 1947 Soviet Famine and the Entitlement Approach to Famines," *Cambridge Journal of Economics* 24, no. 5 (September 2000): 603–30; Filtzer, "Soviet Workers and Late Stalinism," chap. 4; V. F. Zima, *Golod v SSSR 1946–1947 godov: Proiskhozhdenie i posledstviia* (Moscow: Institut Rossiiskoi istorii, 1996).

86. Il'inichna, Mironov, Semenov, interviews.

87. GAGS, f. R-79, op. 2, d. 339, ll. 77–78.

TABLE 5. Infant mortality in Crimea (percentage of total births)

Year	Crimean Oblast (%)	Urban areas (%)	Sevastopol (%)
1946	7.40	9.06	
1947	13.8	18.8	15.2
1948	5.4	6.4	5.1
1949	5.94	6.29	7.38
1950	6.17	6.73	7.85

Sources: GARF, f. A-482, op. 52s, d. 244, l. 232 (1946–48); RGAE, f. 1562, op. 323, d. 2648, l. 211; d. 3157, l. 29; d. 3807, l. 26; d. 4703, l. 183 (1949–50). My thanks to Donald Filtzer for bringing these data to my attention.

Despite years of complaints and petitions from Sevastopol, much of the improvement in public health, as in housing and construction, began with the restructuring and intensification after Stalin's late-1948 order to complete the city's rebuilding in three to four years. Sevastopol was able to build more hospitals, acquire more trash vehicles, provide running water and sewers to many residences, and construct more public bathhouses. However, rapid population increases offset many of these gains. Overcrowding continued, as did the construction of individual residences without facilities.[88] This meant that epidemics continued, but at a less alarming rate. Although we lack clear and comprehensive statistics on infectious diseases in Sevastopol, the fact that only tuberculosis remained a constant topic of discussion suggests that many of the other maladies had become better controlled as housing became less crowded, access to showers and potable water improved, and the population became educated about sanitation and other preventative measures. But even in 1949 and 1950 infant mortality in the city remained a full percentage point higher than the oblast urban average. In the four years between liberation and Stalin's decree on rebuilding the city, local officials and physicians implemented a patchwork program for the local population's health with minimal state resources. Their reports to Moscow consistently showed a city in turmoil.

---

88. Sixty years after the war there was a region near the municipal stadium, disparagingly called "Shanghai," that was still serviced by outhouses.

Beautification, Leisure, and Entertainment

As is easy to see from the discussions of housing and public health, Sevastopol's residents needed something pretty to take their minds off their miserable living conditions. German and Soviet forces had destroyed not only homes but also most of the places of leisure and entertainment like theaters, cinemas, and parks. After a devastating and exhausting war, most people hoped for a few minutes of peace and perhaps some entertainment to escape into a forgotten life. To this end, local urban planners, most often with the encouragement and aid of the local population, sought to rebuild and improve on the network of entertainment and leisure opportunities in the city. *Blagoustroistvo* (the improvement of public services from utilities to transportation to street lights) and *ozelenenie* (greening the city with trees, shrubs, and flowers) served as the foundation of beautification efforts. In many ways blagoustroistvo went hand in hand with improvements in housing stock and sanitation. Water and sewer systems were key to maintaining sanitation and health. But other forms of blagoustroistvo offered aesthetic pleasure and converged with ozelenenie. Tree-lined streets and boulevards provided a much-needed sense of life in a city that had been without meaningful life for so long. Moreover, in a southern seaside city, trees would provide shade in the hot summers and protection from wind and sand the year round. The restoration of 74 hectares, and construction of another 22 hectares, of tree-lined boulevards, parks, and even cemeteries provided natural beauty in a built environment.

Although most people think of green space as a system of parks, it can be more functional. Cemeteries counted as green space in the Soviet system because they were places where people could gather amid nature and receive the health benefits of being outside direct contact with the pollution of the city. The two most prominent green spaces in Sevastopol's center, however, were boulevards: Primorskii and Historical. Both had existed before the revolution as gathering places, particularly on special occasions and for the habitual evening stroll. Primorskii Boulevard, situated at the junction of two bays, served as the traditional place for rest and relaxation in the city long before the Bolshevik Revolution. Although initially reserved for fleet officers and the city's affluent members, it was liberated after the revolution for the use of all. The focal point was the Sechenov Institute, which soon after reconstruction in the 1950s became the House of Pioneers. The facade of the new Lunacharskii Theater closely resembled that of the magnificent neoclassical institute. The broad walking paths provided a venue for painters, holiday performances, and a summer theater. Connected as it was to leisure before the war, preservation of this green space had great importance for local planners and citizens. In short, people fighting for the traditions of the city began to use Moscow's rhetoric of concern and attention to local traditions for their own ends in creating leisure opportunities and preserving tradition.

Although the city center became stunningly beautiful during this period, much of it remained a facade. First, the beauty was not, for the most part, extended to the city's other regions. Construction in the city center was the priority from the beginning. Despite the fact that the first postwar planner, prominent Moscow architect Grigorii Barkhin, had lost his job because of charges of "facadism," administrators in Moscow and Sevastopol insisted that construction groups complete ring-road projects in time for holidays, election campaigns, and other important dates when there would also be abundant food available. The photographs of the progress could then be broadcast via newspapers to the rest of the Soviet Union. Concentrated and efficient construction of a network of government, social, and cultural services served as a much-needed image of urban renewal. However, within the walls of the elaborately designed buildings stood dangerous operating rooms, apartments without services, unhealthy school rooms, and a cinema in which virtually nothing worked as planned.

The first great victory of construction in Sevastopol was the new, two-hall cinema *Pobeda* (Victory). Many buildings had been restored in the first years after the war, but Victory was the first major municipal building designed anew. Its name, purpose, and location on the main ring road of the city center signaled its importance. Victory brought new construction and a much-needed venue for leisure. The symbolism of its construction and completion was for many more important than the quality of the finished product. Accounts of its construction, both at the time and after, hailed the speed and efficiency of workers. Yet the archival documents of city council meetings show that the brilliant white stone facade merely masked a building thrown together in haste with many defects and terrible mismanagement. One contemporary noted that newly trained workers with little experience slowed initial construction. But once a new supervisor, S. D. Almazova, had been named, it took just forty-five days to finish the second half of the building—in time for the anniversary of the revolution.[89] Almazova's recollections were no more accurate. She described the difficult living and working conditions but lavished praise on the party's leadership and the skill of her comrades.[90]

Slava Sevastopolia presented a similar view of Victory, but the private discussions of the city council heaped scorn on the project. The city's main newspaper followed the rush toward completion every day. Articles carried a countdown to completion with heroic tales of overfulfilling daily work targets. When construction ended, workers marched through the streets in the 7 November anniversary parade pulling a float and banners reading "Our gift to the workers of Sevastopol."[91] City officials and residents, both before and after the grand opening, had more honest appraisals. Deputies at city council meetings complained that construction throughout the summer of 1949 remained slow. One official blamed the newly restructured organ for municipal construction for fulfilling only half of its objectives.[92] Two months later the city government condemned the building trust for "wrecking" production schedules, a charge that had landed workers in the gulag throughout Stalin's reign.[93]

When the executive committee reviewed the cinema's operation just after the grand opening, it noted that seats lacked numbers, trash littered the foyer, smokers had no urns on the terrace or outer steps, the entire theater and its surroundings remained filthy, and the reading room and buffet were nearly unusable.[94] Later in the month, city officials had to write to the head of the Stalin Prize committee and decline its offer to nominate the cinema.[95] Condemnation of the building and its operation continued into the new year. The official in charge of cinema in Sevastopol, P. M. Shvetsov, received numerous complaints that shows started late and often without sound, the buffet worked only "from time to time," "uncomfortable"

89. Motorin, *Vozrozhdennyi Sevastopol,* 212–15.
90. Kuzmina, *Vozrozhdenie Sevastopolia,* 94–96.
91. "Do sdachi kinoteatra 'Pobeda' ostalsia 31 den," *Slava Sevastopolia,* 30 August 1949, 1. The photo appeared on the front page of the 11 November 1949 issue.
92. GAGS, f. R-79, op. 2, d. 111, ll. 100–107.
93. GAGS, f. R-79, op. 2, d. 157, ll. 29–40.
94. GAGS, f. R-79, op. 2, d. 157, ll. 89–100.
95. GAGS, f. R-308, op. 1, d. 79, l. 20.

foyers remained dirty and cold, and "hooliganism" reigned in the foyer and viewing halls.[96] By August, only ten months after its opening, the Victory cinema needed major repairs.[97]

Nineteen forty-eight was a turning point for greening the city, as it was for housing and public health, but one with mixed results. The new attention from state organs greatly increased both blagoustroistvo and ozelenenie but with dire consequences. In addition to Sevastopol's receiving new construction directives in 1948, Stalin decreed Union-wide nature preservation.[98] This made the demands to meet targets for planting trees and bushes even greater. Careless construction workers had driven over many saplings, and the inadequate municipal water supply devastated young greenery.[99] The speed of planting after 1948 also resulted in inattention to detail as young trees and bushes blew away in the wind.[100] A successful planting campaign in 1950 along fashionable Bol'shaia Morskaia Street ended abruptly in 1952 when construction workers destroyed the trees and bushes and left their construction waste to litter the area.[101] Moreover, a 1951 city government official chided the militia for not properly protecting green spaces, which suggests that residents might have been stealing young trees and bushes for their own residences or for heating.[102]

The speed-up campaign for construction and planting caused quality to suffer at the hands of demands for quantity. In a state-planning system that relied primarily on numbers, this seems like a logical result. As labor historians have shown from the five-year plans of the 1930s, "storming" seriously undermined the state planning system and quality production, and this seems to have held true for postwar rebuilding as well.[103] The state, ignorant of local progress and conditions, decided by fiat that there

96. GAGS, f. R-79, op. 2, d. 220, l. 39; GAGS, f. R-79, op. 2, d. 220, l. 206.

97. GAGS, f. R-308, op. 1, d. 113, ll. 52–53.

98. See Douglas Weiner, *Little Corner of Freedom,* 88–93.

99. F. Bugaichuk, "Berech' zelenye nasazhdeniia," *Slava Sevastopolia,* 5 November 1947, 2; GAGS, f. R-359, op. 1, d. 29, ll. 61–68; GAGS, f. R-308, op. 1, d. 44, l. 90.

100. GAGS, f. R-79, op. 2, d. 156, ll. 91–94.

101. GAGS, f. R-79, op. 2, d. 340, l. 363.

102. GAGS, f. R-79, op. 2, d. 219, ll. 110–21.

103. Donald Filtzer, *Soviet Workers and Stalinist Industrialization: The Formation of Modern Industrial Relations, 1928–1941* (Armonk, NY: M.E. Sharpe, 1986), 214, 261–69; Hirokai Kuromiya, *Stalin's Industrial Revolution: Politics and Workers, 1928–1932* (Cambridge, UK: Cambridge University Press, 1988), especially chaps. 5 and 6; Siegelbaum, *Stakhanovism,* 300–303.

would be more trees. Not wanting to be blamed for antistate behavior, officials ordered the planting of trees and bushes and blamed their demise on others. When poor state provisioning made one's job impossible, it was easier and politically safer to blame other officials rather than criticize the state and its deficient planning system. Although GASK saw flagrant violations as criminal, historian James Harris's observation that it "was not easy to distinguish incompetence from anti-state behavior" holds true for Sevastopol, too.[104]

In addition to creating a more attractive and healthy environment, local officials sought to provide leisure opportunities for the population toiling to rebuild the city. Trautman's and Alëshina's 1947 revised five-year plan for construction became the key document advocating for the entertainment and comfort of residents and visitors. Three new department stores in the city center allowed people to buy commercial goods. Two shopping complexes planned for the Ship Side and North Side regions encouraged more commerce without requiring people to travel to the center. A yacht club, stadium, and sports club provided venues for "physical culture" beyond the schools and beaches of the city and promoted healthy bodies for labor and war. The yacht club was particularly popular and began to teach the skills necessary to join the fleet in adulthood.[105] Other entertainment and relaxation could be found in the drama theater, concert hall, and three cinemas. For the warmer summer months, local planners also provided two outdoor theaters and two open-air cinemas.[106]

The grandiose drama theater—the new centerpiece of the city—led to a flurry of responses by Sevastopoltsy who challenged both the aesthetics and the location. After Trautman's announcement that he had planned the theater for the central hill, some of the population countered, noting that as planned the theater would prove inaccessible to many residents.[107] Both the theater administration and the audience leveled criticism against the

---

104. Harris, *The Great Urals,* 206.

105. GAGS, f. R-79, op. 2, d. 131, l. 167. In November 1948 the head of the city party and government asked the head of the RSFSR Committee for Physical Culture and Sport to aid in construction of stadiums, swimming pools, sports halls, a track, soccer fields, gymnastics venues, and a yacht club for the "great quantity of young workers" arriving.

106. RGAE, f. 9432, op. 1, d. 241, l. 46.

107. "Vosstanovym rodnoi Sevastopol v 3–4 goda!: Novoe v proekte tsentra goroda," *Slava Sevastopolia,* 26 November 1948, 1.

planned location.[108] Published and unpublished letters to the editor suggested that the climb up stairs to the hilltop in winter would cause many
injuries. Instead, the authors suggested situating the theater on a central
square with bus and trolley access. Unpublished letters from the workers and administrators at the State Khersones Museum wanted the theater
placed near its prewar location on Primorskii Boulevard. The museum
workers also argued for a facade closer to south-shore Crimean traditions,
examples of which they submitted as sketches.[109] Although we have no
records that note why editors chose to publish certain letters, we know
that the unpublished letters to *Slava Sevastopolia* countered the policy of
centralism. Moreover, the drawings challenged prevailing aesthetic trends
of monumentalism, taking localism too much to heart.[110] This illustrates,
however, that local residents cared about their leisure opportunities and felt
emboldened to challenge designs that they felt were contrary to the health
and well-being of city residents and to the seaside aesthetic of Sevastopol.

Raising the Next Generation

From the inception of the Soviet Union, the importance of raising youth in
the proper Communist spirit was paramount. Much of postwar reconstruction planning was aimed at developing an urban environment in which
children could have the happy life for which they thanked Stalin. Care for
society's most vulnerable citizens started at birth by providing medical, nu-
tritional, and financial support for mother and baby. Schools functioned as
the chief venue for intellectual and ideological growth and taught love of
both Motherland and city.

With such a massive loss of life during the Second World War, the USSR
faced a dramatic demographic crisis. The battle for natality was nothing

---

108. B. Gorskii and B. Bertel, "Stroit' teatr na udobnom meste," *Slava Sevastopolia*, 27 November 1948, 1; "Zriteli o stroitel'stve novogo teatra," *Slava Sevastopolia*, 3 December 1948, 1.

109. Four letters have been preserved in the central archives noting the reservations of various groups (RGAE, f. 9432, op. 1, d. 154, ll. 263–68). Workers at the State Khersones Museum, the
archeological museum for 2,500-year-old Greek ruins, would obviously be concerned with tradition and preservation.

110. For a more thorough investigation of the discrepancies between the official press and
unreleased materials see Donald J. Raleigh, "Languages of Power: How the Saratov Bolsheviks
Imagined Their Enemies," *Slavic Review* 57, no. 2 (1998): 320–49.

new in the Soviet Union. During the latter 1930s financial incentives had sought to convince women of their civic duty to have as many children as possible, and abortions were banned. Much of the 1930s' incentives and punishments continued after the war but to little effect in Sevastopol. Likely because young women vastly outnumbered men, the city executive committee routinely allowed marriages of underage boys and girls. Most cases do not give details on the petition except whether the petitioner was male or female and usually how close he or she was to legal age. Most petitioners were female, but males too were usually just a few months shy of their eighteenth birthday. The few cases that state a cause for granting the petition show that the young woman was already pregnant or had just given birth.[111] Because we have no details about individual cases, it is not clear whether pregnancy was the overwhelming reason for early marriages. In any event, exceptions to the law were not uncommon in this age of high demand for future workers and soldiers. In fact, the regime seems to have been advocating premarital sex and single motherhood.[112]

Abortion, although illegal, remained a common strategy of survival for young women unable or unwilling to feed another mouth in a time of great scarcity. Hospital reports show a high percentage of Sevastopol's population having both legal and illegal abortions. Some women went to hospitals and clinics; others chose not too, likely because they feared the consequences of being caught. As in many other spheres of Soviet society, the application of law was uneven. From the scant paper trail, it appears that medical officials or police investigated each known abortion and then forwarded a small number of cases to the procurator for prosecution. A dramatic increase in the ratio of abortions to live births from 1947 to 1951 (0.47 to 1.08) led to greater prosecution of abortion, from 20.6 percent to 42.7 percent (abortions increased over that period from 873 to 2,391) (table 6).[113] To put this in perspective, a 1950 report on abortion in the USSR

---

111. See the following executive committee protocols: GAGS, f. R-79, op. 2, d. 156, ll. 141–50; GAGS, f. R-79, op. 2, d. 78, ll. 2–11; GAGS, f. R-79, op. 2, d. 58, l. 108; GAGS, f. R-79, op. 2, d. 56, l. 85; GAGS, f. R-79, op. 2, d. 56, l. 37.

112. On the postwar dynamics of pronatalism, see Mie Nakachi, "Population, Politics and Reproduction: Late Stalinism and Its Legacy" in Fürst, *Late Stalinist Russia,* 23–45.

113. Data compiled from yearly statistical health reports: GAGS, f. R-59, op. 1, d. 89; GAGS, f. R-59, op. 1, d. 118; GAGS, f. R-59, op. 1, d. 195. In 1951 the regime loosened abortion restrictions, but the number of criminal abortions remained high in Sevastopol.

TABLE 6. Birth and abortion data for Sevastopol

Births or abortions	1944	1946	1947	1948	1949	1951	1952
Live births	261	1912	1844	1906	1278	2205	2527
Premature births	7	92	82	109		92	128
Still births	253	35	41	30	26	56	9
Subsequent deaths	3	24	33	20	22	39	38
Abortions	173	955	873	724	944	2391	
Abortions approved		197	87	79		174	351
Abortions not approved		818	786			2214	
Criminal abortions		70	180	198		953	
Abortion cases referred to procuracy		57	72	198		953	
Abortions per live births	0.66	0.5	0.47	0.38		1.08	
Abortions per pregnancies	0.25	0.33	0.32	0.27		0.51	
Births per 10,000 population	67.3	263.2	236.1	243.6		183.8	

Source: GAGS, R-59, op. 1, d. 12, ll. 1–17 (1944); GAGS, R-59, op. 1, d. 57, ll. 5–22 (1946); GAGS, R-59, op. 1, d. 89, l. 1 (1947); GAGS, R-59, op. 1, d. 118, ll. 10—24 (1948); GAGS, R-59, op. 1, d. 154, ll. 3–10 (1949); GAGS, R-59, op. 1, d. 238, ll. 2–41 (1951); GAGS, R-59, op. 1, d. 290, ll. 23–27 (1951–52). Births per 10,000 population for 1948 are calculated from March 1948 and September 1949 population averages. The exceptionally high number of abortions in 1951 could be a result of the expansion of the criteria for legal abortions in the year. My thanks to Mie Nakachi for bringing this to my attention. Why so many were not approved and deemed criminal is still unknown.

expressed horror that in the large republics of Turkmenistan there were 291 convictions for abortion, in Georgia 626, Uzbekistan 369, and Kirgizstan 416; yet the single city of Sevastopol had 1,021 "criminal" abortions with 953 sent to the judicial system.[114]

Why some abortions became criminal offenses and others did not remains a mystery, but the data show that prosecutions did little to slow abortion rates in Sevastopol. Forty percent of criminal abortions came before the procurator in 1947 and 100 percent a year later. But by 1951 reported abortions had increased. The regime struggled to come to grips with what it perceived as a demographic nightmare. And to some degree it was correct. Of all the ambulance calls for "sudden illnesses," 70.2 percent were responding to abortions. Appendicitis came in a distant second at 12.8 percent.[115] One councilwoman placed the blame not on the underground abortions performed by women with no medical training and in

---

114. GARF, f. 9492, op. 1a, d. 608, ll. 233–36 (resolution "On the Results of a Study of the Judicial Process Regarding Abortions"), cited in E. Iu. Zubkova et al., *Sovetskaia zhizn' 1945–1953* (Moscow: ROSSPEN, 2003), 685–88; GAGS, f. R-59, op. 1, d. 238, ll. 46.

115. GAGS, f. R-59, op. 1, d. 196, l. 176.

unsanitary conditions but rather on the construction organizations that did not create adequate housing for single mothers.[116]

Clearly women were making a choice not to have a child (or another child) when their lives as adults were so precarious. Perhaps the rapid influx of workers in 1949 and 1950 led to new relationships with unintended consequences. Live births and abortions increased in 1951, but live births declined as a percentage of population. This suggests an increase in sexual relationships but also more decisions to terminate pregnancy. Were housing options still too limited to accommodate a growing family? Was provisioning of food and other material goods still too uncertain to make women or couples comfortable with adding dependents? We cannot know how many of these women would have given birth to a second child. As residents of the city, they knew about food scarcity and disease prevalence and likely calculated a low chance of raising a happy, healthy child.

In raising the next generation, no institution was more important to instilling Soviet values than the local schools. In addition to learning Russian, mathematics, sciences, literature, and the other subjects, Sevastopol's school children spent a great deal of time focusing on local history, geography, and flora and fauna in their local studies (*kraevedcheskii*). Education reports to the city government show students studied Sevastopol's history, its founding, the first defense, and the revolutions. They took field trips to sites of the two defenses, to Khersones, and to explore the natural surroundings of the city.[117] Political education went beyond Marxism-Leninism-Stalinism. In what must have been quite a memorable lesson, students learned how in America they "wash dogs in eau de cologne and curl them, but the children of workers die without medical care."[118] In these ways schools sought not only to create more intelligent citizens but also to instill a sense of patriotism and love of city through field trips, projects, and discussions with veterans. The proper understanding of political and international affairs was also paramount.

Sevastopol's educational infrastructure improved and expanded during the reconstruction decade, but its shortcomings created a less than ideal learning environment for the city's youth. Before the outbreak of war,

116. GAGS, f. R-79, op. 2, d. 219, ll. 46–54.
117. GAGS, f. R-102, op. 1, d. 3; GAGS, f. R-90, op. 1, d. 55; GAGS, f. R-90, op. 1, d. 91.
118. GAGS, f. R-90, op. 1, d. 55, l. 44.

Sevastopol's 11,116 students attended twenty-eight schools. Forty-two kindergartens educated another 2,325 children. By the end of 1944, just eight months after liberation, the school-age population was back to half of the prewar total and fourteen schools had been reopened, restoring the ratio of roughly 393 students per school. But by 1948 the average enrollment per school had increased to 485. Pupils per class had shot up from 32.1 to 37.2 between 1945 and 1948 (see table 3 in chapter 1).[119] By every measure, schools became more crowded despite ongoing school construction.

Not surprisingly, student achievement was less than desired. In one quarter during the 1945–46 school year, 22 percent of students failed their exams.[120] Nearly 14 percent (up 1 percent from the previous year) had to repeat a grade after failing end-of-year exams twice (more than 29 percent had failed final exams once).[121] By 1948 the percentage of *vtorogodniki* had fallen to eight.[122] When one considers that few schools had enough heat in the winter, many had no glass in the windows, and all forms of instructional materials were lacking, the students' performance is not hard to understand. The Department of Education noted that much of the turnaround in 1948 came from Sevastopol's new status as a city of republic significance. The increased budget and bureaucratic attention from Moscow brought between eighty and eighty-five thousand textbooks to the city, eight hundred thousand notebooks, and all sorts of other materials (although chalk, pencils, and children's clothes remained scarce).[123]

Despite the educational system's role in instilling discipline, respect, and proper values, starting in the early 1950s, local officials began to focus more attention on the behavior of youth. Although the goal of education in Sevastopol was to raise children "in the spirit of communism, in the spirit of love and devotion to the Motherland, party, leader and teacher comrade

---

119. Data generated from yearly reports of the department of education: GAGS, f. R-90, op. 1, d. 3 (1944); GAGS, f. R-90, op. 1, d. 55–60 (1947–48); GAGS, f. R-90, op. 1, d. 91 (1949–50); GAGS, f. R-90, op. 1, d. 94 (1940, 1945, 1948–49); GAGS, f. R-90, op. 1, d. 118 (1950); GAGS, f. R-90, op. 1, d. 146 (1951).
120. GAGS, f. R-79, op. 2, d. 56, l. 90.
121. GAGS, f. R-90, op. 1, d. 6, ll. 1–3.
122. GAGS, f. R-90, op. 1, d. 60, ll. 1–5.
123. GAGS, f. R-90, op. 1, d. 86, ll. 1–5.

Stalin," reports to the city council show that it was failing. Children bought cigarettes and wine in stores, and sailors directed homeless and neglected children to get them vodka. A militia representative named Chistiakov also noted the names of captains, colonels, and teachers whose children the militia arrested for theft and hooliganism. The report blamed the militia, parents, schools, and even the fleet and city newspaper for not reporting on and curtailing truancy and late-night loitering at movie theaters.[124] A year later the city executive committee forbade children under sixteen to watch films and performances "imprudent" for children. Moreover, on school days a parent, guardian, teacher, or senior Pioneer leader had to chaperone children. Programs for children were to end no later than 8:00 p.m., and admission would be granted for children for whom an adult had purchased a special ticket.

Penalties increased and proliferated as local officials tried to gain control over youth. A 200-ruble fine awaited parents of children exhibiting "street hooliganism" and "mischief." Vendors who sold wine, tobacco, or vodka to minors faced a 100-ruble fine and one month of corrective labor. In order to prevent hooliganism (and improve school attendance in the morning), all children under sixteen without supervision faced a 10:00 p.m. curfew.[125] Of course, there was little hope of improving the situation when some city officials sought an answer to similar behavior in older youth through lectures of interest "on tall buildings, the construction of communism, international affairs, literature and more."[126] Mandatory lectures on topics likely of little interest to most adolescents would reduce their free time to roam the city. But these discussions likely had a negligible effect on improving behavior. Although in the 1940s there were complaints that students, parents, and various organizations in the city did not understand the "importance of instructing the young generation in the communist spirit," only in 1950 did hooliganism become a common problem noted in educational and government institutions.[127] Perhaps sparked by the oppositional

---

124. GAGS, f. R-79, op. 2, d. 219, ll. 27–38. The Department of Education came to similar conclusions in its report on the 1950–51 school year. GAGS, f. R-90, op. 1, d. 115.

125. GAGS, f. R-79, op. 2, d. 339, ll. 218–19.

126. GAGS, f. R-79, op. 2, d. 274, ll. 1–13.

127. GAGS, f. R-90, op. 1, d. 6, ll. 1–3.

youth movement in Leningrad, Cheliabinsk, Voronezh, and other cities in the late 1940s, city officials became more diligent in tracking behaviors that could lead to perceived "anti-Soviet" acts.[128]

Throughout the Soviet period, claims of concern for and accommodation of the population remained. The creation of the Stalin cult in the 1930s rested on the foundation of his image as a father figure guaranteeing the happiness of his family and making life more joyous. While in the 1930s much of this happiness came from parades, films, and increased consumerism, the rubble of the postwar years created additional problems. A November 1945 Council of People's Commissars decree "On Measures for the Restoration of RSFSR Cities Destroyed by German Invaders" called for rapid reconstruction of architecturally valuable structures, city centers, housing, and the "improvement of the everyday conditions of the population of cities."[129] Housing, public health, and beautification are just three of the many categories that could fall under everyday conditions. Proper child rearing and education would create a new generation imbued with a politically minded Soviet and local identity.

Planners ultimately designed urban reconstruction to accommodate the needs of the population. Consistently throughout the postwar decade, local and some central officials reiterated the need for more housing, health care, food, and other social services and condemned the people and organizations that hindered improvement. Time after time Moscow directed new and more resources to the city. Sevastopol and its citizen-sailors were a priority. The failures to bring instant improvement to the city came primarily from a massive lack of resources in the region and country owing to World War II destruction. Cities and the construction industry had been decimated, and the massive loss of life reduced the number of skilled workers in the USSR. After 1948, when industry had recovered and new cadres of trained construction workers filled the city, many of the goals of reconstruction reached fulfillment. Of course, Soviet citizens did not attain everything they wanted or even needed, but numerous parks, cinemas,

---

128. On youth movements, see Juliane Fürst, "Prisoners of the Soviet Self? Political Youth Opposition in Late Stalinism," *Europe-Asia Studies* 54, no. 3 (2002): 353–75; Elena Zubkova, *Russia after the War,* 109–16.

129. GARF, f. A-150, op. 2, d. 20, l. 1.

theaters, and even a circus dotted Sevastopol to bring leisure and comfort to the masses in the hero-city.

When one looked beyond Moscow and Leningrad/St. Petersburg, one saw another side of urban life. When supplies were short in the capitals, they were even more so at the end of the rail lines. While Moscow served as a beacon to which many flocked, the periphery was often starved for qualified labor. (These trends are equally true today.) Whereas discipline in the capitals was often tight, in Sevastopol bureaucratic behavior was more fluid. Local officials and specialists took advantage of their distance from Moscow and their proximity to misery to intervene and to make life a little better for the residents in the rubble. Caught between state planning and the reality of daily life, local powers pleaded, persuaded, and violated the law in order to bridge the gap between the two and to show some real concern for the city's residents. In short, local officials tried to make the Stalinist concern for the individual more than just rhetoric.

The central regime continued to make promises, and local officials and residents demanded fulfillment. Food, housing, health care, and education all appeared at the center of local concerns. As with urban planning, local officials had to carefully negotiate their way through Moscow's failures. Goods bound for Sevastopol were often lost, wasted, or stolen in equally desperate cities. City officials enticed collective farmers to the city, slowly improved the distribution of goods, and tried to protect the quality and safety of food. As more workers arrived to rebuild the city, they found that they had no place to live. Many became squatters in bombed-out buildings, but factory bosses also built barracks in order to prevent their workers from fleeing. Although the construction and the flight of laborers were both illegal, local judicial officials rarely prosecuted offenders. The judiciary knew that central authorities were not meeting residents' daily needs. With the situation in food and housing so desperate for many years, epidemics were an unavoidable part of daily life. Again, local officials stepped into the breach and demanded more medicine, physicians, and diagnostic equipment like X-ray machines, which were vital for containing tuberculosis. Much of the local party, government, and specialist communities worked to protect and provide for residents. Accommodation in city services and housing planned to improve the standard of living of the population, thereby avoiding urban unrest. More important, improved provisioning proved that Marxism-Leninism-Stalinism could provide the best possible life for people.

4

Agitation

Rewriting the Urban Biography in Stone

Sevastopol is a hero-city, city of glorious military and revolutionary tradition, having become famous for immortal feats. By its heroic past Sevastopol personifies the greatness and glory of our people, its love for the Motherland and whole-hearted fortitude in the struggle against its enemies.

KLIMENT VOROSHILOV. Quoted in Zakhar Chebaniuk, *Sevastopol': Istoricheskie mesta i pamiatniki*

Cities in the Soviet Union did more than merely accommodate residents' daily needs; they functioned also as agitational space that sought to transform people's understanding of place and self and link them to the city and Russia. Because of the military importance of Sevastopol and the ever-changing composition of residents in the early postwar years, it was imperative to create a coherent and unified urban biography that stressed sacrifice and duty, especially as the Cold War intensified. Drawing on the lessons from prerevolutionary and World War II–era culture and memorialization, planners focused on sites of identification for Sevastopol—its streets and squares, its memorial parks, and the style of its buildings. In the postwar decade Sevastopol heightened its relational identification with Moscow and its categorical identification as a bastion of naval defense. As plans to accommodate the population's needs developed over time with much negotiation between center and periphery, so, too, did plans to help residents remember the past. At each step in the planning process, local officials and residents challenged Moscow's vision of the city's urban biography and instead fought to maintain local understandings of the city's heritage and its place in Russian history. The agitational spaces that emerged from this contestation became the locations for celebrating and propagating a selective myth of heroic Sevastopol.

The presence of the newcomers in Sevastopol threatened a sense of community that, if allowed to continue unchecked, might have slowed the process of rebuilding the city. In order to encourage sacrifice for the reconstruction effort from new and returning residents alike, naval, municipal, and cultural officials began to focus public attention on Sevastopol's past as a defender against all odds of Russia and the Soviet Union. Historical reference points were essential in a city populated to a great extent by nonresidents who were likely unfamiliar with the city's history but who contributed much to Sevastopol's rapid repopulation in the early years after liberation.[1] German POWs formed one of the largest labor pools, but despite this captive workforce, the scale of destruction demanded much more. Volunteers made up another significant part of the population. These mostly young men and women, often affiliated with Communist youth groups, entered the rubble of Sevastopol with a true desire to rebuild the heroic city. However, because the regime felt it necessary to use POWs and conscripts from once occupied areas of Moldova and Ukraine, one can surmise that the number of true volunteers fell far short of the city's needs. Creating an imagined community was easier still because the scale of damage and the influx of nonresidents also made it easier to create a sanitized community ignorant of the Jewish and Tatar history of the city.

History is constantly used—and not only by authoritarian regimes—to shape an understanding of the past and to help people validate their existence and find their place in a larger, fragmented world. As the modern world moved people away from personal relationships in neighborhoods and villages where they knew the butcher, baker, and postman, dense cities of apartment buildings created a relative anonymity in which many daily social exchanges happened among strangers rather than well-known

---

1. On the preparation of cadres for the Sevastopol construction trust (*Sevastopol'stroi*), see GAGS, f. R-182, op. 1, d. 36, l. 11. The yearly report on the workforce can be found in GAGS, f. R-182, op. 1, d. 37, l. 1.

neighbors. The size and complexity of modern states further disrupt our sense of attachment to one another and to our past. History has become a tool in the modern era that can be used to rebind people to states, neighborhoods, and nationalities. Historical places become "surrogate home towns that contain a familiar and reassuring landscape for people whose points of reference elsewhere have been altered beyond recognition."[2] The demands and structure of the modern world and the greater mobility (chosen or imposed) in life have drawn us further away from the "real" experiences, causing a longing for something "authentic" in order to promote our interests, enhance our sense of self and community, and create (even if imagined) a continuity with the past that provides us with a sense of place. Urban planners, therefore, create sites of identification and symbols.

Sevastopol's planners understood that urban construction had the power to aid in creating local and national identification. Whereas central planners generally favored architectural styles and Soviet memorials common throughout the USSR, local officials understood that a city needed a distinct image. Local planners better honored the city's prerevolutionary heritage and memorialized many of the feats of the nineteenth century that began to write Sevastopol into Russian history. Monuments, streets names, and buildings evoked Sevastopol's deeper history, thereby placing Soviet events in a larger context. Just as important, local planners fought for an urban aesthetic and building materials common to the region. This made the city's vistas distinct from those of other cities. In geographic politics each "symbol stands for something other than itself, and it also evokes an attitude, a set of impressions, or a pattern of events associated through time, through space, through logic, or through imagination with the symbol."[3] The content and style of agitational spaces designed by the local team were unique and more easily identifiable than the standard set of images advocated by Moscow-based planners. Once these local agitational spaces were put in place, Soviet authorities began

---

2. John Fortier, *Fortress of Louisbourg* (Toronto: Oxford University Press, 1979), 19. Cited in David Lowenthal, *The Past Is a Foreign Country* (Cambridge: Cambridge University Press, 1985), xv.

3. Murray Edelman, *The Symbolic Uses of Politics* (Urbana: University of Illinois Press, 1985), 6.

to utilize the space and structure its meaning, as we will see in the following chapter.

From the first draft plans of Ginzburg and Barkhin, agitational spaces that helped to define the city and its place in history had been a prominent part of Sevastopol's new look. The challenges facing Sevastopol and the importance of the city were clear. Creating a stable and content population in one of the USSR's most important military cities required that the residents identify with it and feel a sense of place, especially because accommodation plans often failed. Ginzburg's draft envisioned a grand outdoor museum throughout Sevastopol honoring its past and present victories. Barkhin's winning design centralized and focused Sevastopol's biography in the present. As discussed in chapter 2, Barkhin designed massive monuments to Stalin and glory, among others. However, the context and siting of his projects were equally important in what they tell us about his priorities. In Barkhin's July 1945 revision he explained his use of the artistic device of triangulation, with three monuments to the Crimean War as the points of intersection. Historical Boulevard in the central region, Malakhov Kurgan in the Shipside region, and the Fraternal Cemetery in the northern region created the vertices of the triangle and framed the central hill. Utilizing one of the oldest concepts in urban design, Barkhin planned the most important buildings and monuments on hills and squares and at the junctions of important streets where they could be seen from many places. Various iterations placed statues of Lenin or Stalin or a war museum at the peak of the central hill, on the square of Vladimir Cathedral. Naval clubs, libraries, party and government buildings, and the naval staff were all to be located at the intersections of the city's three main streets around the central hill. Unlike Ginzburg's plan for integrating historical monuments, Barkhin's design marginalized the Crimean War to the vertices of his triangle, which surrounded his centerpiece—the Soviet institutions. He pushed the city's long pre-Soviet history to the background and brought the political present to the fore.

Barkhin redesigned places of leisure in the city center with spaces dominated by war motifs in order to better imbed naval and Soviet identification in the urban form. Barkhin not only sited a complex of naval buildings where people had once enjoyed evening strolls but also planned a series of military monuments. First and foremost, he proposed an enormous statue of Stalin, whom he described as "the great organizer and inspiration for victory."[4] Memorials to war heroes stood in the shadow of Stalin and spread throughout the new garden-park and perimeter of the square. A 110-meter tower of war—four triumphal arches adorned with heroic sculptures—dominated even Stalin's likeness. Barkhin delineated a parade route from Karl Marx Street, along Frunze Street, and into the square and past monuments and the memorial to Stalin. A march along this path would have created a sense of historical connectedness to the past but one that was essentially Soviet. Marchers would have started out on a street named for the father of communist thought, then progressed to one named for the defender of the new Bolshevik state during the civil war, and finally arrived at the square commemorating the war heroes and great father who had saved the Motherland in the latest conflagration. Marx became the alpha to Stalin's omega. In one quick march participants could understand the meaningful past according to Barkhin. Identification in Sevastopol was to be Soviet rather than Russian.

For balance and symmetry, Barkhin planned another equally impressive square on the opposite side of the central hill and stripped it of much of its nonsocialist historical character. He designed Commune Square, as it was called at this stage of planning, to serve not only as a traffic circle for roads coming from the outlying settlements into the center but also as the administrative hub of the city with headquarters for both party and government. Traffic flowing into the center would have to pass the two institutions most important to the regulation of civilian life. Commune Square also evoked the imagery of the ardent French defenders who in 1871 had fought to the death against tyranny. The French communards served as the first great example of the prospects of communism and therefore supported Barkhin's intention to create a Soviet city. The square also served as the entrance to Historical Boulevard. On this site of Sevastopol's Crimean War defense stood the destroyed Panorama and an enormous new statue to Lenin. Until great local pressure forced him to change his plans, Barkhin proposed to strip Historical Boulevard of the Panorama and monuments to the Crimean War. This would have left Lenin, the father of the Soviet system, as the sole historical figure on Historical Boulevard, thereby again shrinking and focusing the city's history.

---

4. GAGS, f. R-79, op. 2, d. 30–a, l. 9.

Barkhin added a third point to the east of the city as a center for memorials and monuments, marginalizing and concentrating remembrance of the Crimea War in one region of the city. With complexes celebrating the latest defense of the city centered on the statues of Lenin and Stalin, Barkhin designed Malakhov Kurgan to become the center of Crimean War memorials. He proposed to relocate the Panorama from Historical Boulevard and rebuild it on Malakhov Kurgan, a key battle site during the Crimean War on which admirals and heroes died. This idea came from his competitor and fellow Moscow architect and professor Moisei Ginzburg, who stated in early 1945 that the "most honorable task in the reconstruction of Sevastopol must be the reflection of the heroic spirit [*geroika*] of the city by the monumental means of architecture and sculpture."[5] The headless statue of Totleben on Historical Boulevard would have been restored and placed alongside new memorials to admirals Kornilov, Istomin, and Nakhimov on Malakhov Kurgan. Barkhin's tampering with local sites of remembrance and homage, however, did not withstand local scrutiny.

A. N. Ivanov and G. A. Lomagin, respectively the heads of the oblast and city architectural administrations, rejected Barkhin's plan in March 1945, which led V. A. Shkvarikov, head of the Russian architectural administration, days later to direct Lomagin to work on a new scheme with Barkhin.[6] Two separate commissions, following the lead of local and regional officials, also rejected Barkhin's general plan because it did not account for the "significance and the natural conditions of the territory."[7] An expert review commission again criticized much of Barkhin's reworked proposal in early April 1945, noting that he had "ignored the specifics of the city."[8]

Barkhin continued to modify his proposal throughout the summer and fall, but the plan for two Panoramas remained, and so did the criticism. Lomagin in July and again in October criticized Barkhin's plan for Malakhov Kurgan. In his latter critique, he suggested that Barkhin preserve the traditional location of existing memorials and monuments and spread new

---

5. RGAE, f. 9432, op. 1, d. 243, ll. 9–11. Quote at l. 11.

6. RGAE, f. 9432, op, 1, d. 242, ll. 93–93ob; GAGS, f. R-308, op. 1, d. 10, l. 12.

7. RGAE, f. 9432, op. 1, d. 154, ll. 148–49.

8. RGAE, f. 9432, op. 1, d. 33, l. 154. Barkhin's second variation on the plan that was supposed to have addressed comments of the review committee was presented to the KA on 5 May 1945. RGAE, f. 9432, op. 1, d. 33, l. 1.

ones throughout the city to mark historical places. Lomagin refused to accept one large outdoor museum and memorial park.[9] Each heroic feat needed its own symbol, and each city region needed monuments to keep the images and messages fresh in viewers' minds. Lomagin believed that his local comrades wanted and needed the reminders all around them and not in a central location like a market, although the latter option would have made sightseeing easier. At the same October meeting one Kvochkin from the engineering department of the fleet criticized numerous plans for monuments and advised Barkhin to consult the political directorate of the fleet for all questions regarding the panorama and memorials. Three days later a naval commission headed by Admiral Oktiabrskii argued that all Crimean War memorials should be preserved in their original locations. Furthermore, the admiral and the commission advised that "the naming of squares and main streets of Sevastopol take into account the historical events and names of the organizers and heroes of the two defenses of Sevastopol."[10] Thus, local architectural and naval officials sank Moscow's plans for a completely new form of commemoration. The local team sought to preserve traditional sites of remembrance and add new monuments to honor the latest sacrifices. The fleet understood how closely its history was bound up with the city and made sure to seize supervisory control over any plans to alter the memorial sites of the city that would have significantly altered Sevastopol's urban biography.

Local and naval officials had constructed a new matrix for the remembrance of history and heroes. In effect, however, they were only articulating a process that had been occurring without planning. From the first days after liberation, monuments and memorials to World War II began to pop up throughout the city, often at the navy's behest, to mark significant battle sites. Municipal officials, who technically had jurisdiction over most of the territory (ports remained controlled by the navy), did nothing to interfere, largely because naval memorialization fostered identification with the city's lore as well.

---

9. GAGS, f. R-79, op. 2, d. 31, ll. 41–44; GAGS, f. R-308, op. 1, d. 7, ll. 6–9ob.
10. GARF, f. A-259, op. 5, d. 279, ll. 16–18.

From Celluloid to Stone

Following the themes of wartime writers and filmmakers, Soviet architects redesigned Sevastopol's postwar urban landscape with a variety of agitational spaces to foster an identification with the city's heroic myth. German bombs and shells had shattered the city's landmarks, so architects set out to re-create Sevastopol's mythology through restoration and new memorial architecture. The conscious German attack on the ships and ports of Sevastopol was more than a military exercise; it was the destruction of a long-held image of the city as Catherine's bastion against the Turks; as the fortress that thwarted the incursion of British, French, and Turkish mariners in the nineteenth century; and as the home of sailors who mutinied for the revolution. Sevastopol's historical significance as an outpost against invasion was clear, and so was its significance as the main Soviet Black Sea port. The theoretical journal of the Academy of Architecture reminded architects that "*[m]emorial architecture* acquires enormous significance in restored cities. Arches, obelisks, [and] monumental memorials will have here not only agitational and memorial significance, but also will play a large role in the creation of an expressive city silhouette."[11] While one might debate the aesthetic merits of much memorial architecture of the Stalin period, its "agitational and memorial significance" cannot be doubted. While monuments served as places of remembrance and mourning, they also served to agitate and instruct. As the author noted, with one design architects could both beautify a city and serve a greater purpose for the Soviet Union by training onlookers to see certain eras and events in a city's history as more important than others. Just as accommodating structures like housing, stores, and theaters could improve the quality of daily life, if designed well they could add to a city's beautification. Ensemble design, then, was crucial and fit well with the Soviet modernist urge to bring order and planning to all sectors of life.

Local aesthetics and historical connections to Russian history were counterparts in redefining the urban biography. Planners realized it was "impossible to ignore the historical appearance of a city when planning

---

11. V. N. Semenov, "Osnovy planirovki vosstanovlivaemykh gorodov," *Problemy sovremennego gradostroitel'stva* 1 (1947): 8 (emphasis in original).

restoration" or "to ignore our [Russian] national heritage."[12] Before and during the war Stalin had conjured up the heroes and institutions of Russia's past to rebuild national unity.[13] In Stalin's USSR the "deployment of Russian national heroes, myths, and iconography was essentially a pragmatic move to augment the more arcane aspects of Marxism-Leninism with populist rhetoric designed to bolster Soviet state legitimacy and promote a society-wide sense of allegiance to the USSR."[14] This was precisely the case for most monuments in postwar Sevastopol, too. The city's naval heritage, highlighted in the wartime press and newsreels, came alive after liberation as old monuments and memorials were restored and new ones were erected alongside them. The same impetus led to memorials and monuments as a foundation for *local* identification.

Architects built monuments symbolizing the heroic defeat of the "fascist invaders" among restored memorials to the heroes of the more distant past. The geographic relation of images, moreover, created a symbolic link between past and present in an effort to create a future image for the city of Sevastopol. In Sevastopol, the outdoor museum culture emphasized the continuity across the revolution and highlighted the city's tradition as part of a larger Russian/Soviet identification. The heroes deployed were Russian and local heroes whose legacies bolstered Sevastopol's relational and categorical identification. Memorial sites tied residents to both Russia's and Sevastopol's pasts and served as an example of ideal behavior for the newest residents battling to rebuild.

Because urban reconstruction quickly became mired in political confrontation, local and military officials (while critiquing the general plans emanating from Moscow) began raising memorials on their own. As President Mikhail Kalinin said, "the contingencies of the moment may justify the omission of certain conveniences in the building of temporary accommodations," but memorialization proceeded without careful planning or central funding.[15] The results were far from temporary. When

---

12. Ibid., 5–6.

13. The most well-known examples are the relative freedom for the Russian Orthodox Church, which raised money for a tank column, and the creation of new medals named for Mikhail Kutuzov, Aleksandr Suvorov, and Aleksandr Nevskii—the great military heroes of the past.

14. David Brandenberger, *National Bolshevism: Stalinist Mass Culture and the Formation of Modern Russian National Identity, 1931–1956* (Cambridge, MA: Harvard University Press, 2002), 4.

15. Mikhail I. Kalinin, "Bol'shaia obshchenarodnaia zadacha," *Izvestiia,* 10 December 1943, 2.

Sovnarkom's decree establishing the KA elaborated on the rubric of architectural structures—"triumphal arches, obelisks, columns, and others"—it signaled a desire for martial and memorial structures throughout Soviet cities. For those like Sevastopol that had been the sites of numerous military exploits, the question became "Which events take precedence?"[16]

In the Soviet Union, the hope was that the massive numbers of memorial sites and the repetition of the "proper" understanding would provide a unitary meaning. As children spoke with veterans or wedding parties paid their respects at monuments to past heroes, each visit to a site was meant to further ingrain a particular message. Memorialization served to connect viewers with a past history of sacrifice for a greater good and provided an outlet for grieving. Like newspapers and films, monuments of all types served to instruct as much as to facilitate remembrance. One could approach a monument in deference to all those lost and remember a loved one at the same time. A viewer could also take the example of sacrifice preserved in stone and apply it to one's daily work in resurrecting the city. No matter how much context is given for a particular site, from plaques to tour guides to guidebooks, the viewer defines the final understanding and use of a memorial site. The location and information around the site can attempt to circumscribe meaning, but each viewer may have a slightly different response based on his or her own experiences.

Central planning continued at a snail's pace, but new administrations at all levels of government designed to oversee the preservation and creation of monuments and memorials began the process of selecting images from the past. On 24 October 1944 the Russian Federation government set forth a statute for lower levels of architectural administration that mandated, among other things, a division for the preservation of memorial architecture and a "bureau of experts."[17] The oblast architectural administration, not to mention the central administration, knew little about what was occurring in Sevastopol. A. N. Ivanov, head of the Crimean Administration of Architectural Affairs, wrote on 18 November 1944 to Vasilii Efremov and Lomagin demanding photographs and texts about all of the city's monuments, especially those commissioned by the military and

---

16. RGAE, f. 9432, op. 1, d. 3, l. 54.
17. GAGS, f. R-308, op. 1, d. 1, ll. 16–17.

Figure 6. Scuttled Ships monument. Photograph by Karl D. Qualls, 2004.

commemorating the second defense.[18] Three days later a similar letter
went out to all Crimean cities requesting a list of monuments of architecture, uses, conditions, and steps for restoration and preservation.[19] Local
officials became empowered by their control of information. From this
moment they not only supplied data but also began to contest and modify
central plans to fit a local heritage.

In late 1945 the Crimean KA finally issued a list of structures to be protected and preserved that shows the power of local influence.[20] Although

---

18. GAGS, f. R-308, op. 1, d. 3, l. 1.

19. Ibid., ll. 3–3ob.

20. GAGS, f. R-308, op. 1, d. 11, l. 5. The complete list included Count's Wharf, the Memorial of
Defense (Crimean War Panorama), Peter and Paul Cathedral, the Fraternal Cemetery, Historical Boulevard, Khersones, the Inkerman ruins (a bridge, fortress, and monastery), the fourteenth-
and fifteenth-century remains of a tower and walls at Balaklava, St. George Monastery and cave
church, ancient structures in Sukharnaia Ravine, the Marmara and Shuldan cave cities, Chorgun
Tower, ruins at Kamyshevaia Bay, the ruins of a fortress near Karan', the church and cemetery at
Belbek Kermen, Byzantine walls near Lapsi, and the ruins on Cape Aiia.

the archival trail is incomplete, one can surmise that the city administration and chief architect heeded the November 1944 request from Ivanov and sent a list of structures to the oblast capital. What was added and deleted we may never know, but in March 1946, when *Slava Sevastopolia* published the oblast committee's decision, four other sites appeared on the list that had not been in the original draft. The four new structures— Vladimir Cathedral, St. Michael's Admiralty Church and the adjacent military-historical museum, and the monument to Scuttled Ships of the Crimean War (figure 6)—were recognized for their architectural and historic importance.[21] Although the latter three were clearly tied to the Crimean War and therefore important symbols of the city's history, Vladimir Cathedral on the central hill was no doubt added because the bodies of Crimean War leaders E. I. Totleben, V. I. Istomin, V. A. Kornilov, and P. S. Nakhimov were interred in the vault below the sanctuary. The unseen crypt made the cathedral historically important. Somewhere in the chain of decisionmaking, likely from the debates over the city's reconstruction, it must have been noted that these additional structures were essential to the city's image and heritage and that therefore even the two churches had to be restored.

The contestation over the fate of the Vladimir Cathedral shows the contested meanings that can be embedded in built space. Barkhin, working for the fleet, planned an outdoor museum that would have razed all the buildings on the central hill, including Vladimir Cathedral, to make way for a new ensemble of buildings for the navy.[22] A local review committee composed of naval and civilian representatives that included architects, engineers, a physician, the head of the city planning bureau, air defense, and fire control met at the end of 1945 and argued vehemently against Barkhin's plan. The local committee stated that the cathedral should be restored and, moreover, that the entire scale of his project was out of line with the city's character.[23] More specifically the committee feared Barkhin's new

---

21. "Okhrana istoriko-arkhitekturnykh pamiatnikov Sevastopolia," *Slava Sevastopolia,* 17 March 1946, 2. The ancient ruins farther from the city center that had no direct relation to the city's heritage as an outpost against invaders either were ignored in the press or had been eliminated from the list.

22. G. Barkhin, "Proekt budushchego: Pochetnoe zadanie," *Slava Sevastopolia,* 18 May 1945, 1; GAGS, f. R-79, op. 2, d. 30–a.

23. GARF, f. A-150, op. 2, d. 52, ll. 1–10.

ensemble would overshadow the Parthenon-like Peter and Paul Cathedral adjacent to the proposed construction. Initial concerns were first couched in terms of scale because this had already been raised as a potential problem. The first plan to preserve Vladimir Cathedral came from the local committee after its initiation in October 1945. Although over one-third of the committee membership came from the navy, it rejected Barkhin's plan to enlarge a naval complex on the central hill at the expense of the Vladimir Cathedral.[24] Local naval and civilian officials were able to alter the plan of the Moscow architect selected to redesign Sevastopol and promote a mutually shared image of the city as a longtime naval bastion. The image of a heroic city was more important to the navy than expanding its own administrative facilities.

There could be three possible reasons that the local team wanted to preserve the cathedral: architectural, memorial, or traditional. Because no one in the debates ever discussed Vladimir Cathedral as a functioning church, we can assume that its religious significance had little bearing on its inclusion in the final list. In their postwar correspondence engineers and military specialists rarely seemed concerned with the aesthetic importance of architecture. Moreover, because the Crimean Committee on Architecture's original 1945 list of important *architectural* monuments omitted the cathedral, one can conclude that it was not highly valued despite being designed by the well-known architect K. A. Ton (best known for designing Christ the Savior Cathedral in Moscow). The cathedral's memorial and traditional significance worked hand in hand to save it. Municipal and naval authorities sought to direct the local community toward a particular history that highlighted heroism, sacrifice, and defense of the city, Russia, and the Soviet Union. Vladimir Cathedral's crypts housed four of the greatest leaders of the Crimean War—the defining moment in the city's history. Despite the more recent World War II feats, the local officials clearly understood that one could not write a history of the city or fleet without direct reference to the Crimean War. Moreover, glorification of past military leaders was likely a surrogate for glorifying World War II military leaders. As early as the 1930s mythmakers had learned it was safer to use examples from the past that had less potential for eventually being purged.[25]

---

24. Ibid., ll. 32–35.
25. Platt and Brandenberger, eds., *Epic Revisionism,* 11.

Memorials and Meanings

Sevastopol had long been a city of memorials and monuments, and maintaining that tradition became paramount in the postwar period. The city's monuments and memorials created visible connections between past and present, and Sevastopol's first monument set the tone for the immortalization of future military engagements.[26] From 1834 to 1839 architect A. P. Briullov, brother of the famous painter Karl Briullov, planned and completed a monument to the ship *Mercury* and its commander, A. I. Kazarskii, and their battle against the Turks. A bronze model of an ancient ship was placed atop a pyramid with the inscription "To Kazarskii. An Example for Posterity" (*Kazarskomu. Potomstvu v primer*) (figure 7). His example, achieving victory despite being outnumbered and overmatched by superior weaponry, would hold true for both of the defenses to come.

Future generations could learn visually about their city's heroic heritage from the countless monuments and memorials throughout the city. The Crimean War in Sevastopol brought death to many in the city, but it also created heroes and heroines who became examples for future generations. Many notables from the Crimean War ringed the facade of the Panorama of the Great Defense of 1854–1855 on Historical Boulevard. Among the trees and bushes stood monuments to the heroes of the war, one young war correspondent (Lev Tolstoy), and the magnificent Panorama with scenes of battle painted on the interior walls. This was as important for agitational reasons as it was to accommodate the population's needs for green space. When strolling with inquisitive children on the weekends or in the evening, parents could transmit the city's history to the next generation. Rather than leave this important educational opportunity to chance, schools also scheduled excursions to important sites of identification throughout the city where students often met with specialists, historians, and World War II veterans. The Panorama and its surroundings provided a vital link in the city's heritage and traditions as a city of glory. From Admiral Nakhimov to Tolstoy to Dasha Sevastopolskaia, all sacrificed their energies, and some their lives, to protect Mother Russia and her people.

---

26. George Mosse also pointed to the importance of past traditions of memorialization before World War I. See especially *Fallen Soldiers,* chaps. 2–3.

Figure 7. Kazarskii monument. Photograph by Karl D. Qualls, 2004.

After the Bolshevik Revolution in 1917, Sevastopol began to erect monuments to its revolutionary heroes, much as it had previously recognized its military heroes. From the 1905 mutinies in the tsar's navy to the Bolshevik Red Army's battle against the old guard White Army in the civil war, new revolutionary heroes joined the obligatory statue of Lenin. In 1935 a pink marble five-cornered star memorialized Lieutenant P. P. Shmidt and his comrades for leading the mutiny of 1905 and subsequently dying in front of the tsar's firing squad on 6 March 1906. Two years later sculptor M. A. Sadovskii honored the "Forty-nine Communards" who participated in the underground battle against the White Army in 1919–20. Throughout the

1930s similar monuments sprang up to honor I. D. Sladkov, military commissar of naval forces during the civil war, and other young communists who brought Soviet power to the city. These revolutionary symbols were not forgotten, but they were soon relegated to a distant third behind the heroes of the two defenses. The victory of the party (1917–22) was relegated to a place behind two events that had a much greater impact on the local community. To this point all the city's memorialization had been Russian and had laid the foundation for Sevastopol's relational and categorical identification for years to come.

Architects, sculptors, and military engineers, taking their cue from over one hundred years of memorializing war heroes, executed an extraordinary number of statues, plaques, and obelisks in the months after liberation from the Nazis. During the first postwar decade, most monuments honored groups of men and women who showed superlative courage and sacrifice under fire and lived up to Kazarskii's example for posterity and the examples of Crimean War and revolutionary heroes. Just a matter of days after the German forces had fled the city in May 1944, naval architects and engineers raised the first monuments to commemorate heroic feats. A. D. Kiselev erected the first monument—a 12-meter-high obelisk to the soldiers of the 318th Novorossiisk Division.[27] The monument's location on Gornaia Heights, at a common grave for the city's defenders, marked the site as virtually holy ground where the blood of soldiers had flowed for Sevastopol's liberation. The obelisk structure, in addition, hints at the lack of money and resources that could be spared as Soviet forces continued their march toward Berlin. The speed with which this task was accomplished suggests a need or desire to make tangible the efforts of the latest group of heroes who had prevailed against all odds. The obelisk was an ancient memorial form, and its simplicity allowed for rapid construction with a minimum of human and financial resources.

Throughout 1944, more obelisks began to dot the horizon, marking sites of battle for reverence and pilgrimage. In July, K. Chankvetadze designed, and soldiers and engineers constructed, a 12-meter-high obelisk

27. Emiliia Doronina and T. I. Iakovleva, *Pamiatniki Sevastopolia: Spravochnik* (Simferopol: Tavriia, 1987), 169–70. Readers can find information on these monuments in the numerous guidebooks discussed in the following chapter or *Sevastopol': Entsiklopedicheskii spravochnik* (Sevastopol: Museum of the Heroic Defense and Liberation of Sevastopol, 2000).

on a common grave in honor of the Second Guards Army.[28] Four months later Lieutenant Commander Zedgenidze erected a 2.5-meter monument on the spot where many of the defenders of the Konstantinovskii Ravelin had been killed. As war continued and resources remained scarce, grandeur and monumentality were reserved for the sites most memorable to the city's new lore. The Victory monument at Cape Khersones, where the last German soldiers had left Crimea, and the Glory obelisk at Sapun Gora, where the Red Army had staged an uphill assault to recapture Sevastopol, both became central sites of identification in the postwar years. The Victory obelisk stands 26.3 meters, and its tetrahedral form, designed by Ginzburg, is faced with pink granite. It is easily visible from throughout the city center and on one's approach from the sea. Fifteen years after the obelisk on Sapun Gora was first erected, a new diorama/museum opened nearby, giving it a significance parallel to that of the Crimean War's Panorama on Historical Boulevard.

With war still raging, money, specialists, and skilled labor could not be utilized for great art. Only after economic recovery could resources be devoted to the much more expensive diorama and museum, but this did not preclude the need and desire for remembrance. The military had taken memorialization into its own hands by marking sites of remembrance that would be examples for posterity. When time and resources permitted, the World War II victory was finally honored with a structure fittingly reminiscent of the memorial of the first defense, to which the second defense was so often compared. The theme of collective action and sacrifice of the two midcentury wars merged well with Soviet themes and continued the glorification of the city and its defenders in a manner consistent with tradition.

Rarely did monuments in the postwar period emphasize the feats of individuals, but when they did, they were given a place of honor and often located close together in cemeteries that could be used as outdoor museums and classrooms. One gunboat sailor, Ivan Golubets, received his own monument because he, better than most, exemplified Kazarskii's example for posterity. In March 1942, Golubets jumped on board a ship engulfed in flames. Fearing the loss of several ships moored nearby, he allegedly began

---

28. Emiliia Doronina and Aleksandr Liakhovich, *Po ulitsam Sevastopolia* (Simferopol: Tavriia, 1983), 80–81.

to throw depth charges overboard to prevent an explosion. His valiant efforts were not fast enough, and he was killed in the ensuing blast. The square-faced obelisk to a Hero of the Soviet Union is topped by a naval symbol and decorated with anchors at its base, a bas-relief of Golubets, and a commemorative plaque. Only a heroic, sacrificial act to protect one's Motherland and comrades could be singled out in an era of an intense personality cult. Furthermore, it harks back to Petr Koshka's daring night raids behind enemy lines during the Crimean War.

More often the military raised monuments to itself (as in most of the above examples) or collectively honored its leaders who had fallen in battle. It is instructive to note that none of Sevastopol's military leaders were so honored during their lives, and even Lenin had to wait until 1957 for his destroyed statue to be replaced. However, dead defenders could be honored and memorialized in busts, plaques, and statues. In November 1946 an Inkerman stone obelisk with bronze bas-reliefs took its place in the Fraternal Cemetery of the Third Anniversary of the Liberation of Crimea, more commonly known as the Cemetery of Communards. The new memorials honored air force generals and Heroes of the Soviet Union N. Ostriakov (aviation commander of the Black Sea Fleet) and F. Korobkov (deputy chief of naval aviation), along with Brigade Commissar of air forces for the Black Sea Fleet M. Stepanenko. All three men died in 1941–42.

The Cemetery of Communards had been constructed in 1923 to commemorate the liberation of the peninsula from the White Army and German forces in the civil war. However, the cemetery, established on the location of the Fifth Bastion, also connected visitors to the city's Crimean War past. This action by the military set a precedent to be followed for decades: important people in the city's history would be buried together, thereby facilitating the instruction of visitors (especially school-age children) in their city's history. Thus military heroes like Oktiabrskii (1899–69), hero-laborers of reconstruction like Evgenii Kolobov (1912–73) and Nikolai Muzika (1927–63), and political figures like wartime First Party Secretary B. A. Borisov (1903–80) were interred side by side. All those who were examples for posterity were honored after their death and served as symbols of people who sacrificed for their city in times of great need. Their proximity to one another allowed for group excursions to see the history of sacrifice in a single trip.

Agitational spaces were only the classroom for educating the public about the city's history and traditions; people had to be instructed in how to read and understand the spaces. As early as November 1944, A. N. Ivanov of the Crimean Administration for Architectural Affairs instructed all municipal architects to give lectures, reports, excursions, and radio and newspaper interviews on the significance of monuments and memorials.[29] Although radio transcripts have not been located, local newspapers were filled with the articles of chief architect Iurii Trautman, stories on the city's history, and coverage of lectures by city officials. Moreover, school-age children took trips to sites as part of the regular curriculum. Veterans, local historians, and educators in Pioneer camps and "children's areas" enlightened them further.[30] Walking the streets of Sevastopol, most of which were named for people and events in the city's history, demonstrated that Oktiabrskii's prediction that the "numberless heroes of the Second defense of Sevastopol [would] be woven into a brilliant fabric of legend" had come true.[31]

Ascribing Meaning to Urban Space

Oktiabrskii's 1945 recommendation that "the naming of squares and main streets of Sevastopol take into account the historical events and names of the organizers and heroes of the two defenses of Sevastopol" also came to fruition.[32] Oktiabrskii's position as head of the fleet and his status as commander during the war obviously was important. Moreover, his desire to immortalize the two wars coincided with a renewed interest by other city

---

29. GAGS, f. R-308, op. 1, d. 3, ll. 3–3ob.
30. As early as 13 July 1944, the Crimean party committee ordered all city committees to organize summer Pioneer camps, GAGS f. R-79, op. 2, d. 7, ll. 76–77. A Gorispolkom report on the 1946 campaign, GAGS, f. R-79, op. 2, d. 63, ll. 64–65ob, further noted that all camp leaders had to attend Komsomol training in order to provide adequate ideological education, which no doubt included information about the city's historic sites to which they were taking the Pioneers. Although the cost for summer camps is unknown, a camp during the winter holidays cost 96 rubles, divided evenly between the city and parents. The poorest 10 percent of the children went free of charge, GAGS f. R-79, op. 2, d. 25, l. 51. For others, children's areas were established in schoolyards during the summer for play and education.
31. *The Heroic Defence of Sevastopol,* 14.
32. GARF, f. A-259, op. 5, d. 279, ll. 16–18.

officials in redefining what "local" meant. Oktiabrskii and urban planners understood that place names helped to ascribe meaning to urban space and create identifications. For Oktiabrskii and other local officials, recasting the city's urban biography by highlighting the city's Russianness, military feats, and unique Greek architectural heritage had to find form in Sevastopol's agitational spaces.

After local architects seized control from Barkhin, they inscribed the city's Crimean War heroes, and much less often Soviet notables, in the names of city landmarks and thereby wrote the past into built space. Trautman and his team set about renaming the city's most prominent streets and squares, likely taking Oktiabrskii's recommendations into account. The naming and renaming of streets, squares, and parks was an integral part of the postwar program of urban agitation and identification, but it was unique to neither Sevastopol nor the USSR.[33]

Name changes suggested political shifts. After the revolution, no one should have been surprised that Catherine the Great's street was renamed for Lenin (as it remains today). The Soviet obsession with making the revolution omnipresent led to assigning the names Lenin, Marx, and Frunze to the three streets of the ring road. During postwar replanning, however, the latter two reverted to Bol'shaia Morskaia (Big Naval) Street and Nakhimov Prospect. When judged as part of a larger plan, this transformation heralded a new emphasis on local identity, historical depth, and national pride. Frunze was essential to Sevastopol's liberation from the Germans and Whites after the revolution, but he was not considered a local hero. Marx, of course, had no direct link to the city, only to its ruling ideology.

---

33. Study of meanings embedded in built space is not new. Richard Wortman has shown the importance of symbolic uses of space and names in the imperial period, and John Murray has documented a similar phenomenon at the end of the Soviet period. John Murray, *Politics and Place-Names: Changing Names in the Late Soviet Period* (Birmingham, UK: Birmingham Slavonic Monographs, 2000); Wortman, *Scenarios of Power,* 10–15; John J. Czaplicka, Nida Gelazis, and Blair Ruble, eds., *Cities after the Fall of Communism: Reshaping Cultural Landscapes and European Identity* (Baltimore, MD: Johns Hopkins University Press and Woodrow Wilson Center Press, 2009) present case studies in post-Communist Eastern European cities in which changes in toponymy were often central. For a more general approach see Diana Agrest and Mario Gandelsonas, "Semiotics and the Limits of Architecture," in *A Perfusion of Signs,* ed. Thomas A. Sebeok (Bloomington: Indiana University Press, 1977), 90–120; Harold D. Lasswell, *The Signature of Power: Buildings, Communication and Policy* (New Brunswick, NJ: Transaction Publishers, 1979); Donald Prezios, *The Semiotics of the Built Environment: An Introduction to Architectonic Analysis* (Bloomington: Indiana University Press, 1979).

Admiral Nakhimov, on the other hand, stood atop the pantheon of heroes from the Crimean War. Bol'shaia Morskaia, much more than Marx, carried the city's image as a naval, both military and commercial, port. Although reverting to prerevolutionary names could be viewed as abandoning socialist goals, the city needed stability and rapid reconstruction. Resurrecting a unique, local character to which residents could attach their ideals and aspirations became one strategy of identification. The lessons of the Crimean War were quite instructive and supported more prevalent Soviet ideals of duty, sacrifice, and fighting against all odds for the Motherland. Therefore, an emphasis on local and categorical traits did not necessarily undermine a relational identification with the Soviet Union, which had become more identified with Russia since the late 1930s.

The names of the city's central squares also went through a radical transformation that likewise promoted the city's nineteenth-century heritage over the Communist Party or more recent events. Nakhimov Square replaced the Square of the Third International, which Barkhin had tentatively called Parade Square. Neither an institution of world socialism nor the martial and functional nature of the square was acceptable; only the name of the city's greatest admiral could adorn the square closest to the sea. Commune Square (the prerevolutionary Novoselskaia) reverted to the name of another naval hero, Admiral Ushakov. Even the Great October Revolution fell victim to the desire to make Sevastopol's naval history ever-present. After World War II, Revolutionary Square took the name of M. P. Lazarev, the commander of the Black Sea Fleet at the end of the eighteenth century. The nomenclature of Sevastopol's streets and squares highlighted the city's prerevolutionary tradition. These most prominent locations in the city center served as hubs for transportation, government, and party administration, celebrations and leisure. Because residents going about their normal routine had to pass by these places and give directions using place names, the new nomenclature likely seeped into their consciousness and became part of their reality and their everyday lives. When one read about the signified events in the newspaper, heard lectures on the radio, took field trips, and then walked the streets, it surely created an air of familiarity and a sense of understanding and belonging. New residents from throughout the USSR would not require much time to understand the history of Sevastopol that had been scripted for them through place names.

For agitational space to be effective, it needs to eliminate or at least marginalize counternarratives. Although the city's historical memory shifted to the previous century, the non-Slavic residents of the city were written out of the urban biography. The rubble of almost complete destruction allowed for a previously heterogeneous city to look and feel more ethnically and culturally united. Two non-Slavic groups had left an architectural footprint in the city center that the war helped to erase. Crimean Tatars had been deported en masse for alleged collaboration with the Nazis, and Crimean Karaite Jews, like most European Jews, suffered under Hitler.[34] Moreover, the postwar period brought renewed anti-Semitism to the USSR, especially after the emergence in 1948 of the new state of Israel and its affiliation with the United States, the USSR's Cold War rival. Thus, postwar planners did not have to give special consideration to Sevastopol's multiethnic heritage in reconstructing the city, and its image as eliminating the remnants of collaborators and "anti-Soviet cosmopolitans" (a catchphrase for Jews) became paramount. The Tatar Settlement (*Tatarskaia slobodka*) became known as Green Hillock (*Zelënaia gorka*). The kenasa, a Karaite Jewish prayer hall, became the Spartak sports club. The Tatar mosque, with minarets removed and the facade "erased" of Koranic inscriptions, became the naval archive, despite one construction unit's request for the building as its new social club.[35]

The turn-of-the-century mosque on Azovskaia Street, like nearly all buildings in the city center, fell prey to artillery and bombs, yet the exterior structure remained intact. The central dome and minaret still towered over nearby buildings much as they had done before the war.[36] Numerous organizations asked municipal authorities for permission to rebuild the structure, but no one petitioned to reopen it as a mosque. The city and oblast governments, as well as the Council on Religious Cults, approved initial plans for the mosque's resurrection as a cinema and club for the Sevastopol

---

34. Crimean Karaites (*Karaim*) differ from the other Karaite Jews because the former developed from a community that spoke Turkic rather than Hebrew, Aramaic, or Arabic. This further separates Crimean Karaites from other Jews in general and other Karaites in particular. Here "Karaite" will refer to the Crimean community.

35. GAGS, f. R-79, op. 2, d. 131, l. 88.

36. GAGS, photos 6411 (1939), 1–11807a and 1–12028 (1944), 3424 and 3332 (1946), and 12483 (1914).

construction trust (Sevastopol'stroi).[37] Yet when the better-connected navy heard that the building was under consideration, it submitted its petition to renovate the building as the city's new naval archive.[38] But not even these organs could spare labor and materials to start anew. Gorispolkom approved the navy's request, but Trautman warned the navy not to waste money trying to "cleanse" the building of the last vestiges of its former owners.[39] He limited them to three points: "Remove all quotations both Arabic and Russian...remove emblems of half-moons, tear down the minaret."[40] Replacing Jews and Tatars with a sports club and a naval building focused the city's image on strength and service. Moreover, it aided in the Russification of the city's biography and image.

Once the city was purged of its cultural diversity, designers also set about unifying and localizing the architectural style that had been an eclectic blend of nineteenth-century neoclassical, constructivist, and early-Stalin-era functionalist buildings. Late-Stalinist architecture, marked in most people's minds by the highly decorative facadism of Moscow's high rise wedding-cake buildings like Moscow State University and the Hotel Ukraine, found no place in Sevastopol. Designers instead reverted to their understanding of Sevastopol's architectural heritage based on the partially preserved Greek ruins of the Khersones Archaeological Preserve. This allowed architects to preserve and restore some of the city's best neoclassical (and often religious) architecture, despite official state atheism.[41] New construction also borrowed heavily from the city's past. The Lunacharskii Drama Theater on Primorskii Boulevard and the nearby Hotel Sevastopol both displayed magnificent Corinthian columns that reflected the influence of the Khersones ruins and served as complements to the former Institute of Physical Therapy that was restored as the House of Pioneers.

37. GAGS, f. R-79, op. 2, d. 56 (Gorispolkom Protocol 35/44); GAGS, f. R-79, op. 1, d. 51, l. 20 (oblast decision); GAGS, f. R-79, op. 2, d. 63, l. 11 (council approval). The oblast's decision noted that 70–75 percent of the buildings had been damaged, but since "at the present time Sevastopol has no believers of the Muslim creed," there was no reason to preserve the building as a mosque.

38. Throughout 1946 various administrations exchanged letters, petitions, and evaluations. Sevastopol's leaders mediated the debate, made rulings, and overturned themselves. GAGS, f. R-308, op. 1, d. 24, l. 23; GAGS, f. R-308, op. 1, d. 20, l. 85; GAGS, f. R-308, op. 1, d. 31, ll. 187–88ob; and GAGS, f. R-308, op. 2, d. 5.

39. GAGS, f. R-79, op. 2, d. 57.

40. GAGS, f. R-79, op. 2, d. 131, l. 88.

41. E. V. Venikeev, *Arkhitektura Sevastopolia: Putevoditel'* (Simferopol: Tavriia, 1983), 67–70.

In addition to the neoclassical motifs, architects chose to include balconies and loggias on nearly all of their buildings in order to take advantage of the seaside character of the city. Likewise, most buildings were plastered in light yellow pastels to contrast with the blue-black sea and to take advantage of the bright sunlight. New buildings after the war were fashioned with Doric, Ionic, and Corinthian columns and massive pediments designed with geometric precision. Unlike Moscow variants on older styles, all new construction in the historic center was kept between three and five stories high. The low verticality separated Sevastopol from the dominant scale of other Soviet cities. Although architects originally argued for this as an aesthetic imperative, their case was better made after the great 1948 earthquake in Ashkhabad, Turkmenistan, revealed that Sevastopol's seismic activity would not permit greater vertical construction with the prevailing building technology and methods.[42] Elimination of cultural diversity permitted a more Russian/Slavic aesthetic, and the choice of style, size, and color created a unique look that spoke to the city's tradition and climate.

Reversion to tradition meant a Russian ethnic identification wrapped in a Greek architectural facade reminiscent of the 2,500-year-old ruins at nearby Khersones, yet devoid of all hints of competing images. The process of renaming and reapportioning buildings also highlighted the historical omissions so important to creating a selective understanding of Sevastopol's history. Planners designed Sevastopol so that its appearance would be as unique as its role within the Soviet Union, and they avoided all European design aesthetics for the next fifty years. Local unity demanded visual and historical unity as well.

The Significance of Style

Repackaging prewar architectural centerpieces expropriated the visual symbols of still-despised religions, and new buildings created future sites of

---

42. The Soviet Union denied the 1948 earthquake until the 1990s. According to the U.S. Geological Survey, it was a magnitude 7.3 with more than one hundred thousand killed, which makes it one of the deadliest on record. See http://neic.usgs.gov/neis/eqlists/eqsmosde.html. The Directorate for the Reconstruction of Sevastopol SSSR discussed the issue in 1949. See RGAE, f. 9432, op. 1, d. 387, ll. 330–35.

identification in Sevastopol. As in other cities around the Soviet Union during the 1920s and 1930s, places of worship in Sevastopol were torn down or given new functions. The Byzantine-inspired Pokrovskii Cathedral suffered severe damage in World War II but was restored by 1950 and held services until becoming a sport hall and city archive in 1959. Another cathedral dedicated to saints Peter and Paul stands on the previous site of a Greek church. It was destroyed during the Crimean War and rebuilt by two merchants in 1889. From the revolution to World War II, it served as the city's archive. In 1946 the city restored it as the Lunacharskii Drama Theater, until it became the House of Culture in 1957. The rebuilding of the churches signaled a return to Russianness in the revival of an architectural style associated with prerevolutionary Russia's most enduring institution, the Russian Orthodox Church. Peter and Paul Cathedral emphasized the localness of the city by copying from Sevastopol's Greek heritage.

Although housing and industry consumed most of the city's meager resources in the early postwar years, new buildings began to rival the beauty of the restored cathedrals. After the decree of October 1948 led to the influx of money and materials into Sevastopol, ground was broken on more creative and symbolic structures. Tents, mud huts, wooden barracks, and caves remained the principal forms of housing, but they deviated from the image of a nation growing stronger by the day. In order to convince the homeless and hungry of Sevastopol and other cities that the Soviet Union had recovered from wartime devastation, the regime needed tangible, grandiose, and visual representations of power, longevity, and authority. Once again a nation turned to ancient styles to legitimize its existence.

The classical styles of ancient Greece and Rome projected the values sought by the regime and its architects. Porticoes and colonnades were "to suggest an ideal reality and to divert attention from the drabness of Soviet life."[43] Beyond the awe-inspiring volume and scale of ancient temples, the classical style demanded geometric proportionality in tune with Soviet dictates for rational planning. Undoubtedly, architects' audiences did not calculate the ratio of height, width, and depth, nor did they care about hypotenuses. Geometric symmetry, however, draws the viewer's attention and immediately creates a sense of permanence and timelessness. Balance,

---

43. Alexei Tarkhonov and Sergei Kavtaradze, *Architecture of the Stalin Era* (New York: Rizzoli, 1992), 182.

symmetry, proportionality, and mathematical exactitude were all desired features of Soviet rational planning.[44] In Sevastopol they were made tangible by architecture.

Since the construction of the first Egyptian pyramids, stone construction has brought permanence to monumental architecture. Moreover, a stone structure attested to the power and influence of its patron. Cost, logistics, and labor conscription demanded a heavy and wealthy hand. So, too, in every society since, governments, nobles, and merchants have raised temples, castles, and seats of power in majestic stone. From the Incas to the ancient wats of southeast Asia to the castles of Europe, stone buildings in enormous proportions have suggested power of the patron or the deity for whom the structure was erected.

Classical style and stone construction were natural for Sevastopol because of the city's unique Greek heritage. Since the ancient Greeks expanded into the Black Sea in the fifth century BCE, stone architecture in the classical style has found a home in Sevastopol. Although little remains of ancient Khersones besides theater seating and the foundations of homes, one can discern meticulous planning. The few Corinthian columns that remain upright attest to Sevastopol's architectural heritage. When postwar Soviet planners chose to erect buildings of local white stone in the ancient style, they could rationalize their decision as local in form, socialist in content. Local history, updated 2,500 years later, provided the regime with its symbols of power and economic rejuvenation, but it also preserved an essential part of local identification.

Nowhere else in the Soviet Union was classical architecture afforded such a prominent role. Architects created variations on classical themes throughout the USSR, but most were more stylized. Moscow's wedding-cake buildings certainly adapted a few elements of classical architecture in both form and purpose. Their vertical lines swept skyward, creating symmetry and proportion. Moreover, the function of Moscow State University and the Ministry of Foreign Affairs recalled the temples of ancient Greece and Rome—loci of power for the state religion. Located on prominent squares and hills, these buildings repeated classical and church planning.

---

44. Rudolf Arnheim, *Dynamics of Architectural Form* (Berkeley: University of California Press, 1977), 217.

The most important structures of the city were most visible.[45] Yet in Sevastopol, classical temple-style architecture came alive in almost unadulterated form. Seismic activity precluded skyscrapers, and tradition mandated the three principal classical orders of Doric, Ionic, and Corinthian.

Architects had clear examples of all three orders among Sevastopol's postwar ruins, but new construction expanded classical symbolism throughout the city center. The Doric order was well represented by Peter and Paul Cathedral and on Count's Wharf. This style, reportedly based on the proportions of a man, often represents power and authority, but as the least decorative of the three orders, it also presents an image of simple elegance, utilitarianism, and inexpensive construction.[46] The Doric order's military symbolism found expression before the revolution in the Panorama to the Great Defense (figure 8) and the entrance to Malakhov Kurgan. Both sites celebrated the military valor and sacrifice of soldiers during the city's siege of 1854–55. After World War II, architects used the robust and aggressive style to express utilitarianism. The first cinema, bank, library, and administrative building in the city center all had Doric facades. Perhaps cost concerns and the lack of skilled stonemasons forced architects into using the least decorative order, but all four buildings also suggested the practical nature of the order. The Victory cinema showed its martial spirit in name and style. The Doric facade allowed the grandiose project to dominate its surroundings. This signified that life was returning to normal. Once again, the simple pleasures of life—movies in this case—could be attained. Gosbank, the Tolstoy Library, and the administrative building at the north end of Lenin Street were designed in the Doric style to represent the serious nature of their work. Conservative yet elegant, facades matched the utilitarian nature of the buildings' functions.

Ionic buildings are often the antithesis of their Doric counterparts. The volutes, or swirls, on column capitals represent the curls of a woman's hair.

45. Charles T. Goodsell, *The Social Meaning of Civic Space: Studying Political Authority Through Architecture* (Lawrence: University Press of Kansas, 1988), 28; Phyllis Ackerman, "The Symbolic Sources of Some Architectural Elements," *Journal of the Society of Architectural Historians* 12, no. 4 (1953): 3–7.

46. Interpretation of the classical orders can be found in Robert Adam, *Classical Architecture: A Comprehensive Handbook to the Tradition of Classical Style* (New York: Harry N. Abrams, 1991); Alexander Tzonis and Liane Lefaivre, *Classical Architecture: The Poetics of Order* (Cambridge: MIT Press, 1986); Vitruvius, *The Ten Books on Architecture,* trans. Moris Hicky Morgan (New York: Dover, 1960).

Figure 8. Crimean War Panorama on Historical Boulevard. Photograph by Karl D. Qualls, 2004.

The narrower stance of the Ionic was based on the slender proportions of an adult woman. By contrast, the Doric column is modeled on the stouter male form. Moreover, the folds of a woman's dress inspired the vertical fluting. The classical interpretation of femininity suggested domestic and more sedentary, docile themes. Today's art museum, originally built in 1899 as a boarding house, contains many ionic elements on its eclectic facade. The Museum of the Black Sea Fleet combines the reflective images of the Ionic order with naval decoration (e.g., anchors, cannons, and flags). The principal examples of postwar Ionic construction include the award-winning housing ensemble along Bol'shaia Morskaia Street and the Sailors' Club on Ushakov Square. Ionic columns, dentils, balustrades, balconies, and loggias decorated the living space of the fashionable district and the place for entertainment and relaxation for the city's naval protectors. Although a naval museum and club could have martial tones, architects rightly distinguished them from the Doric-influenced, agitational monuments of the Panorama and Malakhov Kurgan. Museums and clubs represented relaxation and contemplation. The Panorama and Malakhov Kurgan celebrated heroic self-sacrifice in the face of the enemy with the power and authority of the Doric order.

Corinthian orders decorate some of the most splendid architecture in Sevastopol. As an outgrowth of the Ionic style, Corinthian architecture also is more female than the Doric. The legend of the order's origin, however, brings it into sharp contrast with the Ionic. The famous Athenian sculptor Callimachus came upon the grave of a young Corinthian girl. He noted that a basket of her belongings with a roof tile on top had been placed at her grave. Growing up around the basket were the leaves of the acanthus plant—a form of vegetation often used in Greek funeral rituals. Thus, the placing of acanthus leaves atop a slender column can symbolize death, women, and domestic activity. The highly ornate form also suggested the power, wealth, and prestige of a building's patron. In ancient Greece and Rome, Corinthian temples often praised the power of a deity.

The magnificent Karaite prayer hall and the equally spectacular Sechenov Institute of Physical Therapy remained from Sevastopol's prerevolutionary Corinthian buildings. In its prewar days, the institute represented nurturing and care. When it was turned into a hospital during the war, however, medical care was accompanied more often by death. In the early 1950s, architects began restoring the institute to its original form. As the new Palace of Pioneers, the building contributed to the social well-being of the city's youth (figure 9). The institute's reconstruction began only after a new Corinthian hospital had been built. Facing the new Palace of Pioneers, architects began their most extravagant building project—the new Lunacharskii Drama Theater (figure 10). Its templelike appearance and elaborate ornamentation paid homage to its patron (the socialist system) as well as to its function (the entertainment and education of the population). The Hotel Sevastopol completed the "Corinthian corner" on Nakhimov Prospect (figure 11). A double row of massive columns greeted visitors at the entrance and promised luxury and service to all who entered. The foyer's hand-carved columns with details of the city's monuments matched the hotel's outer opulence and gave the city's guests a glimpse of Sevastopol's richness. The conscious appropriation of classical styles was part of a "specific program, aimed at creating the effect of many centuries of culture in those places where nothing apparently remained."[47]

---

47. Iu. Kosenkova and Iu. Bocharev, "Goroda geroi," in *40 let velikoi pobedy: Arkhitektura,* ed. Iu. P. Volchok (Moscow: Stroiizdat, 1985), 97, quoted in Alexei Tarkhanov and Sergei Kavtaradze, *Architecture of the Stalin Era* (New York: Rizzoli, 1992), 110.

Figure 9. Former Sechenov Institute became the Palace of Pioneers. Photograph by Karl D. Qualls, 2004.

Figure 10. Lunacharskii Drama Theater. Photograph by Karl D. Qualls, 2004.

Figure 11. Hotel Sevastopol. Photograph by Karl D. Qualls, 2004.

Architects designed every element from geographic location and nomenclature to architectural style and memorials in order to give Sevastopol
unique sites of identification and agitational spaces. Although many still
believed in the egalitarian ideals of socialism, the social disruptions of the
1930s had perverted these beyond recognition and led to the abandonment
of what many felt was the true nature of socialism.[48] The men and women
who repopulated the city immediately after liberation in May 1944 set about
rebuilding their homes and lives. The navy and local officials took advantage of the central officials' distractions with war and cataclysmic and widespread destruction throughout the western reaches of the USSR to articulate
and make tangible their vision of Sevastopol's past, present, and future. As

---

48. Zubkova, *Russia after the War,* 4–5, 31–39, 84–85, illustrates the disparity between expecta-
tion and reality in the postwar period. Sarah Davies shows how the same system functioned a decade earlier. Even some true believers criticized the regime in its own language for not meeting
the lofty goals of the revolution. Davies, *Popular Opinion in Stalin's Russia: Terror, Propaganda and
Dissent, 1934–1941* (New York: Cambridge University Press, 1997), 8–9, 186.

the defense of the city collapsed in 1942, military officials and propagandists had already started linking the two defenses of the Crimean War and World War II. After liberation in May 1944 the trend continued, and the military constructed memorials to honor its feats and the lives sacrificed. This continued an established tradition and highlighted the city's heritage as well. Military and civilian officials fought against outsiders who wanted to change the city's identification with Russian history and stressed a continuous local tradition as heroes of the second defense were laid to rest next to heroes of the past. With press coverage, educational excursions, ever-present memorials, and the renaming of streets and squares, residents and visitors alike were steeped in the city's naval heritage while in the agitational spaces.

The "dominant myth," to borrow Amir Weiner's phrase, was military service; Weiner's study showed that one's service during World War II allowed for many sins to be forgiven.[49] But the city of Sevastopol also had a "metamyth," one that sought to project and protect the image of an imagined urban community. The impetus for rebuilding Sevastopol was similar to the revival of past heroic events and people in the late 1930s, which served as a surrogate to a larger Soviet goal.[50] However, for Sevastopol the revival of history was more than merely "russocentrism"; rather, it was based on *local* heroes who had also served a larger Russian/Soviet community through their defense of the homeland. This version of history complemented the objectives of naval and local officials. Thus, a stronger connection with local history and tradition through monuments and renamed streets, often at the expense of glorifying the USSR, likely was much more effective in creating stability and a sense of mission than was abstract Marxism-Leninism-Stalinism.

Iurii Trautman portrayed himself as a local by urging the accommodation of local needs and stressing the importance of preserving local traditions. From an aesthetic perspective, this led him to adopt an architectural style to complement the ruins of Khersones. Like Barkhin, Trautman understood the dominance of the city's naval heritage, but Trautman reached deeper into the city's past to provide a foundation for the World War II

---

49. Amir Weiner, "The Making of a Dominant Myth: The Second World War and the Construction of Political Identities Within the Soviet Polity," *Russian Review* 55:4 (October 1996): 638–60.

50. Platt and Brandenberger, *Epic Revisionism,* 11.

feats that stood at the center of Barkhin's proposal. Most of all, Trautman chose to eliminate Barkhin's grandiose monuments and memorials in favor of restoring Sevastopol's monuments to past heroes. Crimean War leaders became the foundation for the city's historical narrative, and in the ancient Greek styles the city could identify itself with something much older, more awe-inspiring, and more democratic. Neoclassical styling was the norm throughout the Soviet Union, but in Sevastopol it was devoid of most of its Stalinist flourishes and pomposity. The neoclassical forms looked natural in Sevastopol, whereas in most Soviet cities the columns and pediments of new grand structures looked out of sync with local architectural traditions. Thus, Sevastopol looked both Soviet and local at the same time. Although there was no way for the architects to have foreseen it, when the Soviet Union collapsed and cities throughout the former USSR began to change street names, demolish Soviet-style buildings, and re-create an imagined past in the city, Sevastopol was able to avoid the abrupt transition because it had become local decades earlier.

Agitation became a complementary method to create and maintain allegiance and stability after massive dislocation and disillusionment as a result of the war. In Sevastopol, first-time residents needed to be anchored to their new location as the Cold War escalated, and ongoing problems with accommodation called for another strategy. Resource-scarce Sevastopol had to depend on Moscow to allocate nearly all material goods. Moreover, images of the city's naval past (part of its categorical identification) implicitly linked Sevastopol to the Russian Motherland (its relational identification). Strategies of accommodation and agitation both helped to create a relational bond with the center. In return for goods and a preservation of the city's selectively remembered heritage, Sevastopol would continue to defend the Motherland and not rebel as it had in the prerevolutionary period. In essence, a sort of bilateral social contract emerged in which Moscow and Sevastopol defined their roles as material provider and loyal sailor, respectively.

5

PERSISTENCE AND RESILIENCE
OF LOCAL IDENTIFICATION

Having been founded as the base for the Navy, the city of
Sevastopol connected its destiny with the Navy forever. So the Navy
determined its appearance, biography and those severe sufferings
that made Sevastopol world known.

DOBRY AND BORISOVA, *Welcome to Sevastopol*

Since 1991 Sevastopol, an ethnically Russian city in Ukraine, has been
undergoing a reexamination of its heritage. On the eve of the Ukrainian
"Orange Revolution" in 2004, one could see spray-painted graffiti on a yellowed building on Soviet Street on the central hill that read, "Sevastopol is
Russia." While graffiti is a common form of self-expression in most cities,
it is also a political statement. Many if not most of Sevastopol's residents
would likely choose the leadership of Moscow over that of Kyiv. The un-
initiated viewer would likely also be confused by the persistence of the
name Soviet Street, which leads to a large statue of Vladimir Lenin that
towers over the city. Cities throughout Eastern Europe are now Western-
izing by erecting glass and steel skyscrapers while also destroying remnants of the Communist past by tearing down buildings and statues and
renaming streets and squares. Although many post-Soviet cities have
removed traces of the Bolsheviks and Communists, Sevastopol retains
street names, and Lenin's statue still looks down over the city from the
central hill. In fact, Sevastopol's central district is still called Leninskii. Are

Sevastopol's residents and city leaders stuck in the past, or is there another way to explain this Russian-minded enclave nearly twenty years after the fall of the Soviet Union? Why has Sevastopol changed so little and shown less of a concern with creating a new local identity as part of a European community? By not rewriting the city's history as one exclusively tied to revolutionary moments and ideas, Sevastopol's local history has survived in a way that has been virtually impossible for many other cities in Eastern Europe. However, capitalism, tourism, and economic development have combined to (re)define categorical, if not relational, identification in Sevastopol in the twenty-first century. Sevastopol remains a Russian city, but new pages have been added to its urban biography.

From 1954, when Khrushchev transferred Sevastopol to the Ukrainian SSR, to 1991, when Ukraine became an independent country, there was no conflict over a Russian city in Ukraine because the Soviet Union itself had become Russocentric. The newly independent republics and satellite states in Eastern Europe began to assert their national sovereignty and individuality in ways that often eliminated the Russian and Soviet past from the streets of their cities. Sevastopol, however, seems to be an anomaly. Because of the continual reinforcement of its categorical and relational identifications since World War II, it has thus far remained nearly immune to the wave of iconoclasm that has struck much of the region. However, challenges still remain as the lure of capitalism changes the face of the city and has revived the multiethnic character of the region. Moreover, increasing tensions between Russia and Ukraine and the changing relationship between Ukraine and the West have introduced new dynamics and challenges unseen in the Soviet period that may alter identifications in the future.

Identifications are not static; they change over time because of politics, the degree and manner in which agents promote certain identifications, and the changing nature of the city and its residents. This chapter will discuss how and why guidebooks and tourism changed over the last half-century and explore the challenges facing Sevastopol and its sense of self in the twenty-first century. The end of the Soviet period found guidebook writers subtly tweaking the city's biography, but the present century has posed much greater challenges, especially as Karaites, Tatars, and Ukrainians are written back into the city. These changes affect the way that a city is read by a population in the post-Soviet years.

Guidebooks and the Scripting of the Past

The guidebook authors quoted in the epigraph quite rightly noted that the navy, both as an institution and by its mere presence in the city, had an active role in redefining the face of Sevastopol. Moreover, in the act of writing, the authors perpetuated that same connection between city and fleet. In the decades since the completion of reconstruction Sevastopol's visitors have been guided through an understanding of the city. Guidebooks, whether Soviet or post-Soviet, have stressed the city's naval heritage and continued the identification of Sevastopol with heroism. With the collapse of the Soviet Union and the prospects of greater profits from international tourism, the city's image has changed but slightly. Soviet heroes unconnected to World War II are still present in the city's monuments, but visitors are no longer guided to them. Whereas the Second World War temporarily dislocated the Crimean War from the center of Sevastopol's mythology during the Brezhnev years in particular, the post-Soviet tourist industry has now refocused on the earlier conflict. Although Sevastopol is still a city of two defenses, World War II now plays a more secondary role.

Since the end of World War II, the central myth of Sevastopol has undergone minor changes while still staying true to its intimate relationship with the navy and its history. From the completion of reconstruction in the mid-1950s to the early twenty-first century, Sevastopol and the countries of which it has been a part have seen dramatic changes: multiple regime changes, the Cold War and its demise, and most recently, becoming a city in independent Ukraine. One could logically have expected some stasis during the Soviet period, but as the world began to change radically in the late 1980s and early 1990s, cities throughout Eastern Europe began to redefine themselves and throw off the yoke of the Soviet past. Sevastopol, however, maintained the image so consciously created in the wake of war both because it had already subjugated the revolution to war exploits and because the social memory of war had created a vehicle for economic development as independent Ukraine transitioned to capitalism. Throughout the war and postwar decade, mythmakers and urban planners alike worked hard to refashion and keep alive the myth of Sevastopol as a bastion defending the Motherland. But how was this image perpetuated?

Tourism and guidebooks became two of the chief tools to disseminate information and aid in identification creation. Tourists could visit the city and come into contact with the legendary places of Russian military history. They began to experience the city's lore in buildings, street names, and monuments. But even when there were fewer opportunities until 1996 to visit the closed military city freely, guidebooks could still provide readers with the correct understanding of the city's past and its role in Russian and Soviet history. Like guidebooks everywhere, they prescribed and proscribed based on their author's decisions about what merited attention and provided context for the sites to be explored. As time passed and new generations were born with no firsthand knowledge of war, it was important to transmit the mythic images of Sevastopol's past to residents and visitors alike. As the Soviet Union collapsed and opportunities for tourism increased, subtle shifts occurred in the prioritization and presentation of the past in guidebooks. Travel guidebooks remained one of the chief media for introducing and explaining the importance of Sevastopol's place names and 2000 memorials.

Tour guidebooks are one of the most common ways to transmit a sense of place to a touring audience, even in nonauthoritarian regimes. Urban biographies can be found in local history books, but just as often they are condensed in travel guide literature and at sites of memory.[1] In either medium, the urban biography provides readers with a way to identify with the city based on its past. In a free-press society, authors offer images that suit their tastes and that they hope will attract an audience. Whereas one author might highlight cultural opportunities and fine restaurants, another might focus on a city's heritage. But in a censorship regime there is less latitude to refashion local identification, and foregrounding commercial interests like dining and shopping were far from common in the Soviet Union.

---

1. A sampling of approaches can be found in Mosse, *Fallen Soldiers;* Jay Winter and Sivan Emmanuel, eds., *War and Remembrance in the Twentieth Century* (Cambridge: Cambridge University Press, 1999); Rudy Koshar, *German Travel Cultures* (New York: Berg, 2000); Koshar, "'What Ought to Be Seen': Tourists' Guidebooks and National Identities in Modern Germany and Europe," *Journal of Contemporary History* 33, no. 3 (July 1998): 323–40; Anne E. Gorsuch and Diane P. Koenker, eds., *Turizm: The Russian and East European Tourist under Capitalism and Socialism* (Ithaca, NY: Cornell University Press, 2006).

For most Soviet cities, history was key, although some new cities, like Magnitogorsk in the 1930s, highlighted their industrial might. A city's history often had a local and a national aspect. For example, Smolensk's identification centered not only on its ancient origins but also on the city's role in Russia's fight against both Napoleon and Hitler.[2] Novgorod's identification was less divided. While guidebooks made sure to tie the city's history to the revolution, the origins of ancient Russian culture remained at the center of guidebook discussions.[3] This created the anomalous juxtaposition of the atheist state promoting church architecture. But these seeming contradictions were nothing new. Lenin had clearly stated even during the iconoclastic days of the revolution that Russia needed to maintain a link with its past. Moreover, Stalin actively rehabilitated pre-Soviet Russian leaders from Ivan the Terrible to Aleksandr Nevskii because they could be used to argue for a continuous Russian heritage of strong leadership and winning against great odds.[4] Sevastopol's guidebooks maintained a focus on the city's military history, but throughout the second half of the twentieth century the relative weight given to the Crimean War, the October Revolution and civil war, and World War II shifted to reflect the contemporary concern of the authors and the societies of which they were a part.

Through omission and excision guidebooks reinforced the process of forgetting discredited leaders, but they also actively created a selective remembering of the past based on the needs of the present. In addressing the Turkish wars and the Crimean War, authors across the decades remained consistent in the types of sites they highlighted and the language they used

---

2. See the historical framing of the city in *Smolensk: putevoditel'* (Moscow: Moskovskii rabochii, 1974); *Smolensk: Spravochnik-putevoditel'* (Smolensk: Smolenskoe knizhnoe izdatelstvo, 1960); I. Belogortsev, *Arkhitekturnyi ocherk Smolenska* (Smolensk: OGIZ, 1949); I. Belogortsev and I. Sofinskii, *Smolensk* (Moscow: Gosudarstvennoe izdatelstvo literatury po stroitel'stvu i arkhitekture, 1952); G. T. Riabkov, *Gorod-geroi Smolensk: Ocherk-putevoditel'* (Moscow: Moskovskii rabochii, 1988); I. A. Smirnov, *Smolensk: Gorod-geroi* (Moscow: Voenizdat, 1988); I. A. Smirnov, *Smolensk: Gorod russkoi slavy* (Moscow: Moskovskii robochii, 1982).

3. *Novgorod: Putevoditel'* (Leningrad: Lenizdat, 1966); *Novgorod: Illiustrirovannyi putevoditel'* (Leningrad: Lenizdat, 1972); M. Dunaev and F. Razumovsky, *Novgorod: A Guide* (Moscow: Raduga, 1984); Iurii Pokhodaev, *Pamiatniki drevnego zodchestva: Novgorod* (Moscow: Sovetskii khudozhnik, 1969); I. A. Zaitsev and I. I. Kushnir, *Ulitsy Novgoroda: Spravochnik* (Leningrad: Lenizdat, 1975).

4. On the turn in the late 1930s to recognizing pre-Soviet Russian state builders, see Brandenberger, *National Bolshevism,* 43–62; Platt and Brandenberger, introduction to Platt and Brandenberger, *Epic Revisionism,* 3–16.

to describe the themes of heroism and sacrifice. However, coverage of the revolutionary period and World War II varied dramatically among guidebooks as the World War II generation moved into and out of power. Each shift in power helped to redefine the relative importance of military, party, and the Russian masses in Sevastopol's history.

Post–World War II guidebooks emphasized sacrifice, teamwork, unity, and symbolic defiance against great odds, much as the World War II newspapers and newsreels had.[5] In May 1829 Captain Aleksandr Kazarskii decided to blow up his ship's magazine rather than surrender to two Turkish battleships. Author Zakhar Chebaniuk reminded his readers that "in an uneven fight an 18-gun Russian brig won a victory over an enemy that had more than a tenfold superiority in artillery."[6] Emiliia Doronina, writing in the late 1970s and 1980s, called Kazarskii's feat an "example of fortitude to the warriors of the two defenses," which the Soviet Black Sea Fleet was continuing.[7] Doronina not only consciously connected her readers to the past but also showed the continuity of behavior from Kazarskii to the present. A 2001 guidebook noted that the inscription "An example for posterity" on Kazarskii's pedestal came from Tsar Nicholas I, an admission unthinkable in Soviet times.[8] Moreover, Kazarskii now represented a democratic choice because the city's first monument was "dedicated not to an emperor or an admiral, but to a captain-lieutenant!"[9]

The representation of Kazarskii in these three books and periods underscores some of the changing dynamics in the postwar decades. Chebaniuk,

5. In addition to the texts that are cited later in this chapter, see Petr Garmash, *Gorod-geroi Sevastopol': Ocherk putevoditel'* (Simferopol: Tavriia, 1972); Vitalii Olshevskii, *Sevastopol': Spravochnik* (Simferopol: Tavriia, 1977); Vitalii Olshevskii, *Sevastopol': Putevoditel'* (Simferopol: Tavriia, 1981); Nikolai Orlov and Igor Gassko, *Gorod-geroi Sevastopol': Fotoalbom* (Simferopol: Tavriia, 1985); Boris Rosseikin, *Sevastopol': Albom* (Simferopol: Krymizdat, 1960); Boris Rosseikin and Georgii Semin, *Sevastopol': Putevoditel'-spravochnik* (Simferopol: Krymizdat, 1961); Boris Rosseikin, Georgii Semin, and Zakhar Chebaniuk, *Sevastopol': Putevoditel'-spravochnik* (Simferopol: Krymizdat, 1959).

6. Zakhar Chebaniuk, *Sevastopol': Istoricheskie mesta i pamiatniki* (Simferopol: Krymizdat, 1957), 34.

7. Emiliia Nikolaevna Doronina and Tamara Ivanovna Iakovleva, *Pamiatniki Sevastopolia* (Simferopol: Tavriia, 1978), 22–24.

8. Aleksandr Dobry and Irina Borisova, *Welcome to Sevastopol* (Simferopol: Tavriia, 2001), 74. The Russian edition is A. Dobry, *Dobro pozhalovat' v Sevastopol'* (Simferopol: Tavriia, 2000).

9. V. Khapaev and M. Zolotarev, *Legendarnyi Sevastopol': Uvlekatel'nyi putevoditel'* (Sevastopol: Fuji-Krym, 2002), 102.

writing earliest, chose not to interpret the image of Kazarskii too much. He presented the captain as a hero who was willing to die but who instead succeeded in an unequal fight. Doronina, on the other hand, felt obligated to explain to her readers that Kazarskii served as an inspiration to all those who came after him. The post-Soviet texts not only attributed the veneration of Kazarskii to a tsar but also returned to the image of the everyday hero in Sevastopol in which an officer of average rank could become the first symbol of the city.

Veneration of the Crimean War became the first full-scale memorialization project in Sevastopol, with three sites of memory dominating guidebooks: the Monument to Scuttled Ships, Malakhov Kurgan, and the Panorama and Museum of the Great Defense. The latter two, having been saved by local officials from Barkhin's destructive redesign after the war, remained central sites of memory of the first defense. The Monument to Scuttled Ships, which represents the intentional sinking of the Russian fleet in order to prevent the British and French navies from entering Sevastopol Bay, is undoubtedly the most beloved in Sevastopol. It is the "emblem of the city of Russian glory—Sevastopol," and it "reminds everybody of the sorrowful but important event."[10] It continues the legacy of "the sailors [who] served as examples for all participants in the defense" and has become "the emblem of Sevastopol, its visiting card."[11]

Erected in 1905 on the fiftieth anniversary of the Crimean War, the Corinthian column topped with a two-headed eagle holding an anchor and the laurel wreath of glory symbolizes valor and sacrifice. The monument still adorns paintings, book covers, postcards, and numerous city websites. The lone Soviet book chronicling Sevastopol's reconstruction has a photograph of the Scuttled Ships monument standing defiantly as waves crash against its base.[12] The visitor who merely looked on the column and eagle might be impressed with its beauty, but without the aid of guidebooks, tourists would likely not walk away with an understanding of the feat that the monument honored. Moreover, one would not recognize the monument as a symbol of sacrifice to which all were called to aspire. Thus, the

10. Chebaniuk, *Sevastopol'*, 61.

11. Doronina and Iakovleva, *Pamiatniki Sevastopolia*, 54; Dobry and Borisova, *Welcome to Sevastopol*, 45.

12. Motorin, *Vozrozhdennyi Sevastopol'*.

guidebooks in Sevastopol made art into meaningful teaching tools for generation after generation.

The gates of Malakhov Kurgan, the hilltop scene of bloody fighting during the Crimean War that took the lives of several Russian military leaders, appeared on the cover of Chebaniuk's 1955 text. The hill's Crimean War complex remained "one of the most famous places of Sevastopol."[13] Doronina validated the importance of the World War II memorial space at Sapun Gora by noting that its eternal flame was lit from that at Malakhov Kurgan, thereby "symbolizing the continuity of glorious combat traditions."[14] In other words, Malakhov Kurgan and the Crimean War gave legitimacy and historical depth to World War II veneration. Doronina was telling a new generation of readers what their predecessors had learned from wartime media and from building the very structures she discussed. World War II and the Crimean War were two parts of the same whole. Out of losses came victories, and the mettle of the everyday Russian withstood the test and prevented the destruction of the Motherland. By uniting the two wars symbolically, Doronina continued the trend started by wartime writers of positing a clear and direct line of succession from one generation of sailors and fighters to the next. It was as if the anthropomorphized city continued to give birth to men and women willing to sacrifice their lives to protect what they loved most: Russia.

The Panorama building and painting, a "monumental memorial to the heroism of Sevastopol's defenders in the Crimean War" and "the national pride of this country and its people," drew 40 million visitors from 1905 to 2004 and received extensive coverage in all guides.[15] The authors were consistent in describing the events memorialized in the Panorama, its construction, the Nazis' devastation of it, and the postwar reconstruction of the building and the 360-degree panoramic painting on the interior. It is the "main noteworthy site of our city" claimed one post-Soviet author, and "many tourists come more than once to touch the great art and history."[16] As one of the great military feats of the nineteenth century, along with the

13. Khapaev and Zolotarev, *Legendarnyi Sevastopol'*, 126.

14. Doronina and Iakovleva, *Pamiatniki Sevastopolia,* 123.

15. Dobry and Borisova, *Welcome to Sevastopol,* 46–47; V. Kornienko, R. Morzhenkov, and V. Stefaniuk, *Sevastopol': Putevoditel'* (Simferopol: Svit, 2004), 35.

16. Khapaev and Zolotarev, *Legendarnyi Sevastopol',* 111–12.

Napoleonic invasion, the Crimean defense became a defining moment for Russian military and political power, identification, and literature (such as that of Lev Tolstoy).

Like Kazarskii's feat, the scuttling of the fleet and other Crimean War tales served explicitly as examples of fortitude and sacrifice against a superior force; however, the focus on heroes as examples also omits mention of cowardice. The necessity for examples implied a fear that in future conflicts not all would respond with such valor. Here, then, is a process of both forgetting and remembering. How would one read what could be an ambiguous message? Because most people would prefer to be part of something heroic rather than cowardly, tourists and visitors likely chose not to ask whether all sailors lived up to the examples of heroism and sacrifice. Visitors today may see it much differently than their Soviet counterparts did. Do Ukrainian sailors stationed in Sevastopol relate to past Russian heroism and sacrifice in the same way as Russian sailors in the city do? Do they know that the legendary Crimean War sailor Petr Koshka was an ethnic Ukrainian (Petro Kishka)? Do German, British, and American tourists see scuttling as folly, failure, or fortitude? Even in the Soviet period each viewer interpreted through the lenses of gender, age, profession, and more. In the twenty-first century international visitors come from backgrounds that rarely have recognized Russian/Soviet valor and therefore make multiple or muddled understandings more likely. The importance of guidebooks as vehicles for promoting a unified understanding of events is no less important today than it was fifty years ago.

Unlike the Crimean War, the city's revolutionary heritage played a remarkably minor role in guidebooks despite the centrality of many local events to the Soviet revolutionary mythology. The 1905 Revolution and the battleship *Potemkin* are an important part of the city's biography and the residents' heritage. But coverage varied greatly among guidebooks. The November 1905 uprising in which the monarchy arrested and punished hundreds without a trial led to the bloody execution of the leaders. Chebaniuk, writing during the transition between Stalin and Khrushchev, was uncertain about the official interpretation of the revolutionary period after Stalin had rewritten history to give himself a more prominent role. Chebaniuk felt compelled to show that it was the "Menshevik ringleaders," opponents of the Bolshevik Party, who were the cause of failure and that the revolutionaries stood in court with "fortitude...knowing the deep feeling of the many-million masses who were on their side."[17] By placing blame on the Mensheviks, Chebaniuk continued to use Stalin's old foil. To be associated with Trotsky, a former Menshevik, was a free ticket to the gulag in Stalin's era.

Doronina, writing well after Stalin's version of history had been overturned, gave considerably more attention to the revolutionary period, but it was still quite brief in the larger scope of the book (only 23 of 143 total pages). She noted that the First Sevastopol Soviet "endured a drubbing but the revolutionary spirit of the people remained unbroken."[18] Thus death was a perfectly acceptable fate when it led to a greater good. Losses for a cause were merely temporary as the next generation learned from the past. Guidebooks recast momentary losses as ultimate victories and presented courageous men and women who gladly sacrificed for the cause. This understanding of the past also served as a protection against current and future setbacks during the Cold War. When times got hard, residents needed only to redouble their efforts and remember the actions of their forebearers and the ultimate good that came from them.

In post-Soviet Ukraine authors further marginalized the revolutionary tradition, which had lost most of its importance. Aleksandr Dobry lamented that children in 2001 knew little about the revolutionary movement. By devoting only three pages to the revolution, however, he contributed further to its marginalization. Other post-Soviet authors rejected the revolutionary past entirely, noting that it had ushered in "one of the most excruciating periods" of Russian history—the Soviet Union.[19] Another author went further and called the 1917 revolution and civil war a "microscopic, laughable segment of time in the scale of history....Horrible!...Bloody!...Destructive!"[20] He tried to minimize both the duration and importance of the revolution and thereby show that it had had little effect on the longer history of Sevastopol. By casting it as short-lived (and not three-quarters of a century), the author also suggested that it had been grossly out of character with Sevastopol's heroic image and past. In many cities this type of rescripting may have been more difficult. But because

17. Chebaniuk, *Sevastopol'*, 98–101.
18. Doronina and Iakovleva, *Pamiatniki Sevastopolia*, 65.
19. Khapaev and Zolotarev, *Legendarnyi Sevastopol'*, 42.
20. Kornienko, Mozhenkov, and Stefaniuk, *Sevastopol': Putevoditel'*, 22.

mythmakers in the 1940s and 1950s had already given Sevastopol's Russianness predominance over its Sovietness, a new localism that ignored or despised the Soviet period was possible.

Of the only forty-six monuments, plaques, and memorial places dedicated to the events and people of these uprisings, most were erected only after World War II. The timing suggests that memorialization of the events had been an afterthought and not a deeply felt part of the city's character. Erected during a time in which the party-state tried to recapture its dominance and recentralize authority, paeans to revolutionary heroes seemed both hollow and suspect.[21] In comparison, monuments and memorials to World War II began as the war continued. After the end of the USSR, there was no editorial pressure to include what for many likely appeared as an anomaly (and a negative one) in Russian history. Socialism and its revolutions had ceased to be important parts of Sevastopol's urban biography, and guidebooks reflected this fact even though Lenin, the revolution, and other reminders of the Soviet period remained in monuments and place names.

World War II became the defining event for a new generation of Soviet citizens, and guidebooks bear this out. Two-thirds of the sites to World War II activities were erected in the 1960s and 1970s as the war generation moved into power.[22] Not surprisingly, guidebooks similarly began to place greater emphasis on the war. Post-Soviet guidebooks, while still noting the importance of the war in Sevastopol's history, placed World War II exploits in context as one of many moments of valor rather than the most important one, as the war-generation texts had suggested.

In the late 1950s and early 1960s, Chebaniuk focused on individual heroes and thereby personalized the war for his audience. In the first days of the 1941–42 defense, Chebaniuk noted, five members of the naval infantry initiated an "unparalleled duel" as they destroyed sixteen tanks by themselves. In Chebaniuk's favorite phrase, they "fulfilled their debt" as they fought to their death.[23] They were repaying the Soviet system for their upbringing. Doronina, writing in the 1970s, also recounted the feats of the "five daring Black Sea sailors" and their ability to twice repel the German

---

21. Doronina and Iakovleva, *Pamiatniki Sevastopolia*, 64.
22. Dobry and Borisova, *Welcome to Sevastopol*, 64.
23. Chebaniuk, *Sevastopol'*, 113–14.

advance.[24] The seven Communist Youth League members and three Communists in Pillbox No. 11 likewise staged a valiant defense against all odds. Bombarded from the air and on the ground, they held out for more than three days until all but one were dead. Both Chebaniuk and Doronina highlighted their feat and included their oath. Chebaniuk reported the full oath, but Doronina distilled it to its three main points: "Under no condition surrender to captivity. Fight the enemy the Black Sea way [*po-chernomorski*], to the last drop of blood. Be brave, masculine to the end." She conveniently omitted the first point of the oath, which repeated Stalin's infamous directive to take "not one step back." She aided the remembrance of what she viewed as positive, but she omitted reference to Stalin and his order to shoot any Soviet soldier who tried to retreat. Doronina aided the process of forgetting fear and Stalin's brutal repression. She also conveniently forgot that some people did run away from the fight and had to be kept fighting by threats.

Omitting signs of compulsion and relating stories of heroic deeds obscured the heroism that was merely resignation to fate. Stalin's blocking units had been ordered to shoot anyone retreating. Many soldiers may have calculated that if they retreated, their death would be in vain. Some Soviet soldiers likely chose to die by sacrificing their lives in the process of killing the enemy rather than die at the hands of their own state. The hagiographies of the martyrs for a good cause were intended to stimulate similar actions all across the battlefield. The World War II generation wanted to ignore the fact that some of those too frightened to fight had been compelled to do so. The younger generations reading these texts were to be told that all were brave and all were heroes. When the time came, Sevastopol and its defenders would emulate those feats and fulfill their debt to future generations. Like Kazarskii over a century earlier, World War II had its examples for posterity. A dying soldier named Kaliuzhnyi wrote, "My Motherland! Russian land! ... I kept my oath. Kaliuzhnyi."[25] Not surprisingly for a city already near the center of Russian national lore for two great defenses, Kaliuzhnyi's sacrifice was for his "Russian land," not the Soviet Union. Soviet memorialization is not unique—would any country erect monuments to those who had panicked and fled from battle?

---

24. Doronina and Iakovleva, *Pamiatniki Sevastopolia,* 103–4.
25. Ibid., 104–5.

Doronina and Dobry generally omitted detailed discussion of individual heroes and instead directed readers' attention to the larger complexes of communal remembrance that became more common during Leonid Brezhnev's reign. Perhaps as a reaction against the cult of personality of the Stalin years, monuments from the 1960s on highlighted groups more often than individuals. Doronina and the post-Soviet authors followed suit and spread the umbrella of heroism over a broad audience. Doronina focused on monuments to military divisions; post-Soviet guides concentrated on events like the storming of Sapun Gora. The most recent guides have omitted all monuments to individual World War II heroes. Instead they highlight larger groups, as in the Monument to Young People, the Monument to the Defenders of Sevastopol, and the Monument to the Aviators of the Black Sea Navy. Individuals from the Crimean War, however, are still honored.

The location of the monuments that Chebaniuk had favored, which are located at the site of action in the city's outskirts, are too far off the beaten path for today's tourists. Also, authors may have judged that contemporary tourists were too detached from the war to know or care much about the individual feats. Instead, twenty-first-century guidebooks have accommodated the time-sensitive tourist by including centrally located monuments. The Memorial to the Heroes of the Defense on the chief square and traffic node of the city lists various heroes of the Soviet Union. With its eternal flame it honors all who fought and died for the city. The Hero-City Obelisk and Monument to Victory honor the city and all who fought for it. The Sapun Gora complex is the only World War II site outside the city center to merit inclusion and significant commentary in post-Soviet guidebooks.

Why this shift? It could be that the luster of hagiographic images has dulled and that guidebook authors are content with providing a few examples. As the demystification of wartime heroes like partisan Zoia Kosmodemianskaia has continued in the post-Soviet period, it has certainly raised questions about all individual hagiographies. Without state censorship and subsidies, authors are free to include what they choose and must be selective in order to minimize the size of the texts and thereby manage profitability. Rather than laboriously cover each example of heroism, guidebook authors have opted for portraying the overall collective heroism of the defenders of World War II. The explosion of commemoration in the last quarter century that added roughly five hundred monuments to the city landscape has made comprehensive coverage impossible and likely seems excessive for generations with no direct contact to the war.[26] Besides, as one guidebook noted, "one must judge that many monuments are either excessively grandiose or simplistic [*prostovaty*]."[27]

With the war generation long out of power, post-Soviet monument construction has slowed and authors are taking a more balanced approach to the city's military past. Recent guidebooks honor the war and the valor of fighting. But individual heroes have less meaning for them and their readers. With the passing of many World War II veterans, municipal officials have decided it is time to honor other servicemen in a collective fashion. For example, in 1999 a large cross atop a star represented the Sevastopol citizens who fought against the CIA-backed muhajadeen in Afghanistan.[28]

The strategies of identification have been built into Sevastopol's streets, squares, buildings, and monuments, and guidebooks retain the narrative of the city's relational web with Russia. But this does not mean that Sevastopol is still mired in the Soviet period. The prospect of renewed tourism since the lifting of travel restrictions in 1996 has brought early signs of change.

With the collapse of the Soviet Union and the emergence of Sevastopol as part of independent Ukraine, yet with the Russian Black Sea Fleet still inhabiting the vast majority of the ports, guidebooks and the tourism industry began a rather dramatic shift in style and emphasis while maintaining the image of Sevastopol as a city of heroism and valor. For almost a decade the Ukrainian economy stagnated under the weight of corruption and post-Soviet mismanagement.[29] The economic boom, starting in 1999, created investment opportunities in the infrastructures of tourism (e.g., hotels and restaurants) that could generate even greater capital, especially from foreign tourism. Sevastopol and much of the Ukrainian hinterland has developed more slowly than Kyiv, but relative prosperity may be in sight. In the early years of the twenty-first century, Sevastopol and the surrounding region began what could be a new economic industry to

---

26. In 1978 Doronina counted 739 monuments, and in 1999 there were 2,015 monuments registered with the city. See Doronina and Iakovleva, *Pamiatniki Sevastopolia*, 3; Dobry and Borisova, *Welcome to Sevastopol*, 46.

27. Kornienko, Mozhenkov, and Stefaniuk, *Sevastopol': Putevoditel'*, 37.

28. Ibid.; Khapaev and Zolotarev, *Legendarnyi Sevastopol'*, 95.

29. Jason Bush, "Will the Boom Last in Ukraine?" *Business Week*, 8 November 2004, 62.

complement the fishing, winemaking, and ship construction and repair industries that have been central to the region for so long. In 1996, after roughly six decades as a closed city, Sevastopol began to welcome tourists freely from the former Soviet Union and abroad. One guidebook listed its first chapter "Sevastopol-Open City!"[30] Approximately five hundred thousand tourists visit Sevastopol each year; about fifteen thousand visitors came from outside the former Soviet Union.[31] Although the gains so far have been modest, Sevastopol appears ready to tap into several tourism markets.

Early twenty-first-century guidebooks, while retaining the focus on the city's heroic past, have started to cater to a new audience. As one guidebook noted, "Sevastopol is neither only a fleet nor only a museum. It is an incomparably beautiful and affable city, welcoming guests with its glow."[32] Three things separate most post-Soviet guidebooks from their predecessors: less attention to the individual heroes of World War II, greater elaboration on opportunities for leisure beyond historical tourism, and more discussion of ethnic and religious diversity. The city's premier symbols, like the Monument to Scuttled Ships, Kazarskii's memorial, and the Crimean War Panorama, remain the focal points of post-Soviet guidebooks and carry on the tradition of noting the heroism, courage, and sacrifice of the city's defenders. The trends continue of placing sacrifice at the center of Sevastopol's mythology while avoiding mention of disasters that could not be redeemed by leading to an ultimate victory or greater good.

The change to profit-driven publication also has greatly decreased the length of guidebooks, which necessitates an even more selective portrayal of the past. Tourist-consumers are demanding more attention to the comforts that they now associate with vacations. With the opening of the city came a need for guidebooks to tell nonresidents about transportation, accommodations, and leisure. Some books reproduced extensive train schedules

---

30. Kornienko, Mozhenkov, and Stefaniuk, *Sevastopol': Putevoditel'*. Prior to 1996, one had to receive permission from the Ministry of Internal Affairs to visit the city, an honor reserved primarily for family members of residents and package tours for veterans, workers, students, and other groups coming to pay homage to the hero-city. The new 1996 law did not stop police and border guards during the winter of 1996–97 from repeatedly asking for the author's residency permission. Soviet tourists looking for pleasure went instead to Yalta or the other nearby resorts of the South Shore.

31. "Travel Ukraine," 2004, http://www.ukrtravel.com/sevastopol/main.htm.

32. Khapaev and Zolotarev, *Legendarnyi Sevastopol'*, 3.

and maps of train, bus, and fixed-route taxi lines.[33] Rarely does one find this level of detail in Soviet-era guidebooks because touring agencies arranged group transport in advance. The list of excursions in Sevastopol's guidebooks often included trolley numbers for various destinations, but as a rule these guides contained no detailed maps for reasons of military security. In a shift from the emphasis on physical activity and learning, post-Soviet guidebooks also paid much more attention to restful places like beaches and highlighted the natural beauty of the city and region. With a nod to more consumer-driven tourism, guidebooks provided locations and working hours to markets, souvenir stands, restaurants, and stores.[34] Several guidebooks told readers about vineyards and retailers.[35] Authors noted the location, sometimes with maps, of the city's various beaches and enumerated some of the amenities of each.

Beaches in Sevastopol were wildly popular with locals in Soviet times, but they were rarely mentioned in guidebooks because the focus remained on knowledge, not pure pleasure in Sevastopol.[36] Soviet guidebooks focused on educating rather than entertaining. In Sevastopol, which was not, like Yalta, a major Black Sea resort city in the Soviet period, fun rarely surfaced in guidebooks. Post-Soviet authors seemed to understand that many tourists wanted to relax, and they therefore promoted Sevastopol's beaches in an attempt to lure tourists away from Yalta. The city government aided the tourism industry by beautifying recreation areas for the foreign visitor.

The city government is now actively engaged in marketing Sevastopol's historical past for consumption by domestic and foreign tourists. In 2004 city officials began the process of demilitarizing Balaklava, the site of much Crimean War tourism, and cleaning up ordnance and other ecological dangers "for further development of Balaklava as a resort-recreation zone."[37] Here is one way in which the old and new Sevastopol merge.

---

33. Ibid., 152–57.

34. Kornienko, Mozhenkov, and Stefaniuk, *Sevastopol': Putevoditel'*, passim; Dobry and Borisova, *Welcome to Sevastopol*, passim; Khapaev and Zolotarev, *Legendarnyi Sevastopol'*, passim.

35. Kornienko, Mozhenkov, and Stefaniuk, *Sevastopol': Putevoditel'*, 88–89; Dobry and Borisova, *Welcome to Sevastopol*, 118–22.

36. Beach restoration and maintenance were key points in the accommodation plans of postwar reconstruction. For one such discussion see RGAE, f. 9432, op. 1, d. 387, ll. 371–75.

37. "Demilitarizatsiia Balaklavskoi bukhty uspeshno vypolniaetsia," *Sevastopol'skaia gazeta* 44 (2004): 3.

Knowing that few modern travelers will tolerate a lack of entertainment outlets, city officials have set out to reclaim beaches, develop docks for sailing, and open up the surrounding countryside for hiking, biking, and rock climbing. Much like Baltimore, Cleveland, and other industrial cities in the United States that undertook port reclamation projects in the 1990s, Sevastopol faces a great challenge from industrial and military pollution that has created large dead zones in nearby waters.

From the outset, post-Soviet guides made natural beauty a complement to the city's historical attractions. After noting that "Sevastopol, 'where each stone is history,' is a unique museum under an open sky," one publisher asserted that it has everything for "any taste and purse."[38] The nod to consumerism was not only unmistakable but also a stark change from Soviet times. He described the bays, hills, numerous cafes and shops, tree-lined streets, and more. Not wasting a chance for hyperbole, another author concluded that "Sevastopol is one of the most beautiful cities in the world....It is right to consider Crimea the most museum-like region of Ukraine, and in Crimea it is Sevastopol."[39] The chance for romance was a new lure for tourists too: "The incomparably romantic aura of this city penetrates the soul and remains there forever. It wants to come back in order to breathe this velvet air, dip into the waves of the tender sea and look at the silhouettes of the ships."[40]

This type of boosterism was imperative as Sevastopol fought for tourist dollars. "Sevastopol," lamented one guidebook, "is almost unknown to the wider resort public." Most view it as a "military city, the great port of Crimea, a city of ships and sailors. Not more than two of one hundred people identify Sevastopol as a resort."[41] The author even tried to personify the city, asking the reader to "feel its pulse, its vibration, its breathing."[42] The authors recognized the success of postwar memorialization of the city's military heritage that had come to dominate people's understanding of the city. In their view, the city now had to struggle against past perceptions in order to gain a larger tourist audience. They also seemed to suggest that

---

38. Khapaev and Zolotarev, *Legendarnyi Sevastopol'*, 1.
39. Kornienko, Mozhenkov, and Stefaniuk, *Sevastopol': Putevoditel'*, 26.
40. Khapaev and Zolotarev, *Legendarnyi Sevastopol'*, 1.
41. Kornienko, Mozhenkov, and Stefaniuk, *Sevastopol': Putevoditel'*, 76.
42. Ibid., 26.

the draw of a historical city could not compete with the pure leisure travel offered by resorts like nearby Yalta. Sevastopol had begun to adapt to an era in which travel no longer had to be useful, as was the dictate of Soviet times. Blending history with pleasure appeared to be the city's new niche.

Despite these changing images of Sevastopol, recent years have brought little physical change to the city that would challenge the local identification fostered in the wake of World War II. Except for new dachas and the commercialization of ground-floor storefronts on the central ring road, one would notice little change in the cityscape over the last decade. The relative continuity in Sevastopol's built environment is a result of a well-defined and long-lasting local identification process developed before, during, and after World War II. Moreover, the identification was easily adapted to the post-Soviet transformation and thus mitigated the need to redefine the city as had been so common elsewhere.

Sevastopol's lore transcended the Soviet Union and continues to frustrate attempts to develop an identification with Ukraine. Because the Russian Black Sea Fleet is still based in the city and most of the sites of memory created in the twentieth century highlight the contribution of Russians, political affinities tend toward Moscow rather than Kyiv. Whereas other Eastern European cities saw great transformation, none shared Sevastopol's demography nor maintained as strong a connection to their pre-Soviet roots throughout the twentieth century. Because the city had not been created as specifically Soviet after World War II, but rather also relied on its prerevolutionary Russian heritage, the transformation after 1991 was less traumatic and dramatic than in those cities that had had their pre-Soviet history expunged during the twentieth century. Postwar urban planners had already placed the city's nineteenth-century heritage ahead of the Soviet revolutionary tradition. Therefore, with the collapse of the USSR, Sevastopol could easily revert to its Russian orientation despite its place within independent Ukraine.

Ethnicity, Tourism, and the Redefinition of Space

The most striking change in twenty-first-century guidebooks, beyond downplaying Soviet-era politics, is their treatment of Sevastopol's multiethnic past. Soviet guidebooks minimized or excluded the understanding of the city's ethnic past. Post-Soviet guidebooks have embraced much of this diversity and even expanded their coverage beyond the perceived borders of the city in order to incorporate nearby Tatar and Karaite sites. While this could be seen as finally admitting the non-Slavic past of the region, it appears to be motivated more by profit than by a desire for reconciliation. Guidebooks, in short, have begun to meet the needs of the developing capitalist tourist industry and the various travel cultures it has engendered. Renewed attention to non-Slavs may draw visitors hoping to reclaim some of their own past and others who desire a sense of the exotic, for which Crimea has been known since Aleksandr Pushkin's famous 1824 poem "The Fountain at Bakhchisarai."

Most post-Soviet guidebooks recognized the city's multiethnic, multiconfessional character. Taking advantage of the near absence of ethnic diversity after the slaughter of Jews and the repression and deportation of Tatars, Greeks, and others in World War II, Soviet authors initially omitted or at least minimized the past influence of non-Slavic groups. It was only after the collapse of the Soviet Union that many people rediscovered Sevastopol's multiethnic past. "The history of the defense of the city," according to a 1995 memorial book, "is full of examples of the massive heroism of its defenders—sons and daughters of a variety of people."[43] Post-Soviet guidebooks became more explicit in retelling part of the history of the "small peoples" of Sevastopol and its region. One book, for example, included a discussion of the Crimean Khanate in its "Great History" section, something that could not have happened while the supposed war collaborators still languished in their Soviet-imposed exile. Authors also provided an extended discussion of Sevastopol's Karaite tradition, even noting that several prerevolutionary Karaites "played a significant role in the fate of the city, becoming honorific citizens."[44] This did not prove that anti-Semitism was any less virulent in post-Soviet Ukraine, but the reinclusion of the Karaite legacy was an admission of the group's importance to the city's development and growth up to 1941.

At more than 10 percent of Crimea's population at the beginning of the twenty-first century, following Russians and Ukrainians, Tatars are now

---

43. *Gorod-geroi Sevastopol': Kniga pamiati* (Simferopol: Tavriia, 1995) 2:14–15.

44. On the Crimean Khanate see Khapaev and Zolotarev, *Legendarnyi Sevastopol'*, 17–19, 86–87.

poised to become a significant part of the region's economy, politics, and culture, as they had been for five hundred years.[45] The Crimean Khanate grew from the fifteenth to the eighteenth century as the dominant force on the peninsula from its capital at Bakhchisarai. However, in 1783 Catherine II began the Russian conquest of the region. Throughout the nineteenth century to the 1920s, the Crimean Tatars were of great ethnographic interest. On 18 May 1944, however, Stalin ordered that they all be deported for alleged collaboration with the enemy. While a few thousand Tatars wore Nazi uniforms, tens of thousands fought in the Red Army. The deportation in closed railcars and the squalor of their new residences killed roughly half of the deportees. When Khrushchev rehabilitated Stalin's "punished peoples" in the 1950s, the Crimean Tatars remained one of only three groups (together with the Volga Germans and Meskhetian Turks) denied the right to return to their homes.[46]

For the rest of the Soviet period Tatars continued to demonstrate for the right of return, and at the end of the Soviet period they finally realized their dreams.[47] But in the wake of the political and economic collapse of the Soviet Union, many families were unable to make the long trip back. Sporadic attacks against Crimean Tatar enclaves and leaders have continued to the present. But public goodwill is also evident. Sevastopol's city administration congratulated the city's Muslims on the holiday of Kurban-Bairam, one of the most important festivals of the hadj, and the members of the Muslim society Miunevver in turn wished health, peace, and neighborliness (*dobrososedstvo*) to all city residents.[48] But the return of Tatars is more important than merely reinstituting confessional diversity.

Much of Sevastopol's commercial and economic expansion no doubt came from ethnotourism that highlighted the region's complex ethnic heritage. After a harsh decade of dramatic economic decline, some entrepreneurs in Sevastopol and Crimea realized that there was money to be made in tourism, and ethnotourism took hold. Travel packages highlighted

45. Askold Krushelnycky, "Ukraine: Ethnic Tensions in Crimea Bubbling Over," *RFE/RL*, 11 February 2004.

46. Alexander Nekrich, *The Punished Peoples: The Deportation and Fate of Soviet Minorities at the End of the Second World War*, trans. George Saunders (New York: Norton, 1978), 133, 172–73.

47. David Remnick, "Soviets Say Crimean Tatars May Return to Homeland: Commission Rejects Restoration of Autonomy," *Washington Post*, 10 June 1988, A1.

48. "Mira i dobra vam, liudi!" *Slava Sevastopolia*, 22 January 2005, 1.

the rich ethnic heritage of Sevastopol and its nearby suburbs. Although the city's military heritage remained the central theme of most Sevastopol tours, ethnotourism became increasingly popular.[49] One- to five-day tour packages included a walking trip around the central ring road and its monuments and the Crimean War Panorama and Museum on Historical Boulevard. Some itineraries included an excursion to the diorama museum of World War II at Sapun Gora. Prepackaged itineraries provided visitors with a quick introduction to the city's military and naval past. For those who could spend more than one day, packages usually included a discussion of the city's Greek heritage at the Khersones Archaeological Preserve. At Khersones one can walk the ancient streets and through the foundations of what were once homes and stores. The museum contains a staggering array of artifacts from the various groups (Greeks, Romans, Tatars, and Turks) who at one time controlled the area. Many longer tours also began to include side trips to Bakhchisarai and Chufut-Kale. These two sites, located about one hour outside the city center, highlight the region's Tatar and Karaite heritage, respectively. At Bakhchisarai one can tour the palace and its grounds and view both permanent and rotating exhibits of Tatar life, art, and craft work. Walking the former streets of the Chufut-Kale cave city is more treacherous, and archaeological exploration has only just begun.

Sandwiched between Bakhchisarai and Chufut-Kale is the Russian Orthodox Uspenskii Cave Monastery. The additional attention paid to Orthodox sites like the Uspenskii Monastery, the site of Vladimir the Great's baptism at Khersones, and the various other monasteries built into the hillsides surrounding the city brings a new dimension to Sevastopol tourism that one could not have experienced in the Soviet era. Highlighting the Russian Orthodox Church as well as the Tatars and Karaites illuminates the centrality of Crimea to all these groups and separates the peninsula demographically and religiously from surrounding regions. The uniqueness of the city and region further pulls Sevastopol away from Europe, toward which Ukraine and much of the former Soviet bloc have been moving

---

49. For a sampling of sites (content accessed December 2004), see http://www.tourism.crimea. ua/ (the official site of the Ministry of Resorts and Tourism of Crimea); http://sevtour.by.ru/ (Unforgettable Rest in Crimea); http://www.dreamland.crimea.ua/; http://rest.crimea.ua/; http:// www.tour-ethno.com.

since independence. In response to the new tourism market, however, the boundaries of Sevastopol have been shifted geographically and topically. Identification with the city's military heritage remains most important and still dominates the center of the city most frequented by tourists. The optional packages outside the city center show a non-Russian identity little discussed in the Soviet period. It seems implausible, however, that other ethnic groups will pose a serious challenge to Sevastopol's Russian-centered identification as long as current demographic trends hold, which are likely as long as the Russian Fleet remains.

Commercialization of Post-Soviet Space

Although agitational spaces and sites of memory have remained relatively unchanged since the end of the Soviet Union, newly commercialized space has created a drastic juxtaposition between old and new. The twenty-first century has brought commercial storefronts to the ground floors of buildings along the central ring road. Unlike the city of the mid-1990s, Sevastopol today boasts several fashionable restaurants (and unfashionable ones like McDonald's), jewelers, clothing stores, and more. Many stores promote foreign products with foreign advertising, but even stores for local Russian and Ukrainian products have transformed the aesthetic of the urban environment. The contrast between old and new is clear to any observer. Many ground-floor shops sport modern glass display windows and steel entryways with newly painted plaster facades. The upper residential floors show the wear of the years since the buildings rose out of the rubble of the Second World War. On the upper floors, which are primarily residential, yellowed and grayed plaster remains and ferro-concrete balconies and loggias crumble. Although residents live in the old Sevastopol, tourists and wealthy residents shop in the new.

Two stores on Bol'shaia Morskaia Street, the most fashionable shopping area of the city, show the contrast between the traditional Soviet use of built space and the new commercialization of post-Soviet space. Megasport became the largest sporting goods store in the city center. The large, heavy, Soviet-era wooden doors greeted visitors as they walked beneath the English-language store sign. Brightly colored placards (also in Latin characters) promoting Reebok, Nike, Speedo, and Adidas flanked the entryway down

Figure 12. Megasport sporting goods store. Photograph by Karl D. Qualls, 2004.

the length of the sidewalk. Two large color posters of male athletes hung on either side of the doorway with text in Ukrainian and store hours in Russian. Thus we have a multilingual storefront promoting an all-foreign line of sporting goods. Moreover, the plaster wall facades were painted a bright white, offsetting the color of the promotional material. Juxtaposed with the bright, colorful lower floor were the essentially untouched upper two floors. The plaster walls had grayed, and the faux balustrade immediately above the store appeared particularly shabby when set off against the new white paint (figure 12).

On the opposite side of the street, the women's clothing store Fete and its neighboring casino showed an even greater juxtaposition between old and new (figure 13). A new arched doorway cut in the stone facade had been reinforced with highly polished steel. The glass door and display window had been topped by a similar glass arch. Clean, modern lines dominated the interior and exterior, but the balcony and the Doric-style balustrade that served as a railing on the floor above were disintegrating. In one section

Figure 13. Fete store. Photograph by Karl D. Qualls, 2004.

of six balusters, five were missing. The newly painted facade, much like Megasport's, set off the new commercial floor from the older, dilapidated residential floors above (figure 14). The casino, something strictly forbidden in the Soviet period, beckoned a new generation of residents with disposable income or those in desperate hope for a better future.

The juxtaposition of wealth and poverty was also visible in other places along this stretch of street. A broad consumer products store with painted white facade lurked below a second-floor balcony that had rotted through and showed clear signs that the apartment owner had tried to keep it

Figure 14. Store and apartments on Bol'shaia Morskaia. Photograph by Karl D. Qualls, 2004.

fastened to the building with cement. Directly above this dangerous balcony was a loggia with Ionic columns, also painted stark white, which contrasted starkly with the neighboring apartment's unpainted and enclosed loggia. Sevastopol's commercial and tourist development had created a wealth gap that catalyzed urban transformation and changed the original use and appearance of buildings.

Only one store in the center was designed as unabashedly Western in every way. Situated at Lazarev Square nearly equidistant from the city's main theater and cinema, McDonald's, although small, resembled a McDonald's anywhere in the world save for its Russian-language menu. The decor, food, and service were completely out of place in Sevastopol. The life-size Ronald McDonald placed outside beckoned to the passing crowd. Whereas Fete and Megasport sent mixed messages, McDonald's left no doubt that it is *the* symbol of Westernization. These new modern structures and businesses in twenty-first-century Sevastopol began to equate Europe and the West with modernity and affluence, but they also created and represented economic inequality.

However, some commercial interests in the city began to embrace the Russian past. The most well-known restaurant, Traktir, was named for the 1855 Crimean War battle that attempted to remove the French from the city, and the interior designer covered walls with paintings on nautical and military themes. All the servers, although they are women, dressed as Imperial Russian sailors. Ironically, the restaurant became known for the best and most authentic Russian cuisine in the city, but its borsch was Ukrainian. This did not seem to matter to the Russian marines and sailors, tourists from Europe and North America, and civilian residents who frequented the restaurant. Visitors and city residents were transported into Sevastopol's heroic past (although very superficially) during their meal.

Advertisers also learned to target local consumers by associating their products with the city's past. The meat products firm KAMO placed billboards around the city stating, "There are Sausages. And there are KAMO Sausages." The background to this unimaginative slogan was the Monument to Scuttled Ships, the most beloved monument in the entire city. In short, such advertisers drew not only on the city's Russian past but also on the residents' sense of local patriotism and identity. The intent was to associate KAMO with the city and create modern brand loyalty. As Sevastopol adapts to the world of capitalism, its image as a stalwart defender of the Motherland is strengthened through advertising and marketing of its past, but it is also diluted through the multiple images that city leaders and entrepreneurs are projecting about leisure and ethnic tourism.

The Tensions of Post-Soviet Ukrainianization

Tourism and capitalism have begun to challenge parts of Sevastopol's biography, but the shift to Ukrainian jurisdiction since 1991 poses the most significant test to the narrative established in the postwar decade. When the Soviet Union imploded and an independent Ukraine emerged, the overwhelmingly linguistically Russian population of Sevastopol wondered what would become of them, the city's Russianness, and its privileged position vis-à-vis the state of which it was a part. In addition to its cultural dissimilarity with western Ukraine, Sevastopol had also had a special distinction as a "city of republic subordination" since 1948.[50] Simply put, the city had much more autonomy and a direct relationship with the Soviet capital that often bypassed the regional governments. Because of its military importance, it was better provisioned than other Crimean cities and most other Ukrainian cities, too. When Soviet largesse came to an end, many wondered if independent Ukraine would continue to support Sevastopol in the same manner. Moreover, as Ukraine started a dialogue with the North Atlantic Treaty Organization (NATO) and the European Union (EU) about future alliances, the Russian fleet and pro-Russian population that shared Moscow's disdain for these links to Europe saw their worldview challenged.

The mid-1990s were a tumultuous period in which much of Crimea sought to establish its independence from Ukraine. What had seemed like an empty gesture by Nikita Khrushchev in 1954 became a central factor in growing Russian-Ukrainian tensions. Khrushchev gave Crimea to Ukraine in that year as a gift on the three hundredth anniversary marking the union of Ukraine and Russia in the Treaty of Pereislav. The administrative transfer meant little in the centralized Soviet system, but in 1991 it meant that Russia no longer had its home port on the Black Sea. Sevastopol and Moscow sought reunification, and the Black Sea Fleet stood divided between Russia and Ukraine.

In 1994 Iurii Meshkov, the pro-Russian separatist president of the Crimean Autonomous Republic, came to power, and Sevastopol's city council declared itself a Russian territory.[51] On 17 March 1995 the Ukrainian parliament, backed by President Leonid Kuchma, eliminated the presidency of Crimea and revoked its constitution, which left Meshkov without power or a position. Russia, which immediately after the Soviet collapse protested that Sevastopol was still Russian territory, could say little while still fighting a war against secessionist Chechnya.[52] Two years later, after

---

50. When in 1948 the Council of Ministers ordered that the reconstruction of Sevastopol be completed in three to four years, it raised Sevastopol to a "city of republic subordination," which meant, among other things, that its budget and orders came directly from the Russian Federation, not the Crimean Soviet Socialist Autonomous Republic. See GAGS, f. R-79, op. 2, d. 103, l. 221.

51. "Crimea: Who's in Charge Today?" *Economist* 332, 17 September 1994, 56–57.

52. For more on the separatist movement and the fall of Meshkov see Vyacheslav Savchenko, "Crimea Is Shaken by President-Parliament Clash," *Current Digest of the Soviet Press,* 12 October

protracted negotiations, Russia and Ukraine signed the Treaty of Friendship and Cooperation in which Russia agreed to recognize Ukraine's territorial boundaries, including Crimea.

For Sevastopol, the disposition of the Soviet Black Sea Fleet was clearly
the most important Russo-Ukrainian conflict, and it has dramatically affected the city's vistas. Since 1991 the former Soviet fleet had flown the flags
of both countries. Commanders, however, usually followed orders from
Moscow, which paid most salaries. As the Crimean government fought to
secede from Ukraine, the issue of the fleet was a powder keg. Bloody fights
between Ukrainian and Russian sailors lessened after 1995 when Russia
received 82 percent of the fleet and promised to lease the city's naval facilities for twenty years.[53] But NATO exercises in the Black Sea enraged
many Russians, who saw them as a provocation and an attempt to woo
Ukraine away from its Slavic brother. For four years the two fleets had
looked at each other with contempt, suspicion, and animosity, each blaming the other for poor maintenance, inadequate funding, and nationalist
pretensions.[54] In one famous incident, Ukrainian commandos stormed a
Russian naval base in Odessa and arrested three officers. Russian authorities said that even the officers' children were beaten. Ukraine argued it was
retaliating for the theft of $10 million in navigation equipment aboard the
Sevastopol-based ship *Chekelen*. When two Ukrainian ships tried to inter-
cept the *Chekelen*, the Russian navy sent an attack group from Sevastopol
that chased the ships away. Ensuing Ukrainian seizures of former Soviet
bases led Moscow to place its warships on full alert.[55]

After the division of the fleet, the number of Russian sailors and housing units rose dramatically. The navy started carving up parts of the city

---

1994, 5; "Ukraine: Time to Scratch," *Economist,* 25 March 1995, 58; "Crimea: Guess Who Won,"
Economist, 15 July 1995, 33.

53. The author personally witnessed two Russian sailors bloodying a Ukrainian sailor in 1997.
Russian hegemony was also apparent during the military parade celebrating the city's liberation
from Nazi Germany when most onlookers left the sidewalks after the Russian forces marched by,
leaving near-empty streets for the Ukrainian fleet. In 2004, both fleets garnered sizable audiences.

54. Richard Boudreaux, "Russia and Ukraine Seek Sea Change in Sevastopol Politics: Control over City That Is Port to Black Sea Fleet and Kiev's Navy Is a Sticking Point between Two
Nations," *Los Angeles Times,* 23 April 1995, 4.

55. Julian Borger, "Moscow Puts Warships on Full Alert," *Guardian,* 15 April 1994, 11; Lee
Hockstader, "Ukraine Detains Officers After Russia Grabs Ship, as Fleet Conflict Escalates,"
Washington Post, 12 April 1994, A16.

near the ports for dacha-style housing. Sevastopol was becoming a home and not merely a military posting.[56] In 1997, Moscow Mayor Iurii Luzhkov fanned the flames by financing and building apartments for Russian sailors in Sevastopol. With new housing dominating the western skyline, Luzhkov's popularity skyrocketed in Sevastopol and led one resident to say, "Luzhkov is right. Sevastopol is a historic military city of Russia. All its major events and achievements are important chapters in Russian history."[57] One and a half years later Luzhkov continued to insist that "Crimea must be returned to Russia."[58] On a Moscow television program Russian rear admiral Vadim Vasyukov noted that it is "hard to overestimate the contribution of the Moscow municipal government and Iurii Mikhailovich Luzhkov personally" to the work of the Black Sea Fleet.[59] Luzhkov continued the Russian presence in the city by signing an agreement to aid Sevastopol in economic, cultural, and technical matters through 2005.[60]

Cultural treasures and the ownership of history also remained points of tension between Russia and Ukraine. The St. Vladimir Cathedral at Khersones, rededicated in 2001 with Russian and Ukrainian presidents Vladimir Putin and Leonid Kuchma in attendance, once again dominates the skyline of the architectural preserve.[61] Erected in 1891 on the spot where Vladimir the Great is said to have accepted the Byzantine faith and thus brought Christianity to the East Slavs of his kingdom, it functioned only twenty-three years before the Soviet government closed it. Nazi bombing

---

56. Mary Mycio, "Regional Outlook a Dacha Duel in Crimea between Russia, Ukraine: Under Cover of Political Chaos, a Land Grab Rages in Sevastopol, Home of the Black Sea Fleet," *Los Angeles Times,* 24 May 1994, 6.

57. Carol J. Williams, "Ribbon Cut on a New Crimean War: An Apartment House, Built by Moscow's Mayor, Opens in Sevastopol. And as Russians Move in, So Enters a New Jab at Black Sea Fleet Deal," *Los Angeles Times,* 5 October 1997, 13.

58. Lev Ryabchikov, "Moscow Mayor Insists That Crimea Be Returned to Russia," ITAR-TASS News Wire, 19 March 1999, 1.

59. "Russian Black Sea Fleet's Flagship Back in Service Thanks to Moscow Mayor," BBC Monitoring, 9 April 2000, 1.

60. "Moscow Mayor Signs Cooperation Agreement with Ukrainian Sevastopol," BBC Monitoring, 21 March 2002, 1.

61. In addition to the Sevastopol encyclopedia entries for these sites see Venikeev, *Arkhitektura Sevastopolia;* E. V. Venikeev, *Sevastopol i ego okrestnosti* (Moscow: Iskusstvo, 1986); Vladimir Shavshin, *Bastiony Sevastopolia, Pamiatniki i polia srazhenii Krymskoi voiny* (Simferopol: Tavriia, 2000); Kornienko, Mozhenkov, and Stefaniuk, *Putevoditel': Sevastopol',* 5. The latter suggests that the reopening of the cathedral is central to the city's plan to remake its image as a tourist center by 2010.

and local looting of stone rubble for housing left the structure in ruins after World War II. In 1992 the church reclaimed the building, and in 2004 Sevastopol's mayor handed this magnificent structure to the Moscow patriarchate because Russian Orthodoxy was the "largest confession in the region."[62] The presence of Putin and Kuchma signaled the importance of the common heritage of the two states. However, the mayor's gift of control to Moscow suggested that Vladimir the Great and his capital at Kyiv were more a part of Russian history than Ukrainian, which was consistent with much Russian national historiography that traced the Russian state to Kyiv.

Because Luzhkov and the Russian fleet have guaranteed a strong Russian presence demographically and politically until the fleet's lease expires in 2017, Sevastopol's identification as a Ukrainian city is still not imminent. It is also clear when one visits the city, however, that Sevastopol is in a state of flux. As Ukraine tries to position itself for NATO and EU membership, Russia feels threatened with the loss of its former sphere of influence. For some in the population, the encroachment of the West into the former Soviet Union pushes them closer to Russia as a bulwark against Western domination. For others who see economic opportunity in closer ties to Europe, identification of Sevastopol as a Russian city is still important, but servility to Moscow is not. Few in the city see a wholesale redesignation of the city as Ukrainian as a positive and viable option. The myth of Sevastopol as a defender of the Russian Motherland from Kazarskii and Tolstoy through the Second World War has been too lasting and pervasive to be changed casually and quickly.

Politicized Space in Sevastopol's 2004 Presidential Campaign

Russian-Ukrainian conflict in the 1990s came into full view during the 2004 Ukrainian presidential election campaign, which highlighted the juxtaposition of old and new, Russia and Europe in Sevastopol. Traditionally, Nakhimov Square, one of the oldest parts of the city, has been the site of demonstrations and parades. Sevastopol celebrated all major holidays with parades and marches around the ring road that started and

---

62. "Vladimirskoi sobor peredan tserkvi," *Sevastopol'skaia gazeta,* 5 November 2004, 3.

ended at Nakhimov Square.[63] It is not surprising that communist and socialist parties in the 2004 presidential campaign used this area for their
demonstrations with speakers, megaphones, songs, and marches. One of the
communist parties held a nearly daily vigil at the entrance of Primorskii Boulevard, the city's traditional and still most popular leisure area, into
Nakhimov Square. Along the wrought-iron garden fence the communists
placed placards, all in Russian, decrying capitalism, nationalism, and Ukrainian participation in the occupation of Iraq. This older geographic space became the location for the older residents' political stand.

Viktor Yushchenko's younger and distinctly Ukrainian "Orange Revolution" was not well received in overwhelmingly Russian Sevastopol.[64] His
supporters chose a location that could not have been more different from
the communists' choice. A lone Yushchenko information tent stood along
the central ring road directly in front of McDonald's. None of the twenty-
somethings I talked to who were working for Yushchenko's campaign
knew whether the location had been selected for a particular reason. There
is a great deal of foot traffic in the area, including both residents and tourists. Moreover, McDonald's, as in many countries, serves as a meeting place
for the city's youth. Because the Yushchenko campaign targeted youth in
particular in eastern and southern Ukraine, McDonald's seemed to be a
perfect location to bring his message to the youngest voters in the city.

It is likely that the symbolism of this location was intentional. Closer
ties to Europe and greater economic integration and development formed
the base of Yushchenko's campaign; therefore, an information tent in front
of one of the largest global corporations based in the West would link
Yushchenko with economic vitality and modernization. Contact with the
EU and NATO stood near the top of his international agenda, but the
local press decried Yushchenko's plans to prepare Ukraine for entry into
the EU as the harbinger of "national catastrophe" that would create conflict with Russia, as happened in Georgia after its revolution.[65] Questions

63. Many specialists reviewing the initial reconstruction plans after World War II noted that
all redesign of the square had to account for its central function as an agitational space. See RGAE,
f. 9432, op. 1, d. 243, l. 13.

64. In the first round, he garnered only 5.98 percent of the vote in Sevastopol. "Predvaritel'nye
rezultaty vyborov," *Sevastopol'skaia gazeta,* November 4, 2004.

65. A. Tikhii, "Gruzinskoe ruslo ukrainskoi evrointegratsii," *Slava Sevastopolia,* October 22,
2004.

of illegal campaign contributions and U.S. interference on his behalf were also common.[66] The contrast between old and new could not have been clearer between Yushchenko's campaign center and the communist-defined space on Nakhimov Square and its statue to the Crimean War admiral P. S. Nakhimov.

Yushchenko's opponent, Viktor Yanukovich, moved unhindered throughout Sevastopol's built space, unlike Yushchenko, who rarely ventured past Simferopol's airport, about 100 kilometers from Sevastopol. Yanukovich's overwhelming popularity among the largely Russophile residents allowed him and his supporters to roam freely throughout the city. His placards and information kiosks dotted the urban landscape. Yanukovich's dominance was most clearly reflected at the newspaper kiosk. In addition to large posters of a smiling Yanukovich in the kiosk windows, local newspapers consistently carried pro-Yanukovich articles and scathing exposes of Yushchenko and his policies. Journalists portrayed Yanukovich as the champion of the poor and downtrodden and Yushchenko (especially during his time as prime minister) as taking money from invalids and families with children.[67] In both cases, Yanukovich was careful to play on Sevastopol's existing identity and pledged to support it. He made appearances at war memorials to praise the city and its heroes and promised 10 million hryvnias from the central Ukrainian budget for a new war memorial and museum.[68]

The political campaigns used the traditions and innovations inscribed in the urban fabric for their purposes. As long as the boundaries of tradition were maintained, the electoral campaign remained civil. Even though communists were a distinct minority, they played a role familiar to the city's past in an area long used for demonstrations. Yushchenko's nationalist, pro-Western campaign, however, violated Sevastopol's traditional identification as a protector of Mother Russia and thus had less access to

66. A. Artemenko, "Kriminal'nye avtoritety sobiraiut den'gi na prezidentskuiu kampaniiu 'messii?'" *Slava Sevastopolia,* May 27, 2004; P. Ivanits, "Posol SShA Dzhon Kherbst kak agitator kandidata v prezidenty Viktora Iushchenko," *Slava Sevastopolia,* July 21, 2004.

67. Ia. Stetsenko, "Bor'ba s bednost'iu—glavnaia zadacha Viktora Ianukovicha," *Slava Sevastopolia,* October 22, 2004.

68. "Blagodaren sevastopol'tsam za to, chto segodnia veriat vlasti," *Slava Sevastopolia,* October 29, 2004.

the public spaces of the city. Verbal abuse against Yushchenko's supporters was commonplace in public and in private and ranged from old women screaming about how a Yushchenko victory would undo all their sacrifices in World War II to the scolding of young men and women trying to distribute campaign literature. One clever middle-aged man commented that the life-sized Ronald McDonald statue directly behind the campaign tent would be a better president than Yushchenko and also wondered if it was a statue of Yushchenko's American wife. Had the Yushchenko campaign tried to organize at Russian military sites of memory, the local response might have been more violent.

By staying in the most commercialized region of the ring road, the campaign aligned Yushchenko with economic progress, although one could clearly also read McDonald's as a symbol of the destruction of the past. Communists remained true to the past both in the language and the location of their political campaign. Yanukovich, who was portrayed as a protector or savior for the city and its residents, roamed freely throughout the city, crossing the boundaries of old and new, poor and rich, military and civilian. Ultimately, however, Yanukovich's popularity in Sevastopol was not enough to overcome Yushchenko's majority nationwide.

Like the ever-changing nature of memory and identification, Sevastopol will no doubt endure further change. Some may come sooner than both Russians and Ukrainians would like. After a U.S. warship docked in the Crimean port of Feodosiia during joint naval exercises with Ukraine in 2006, the Crimean parliament designated the peninsula a "NATO-free" zone.[69] A local Ukrainian representative, Volodymyr Arabadzhy, encapsulated the dilemma perfectly: "If we go towards NATO, the Russian fleet will have to leave Sevastopol. If the Russian Fleet is in Sevastopol, Ukraine cannot be in NATO. . . . Our people in Sevastopol have many traditions—mostly close to the navy fleet, because Sevastopol was born as a naval base 225 years ago."[70] Arabadzhy's statement reveals the power of the postwar rebuilding process in creating a stronger identification with Moscow.

---

69. Richard Weitz, "Moscow Mayor Inflames Russian-Ukrainian Differences over Sevastopol," *World Politics Review,* 27 May 2008; "Moscow Says Ukraine's Black Sea Fleet Decree Erodes Trust," *Russian Courier,* 22 May 2008.

70. "Fleet Gives Russia Crimean Clout," BBC News, 12 February 2008.

With the anniversaries of the end of the Second World War, the liberation of Sevastopol and Crimea, and the founding of the Black Sea Fleet all coinciding in early May 2008, new salvos were fired in the ongoing battle for Sevastopol. In April 2008, Alexei Ostrovsky, head of the Russian State Duma committee on the affairs of the Commonwealth of Independent States, said that Russia could reclaim Crimea if Ukraine joined NATO. A month later, during a visit to Sevastopol to mark the 225th anniversary of the Black Sea Fleet, Moscow mayor Iurii Luzhkov again stoked the flames of the conflict by noting that Khrushchev's gift of Crimea to Ukraine in 1954 had had no impact on the disposition of Sevastopol. He stated that Sevastopol was at the time of the transfer a federal city with special administrative status; therefore, the city could not have been part of the gift to Ukraine. The following day the Ukrainian Security Services issued a statement: "Russian citizen [Iurii] Luzhkov has been barred from entering Ukraine, starting on May 12, because, despite warnings he continued to call for actions that threaten Ukraine's national interests and territorial integrity."[71]

Less than two weeks later Viktor Yushchenko requested draft legislation to end all international relations regarding the Russian fleet's presence in Crimea. In a separate address Yushchenko called for the removal of all symbols of the Soviet past and totalitarian repression. While not mentioning Sevastopol specifically, the implications were clear. Sevastopol's chief newspaper reported the plan to tear down monuments and rename streets and pointed out what this would mean for Sevastopol. The author noted that not only would it purge the city's Soviet history, but it also would likely encourage further attempts to Ukrainianize the urban landscape. The six residents who responded to the article showed a diversity of opinions, from the view that it was acceptable to rid cities of some vestiges of the past, especially those that were of little artistic merit, to the opinion of a World War II veteran, who said, "It is impossible to touch the monuments. They are signs of our history."[72]

---

71. "Moscow Mayor Barred from Ukraine," *Russian Courier,* 12 May 2008; "Eurasian Secret Services Daily Report," 12 May 2008; Michael Schwirtz, "Russia and Ukraine Pick a New Fight over an Old Naval Base," 23 May 2008.

72. Klim Kostner, "Mazepa? Velikii? Nam put' ozarit?" *Slava Sevastopolia,* 21 May 2008.

What Might the Future Hold?

Although it might appear counterintuitive, local identification was one strategy of reimposing central authority, which was the key to all political intriguing at the center of power in the postwar decade. Disoriented and homeless citizens needed somewhere to root themselves after a traumatic era. As long as an urban biography showed the unique local role as part of the larger Russian/Soviet state, then the process of local identification posed little threat to the central regime. With the Soviet Union forming a Russocentric identification, Sevastopol was free to reach back to its nineteenth-century heritage to construct a mythology that trumped even the October Revolution. The construction of an urban biography was both a reflection of and a catalyst for local identification. Authors, artists, architects, and other creators of urban biographies did not start from a tabula rasa; they selectively remembered the past and transformed it to meet contemporary conditions and to promote their own values and beliefs or those of their patrons.

Although scholars often give preference to the power of the written word in describing the genesis of urban biographies, monuments, street names, and architectural aesthetics can also tell a local story. Parades, festivals, and other celebrations reiterate the narrative, allowing participants to reenact and reimagine local and national events. The city's urban identity was manufactured for travelers but also for new arrivals to the city in order to direct them to what it meant to be local. In a city like Sevastopol that had almost ceased to exist during World War II, many of the people who inhabited the rubble after liberation and rebuilt the city came from elsewhere. In order to mobilize, settle, and motivate the new labor force for reconstruction, various strategies of local identification became common.

Agents embedded identification in a series of narratives, from travel guides to memorials and the built space of the city itself. Memorials, architecture, and place names acted as a public narrative that was often unmediated and therefore could be interpreted in many ways. The public narrative also functioned to perpetuate identification that the censorship regime had scripted. Once the planning and press coverage subsided, sites of identification continued as reminders of a constructed past. Although Rogers Brubaker and Frederick Cooper do not discuss urban identification in their article "Beyond 'Identity,'" it is clear that Soviet urban reconstruction resembled their "relational and categorical modes of identification."[73] The agents of identification in Sevastopol created a relational web with the city and its population serving as defenders of the Motherland. It was Moscow to which city leaders had to appeal for accommodation. Moscow directed the resources—however belatedly—that allowed Sevastopol to be reborn. And even though Moscow architects initially fought to change the city, it was the architectural and planning agencies in Moscow that had to give final approval to the local plan that prevailed in the end. All this means that much of Sevastopol's perceived place in the world was connected to Russia and the USSR. As one of the first designated hero-cities, Sevastopol carried a categorical identification initially shared only with Leningrad, Stalingrad, and Odessa. Because the categorical, but especially the relational, mode of identification tied Sevastopol to Russia, the city's incorporation into the post-Soviet independent state of Ukraine has been fraught with challenges.

The developments during Sevastopol's postwar decade are as important in the twenty-first century as they were during the Soviet period. The physical rebuilding of the city was long ago completed. Homes and hospitals replaced rubble, but the city's struggle with its past continues. As we move into the second decade of the twenty-first century, the myth of Sevastopol may be challenged more than at any point in its history. The pressures of capitalism and tourism could displace history in favor of recreation and resort tourism. What history remains could challenge the primacy of the Russocentric narrative as ethnotourism gains in popularity. Even after the Cold War, Sevastopol is still central to geopolitical conflicts. NATO expansion and Russian-Ukrainian conflicts are more than just topics of conversation in Sevastopol; they are potential threats to residents' long-held identification as a Russian naval city. Although it is building a new naval base in Novorossisk, Russia needs to maintain its presence in Sevastopol because of its ties to the city's religious and military heritage. Ukraine, on the other hand, needs to take sovereignty of its territory. If Ukraine forces the Russian fleet out of Sevastopol and the rest of its bases in Crimea, it will have a dramatic effect on the local economy. Just as important, Ukraine

---

73. Brubaker and Cooper, 16.

would have to begin to pay its debts to Russia. Russia forgives between 90 and 100 million dollars of Ukraine's debt in return for the lease of Sevastopol. Russia has already shown its willingness to use energy as a political tool. If Russia is removed from the Crimean Peninsula, Ukraine will have little leverage to demand delivery of oil and gas.

Although Yushchenko has signaled his intentions to rewrite history, it is difficult to see how Sevastopol's relational identification toward Kyiv could change without changing its categorical identification. Even if the Russian fleet is removed, the city will still be home to the Ukrainian navy and therefore maintain its categorical identification as a naval port. However, except for the common experience of World War II, it is not possible to tie Sevastopol's naval past to Ukraine. Catherine the Great established the modern city as the empire's southern naval port. Ukraine and Russia shared the trauma of the war, but it is not possible to write Ukraine into the Russo-Turkish or the Crimean war.

The postwar strategies of identification forged an urban biography that has proved remarkably resilient into the twenty-first century. If Ukraine is to capture the allegiance of the citizens of its most important naval city, it would do well to learn from the postwar process of accommodation and agitation. Iurii Luzhkov has understood and reaped the benefits of spreading his largesse throughout the city. Ukraine would need to invest heavily in projects the local community deems important. If the Russian fleet left the city and unemployment increased, Ukraine would face one of its greatest domestic challenges since independence. It would not have to rebuild the city as in 1944, but it would no doubt find it more difficult to rewrite the city's urban biography without the ruins that allowed for so many possibilities. Without a nationwide tragedy like World War II, the city's residents would see no reason why the state should not accommodate their needs immediately. Further, the recent history of Moscow's heavy investment in a Ukrainian city would surely provoke questions as to why Ukraine would not do the same. Officials in Kyiv would be well advised to start recruiting their own locals from whom they can gather good information about the needs and wants of residents. They must also be ready to invest large sums of money to show their concern for the populace. Last, they should be cognizant of local identifications. Any extensive purge of the past, even the much-maligned early-Soviet period, could lead to a retrenchment into Russian nationalism for the nearly three-quarters of the population that is ethnically Russian.[74]

In the end, Sevastopol became what it is largely because of the efforts of those local officials and citizens who had learned well how to negotiate the Soviet system to their advantage and leverage attention and resources to fulfill *their* plans rather than those drawn up exclusively in Moscow statistical bureaus and urban planning workshops. This was not a community that appeared spontaneously. Instead, it was consciously crafted and created as an imagined or invented community whose social or collective memory could easily merge national and local identifications. One has to wonder whether the little girl who lived in the bank vault after the war or her friends who grew up in caves and dugouts will now challenge Kyiv and continue to fight for local narratives that may not merge easily with Ukraine. It appears that the quality of Sevastopol's memory project outlasted that of the buildings from the reconstruction years. As balconies crumbled, Sevastopol's Russian military heritage stood fast. It has so far withstood challenges from tourism and capitalism and simply marginalized the memory of its Soviet feats. The deeper history of the nineteenth century, so clearly tied to Russian state building, remains central.

When Russia's lease of Sevastopol's ports ends in 2017, the World War II generation will have passed and the direct connection to the last great defense will be severed. At this point there may be an opportunity to inject Ukrainian identification into Sevastopol and move it toward a European orientation. However, it seems implausible that memory of the Crimean War and World War II can be fully Ukrainianized in the near future. Although the memory of World War II could bring the city toward Ukraine, which also suffered greatly in the war, Sevastopol has been distancing itself from the mid-twentieth century by refocusing on the Crimean War instead. Unless another catastrophe levels the city and provides a tabula rasa for Ukrainian planners, Sevastopol likely will remain in part a Russian city, even if only in the historical imagination. And as long as the Russian Federation continues to see itself as separate from Europe, most of Sevastopol's residents will likely do the same. The city council seems hesitant to

---

74. As of 2001, 74 percent of Sevastopol's population was Russian and 21 percent Ukrainian; Belorussians, Crimean Tatars, Jews, Armenians, Greeks, Germans, Moldovans, Poles, and other groups made up the other 5 percent. Dobry and Borisova, *Welcome to Sevastopol,* 5.

change street names en masse or to introduce new Ukrainian monuments unconnected to military themes. City leaders and entrepreneurs seem to be steering a middle course—one that allows them to reap the economic benefits from tourism while still promoting their Crimean War heritage above all else.

Selected Bibliography

Newspaper and Journals

Arkhitektura SSSR
Arkhitektura i stroitel'stvo
Izvestiia
Krasnyi Chernomorets
Pravda
Problemy sovremennogo gradostroitel'stva
Slava Sevastopolia
Sevastopol'skaia gazeta
Sevastopol'skaia pravda
Sevastopol'skii stroitel'
VOKS Bulletin
Za Rodinu!

Archival Sources

Gosudarstvennyi arkhiv goroda Sevastopolia (State Archive of the City of Sevastopol)
    (GAGS)

f. R-13, Department of Soviet Provisioning
f. R-38, Municipal Committee of the Union of State Trade and Catering
f. R-59, Municipal Department of Health Maintenance
f. R-79, Executive Committee of the Sevastopol City Soviet of People's Deputies
f. R-90, Municipal Department of People's Education
f. R-109, Department of Cultural-Instructional Work
f. R-160, Trust of Cafeterias and Restaurants
f. R-184, Municipal Housing Administration
f. R-257, Administration of Trade of the City Executive Committee
f. R-294, Organ of Professional-Technical Education
f. R-308, Administration of City Building and Architecture
f. R-359, City Planning Commission
Gosudarstvennyi arkhiv Rossiiskoi Federatsii (State Archive of the Russian Federation) (GARF)
f. 5446, USSR Council of Ministers
f. A-150, State Committee of the Council of Ministers RSFSR for Construction and Architectural Affairs
f. A-259, RSFSR Council of Ministers
f. A-374, Central Statistical Administration RSFSR
f. A-471, Institute of City Planning of the State Committee of the Council of Ministers RSFSR for Construction Affairs
National Archives and Record Administration (NARA)
Record Group 208, Records of the Office of War Information
Record Group 111, Records of the Office of the Chief Signal Officer
Record Group 242, Collection of Foreign Records Seized
Record Group 373, Records of the Defense Intelligence Agency
Rossiiskii gosudarstvennyi arkhiv ekonomiki (Russian State Archive of the Economy) (RGAE)
f. 293, All-Union Academy of Architecture
f. 1562, Central Statistical Administration
f. 9432, Council of Ministers Committee on Architectural Affairs
f. 9510, Ministry of City Building
Rossiiskii gosudarstvennyi arkhiv literatury i iskusstva (Russian State Archive of Literature and Art) (RGALI)
f. 674 Union of Soviet Architects

Primary Sources

Almazova, S.D. "Etazh i liudi." In *Vozrozhdenie Sevastopolia: Sbornik,* compiled by Vera Kuzmina. Simferopol, 1982.
Andreev-Khomiakov, Gennady. *Bitter Waters: Life and Work in Stalin's Russia.* Translated by Ann E. Healy. Boulder, 1997.
Belogortsev, Igor D. *Arkhitekturnyi ocherk Smolenska.* Smolensk, 1949.
Belogortsev, Igor D., and I. Sofinskii, *Smolensk.* Moscow, 1952.

Borisov, Boris Alekseevich. *Podvig Sevastopolia: Dokumental'naia povest'.* Moscow, 1952.

———. *Sevastopol'skaia byl.* Simferopol, 1968.

———. *Shkola zhizni.* Moscow, 1971.

———. *Zapiski sekretaria gorkoma.* Moscow, 1964.

Chebaniuk, Zakhar. *Sevastopol': Istoricheskie mesta i pamiatniki.* Simferopol, 1955.

———. *Sevastopol': Istoricheskie mesta i pamiatniki.* Simferopol, 1957

Doronina, Emiliia, and Tamara Ivanovna Iakovleva. *Pamiatniki Sevastopolia.* Simferopol, 1978.

———. *Pamiatniki Sevastopolia: Spravochnik.* Simferopol, 1987.

Dobry, Aleksandr. *Dobro pozhalovat' v Sevastopol'.* Simferopol, 2000.

Dobry, Aleksandr, and Irina Borisova, *Welcome to Sevastopol.* Simferopol, 2001.

Dunaev, M., and F. Razumovsky, *Novgorod: A Guide.* Moscow, 1984.

Ehrenburg, Ilya, and Konstantin Simonov. *In One Newspaper: A Chronicle of Unforgettable Years.* New York, 1985.

Garmash, Petr. *Gorod-geroi Sevastopol': Ocherk putevoditel'.* Simferopol, 1972.

General'nyi plan rekonstruktsii goroda Moskvy. Moscow, 1936.

Gol'ts, G. "Smolensk: K proekty vosstanovleniia goroda." *Arkhitektura i stroitel'stvo* 10 (1945): 3–6.

The Heroic Defence of Sevastopol. Moscow, 1942.

Irin, L. "Restoration Plans for Fifteen Cities." *USSR Information Bulletin* 4, no. 2 (April 1946): 277.

Istoriia goroda-geroia Sevastopolia, 1917–1957. Kyiv, 1960.

Kaganovich, L.M. *Za sotsialistichskuiu rekonstruktsiiu Moskvy i gorodov SSSR.* Moscow, 1931.

Kandinsky, Wassily. *Concerning the Spiritual in Art.* New York, 1947.

Kornienko, V., R. Morzhenkov, and V. Stefaniuk, *Sevastopol': Putevoditel'.* Simferopol, Svit.

Krovavye zlodeianiia nemtsev v Sevastopole. Sevastopol, 1944.

Levchenko, Ia. P. *Planirovka gorodov: Tekhniko-ekonomicheskie pokazateli i rascheti.* Moscow, 1952.

———. *Tekhniko-ekonomicheskie osnovy planirovki poselkov.* Moscow, 1944.

Narodnoe khoziatstvo krymskoi oblasti. Simferopol, 1957.

Notes and Statement by the Soviet Government on German Atrocities. Moscow, 1943.

Novgorod: Putevoditel'. Leningrad, 1966.

Novgorod: Illiustrirovannyi putevoditel'. Leningrad, 1972.

Olshevskii, Vitalii. *Sevastopol': Putevoditel'.* Simferopol, 1981.

———. *Sevastopol': Spravochnik.* Simferopol, 1977.

Orlov, Nikolai, and Igor Gassko. *Gorod-geroi Sevastopol': Fotoalbom.* Simferopol, 1985.

Pokhodaev, Iurii. *Pamiatniki drevnego zodchestva: Novgorod.* Moscow, 1969.

Putevoditel': Sevastopol'. Simferopol, 2004.

Riabkov, G.T. *Gorod-geroi Smolensk: Ocherk-putevoditel'.* Moscow, 1988.

Rosseikin, Boris. *Sevastopol': Albom.* Simferopol, 1960.

Rosseikin, Boris, and Georgii Semin. *Sevastopol': Putevoditel'-spravochnik.* Simferopol, 1961.

Rosseikin, Boris, Georgii Semin, and Zakhar Chebaniuk. *Sevastopol': Putevoditel'-spravochnik.* Simferopol, 1959.

Sevastopoliu 200 let, 1783–1983: Sbornik dokumentov i materialov. Kyiv, 1983.

Sevastopol: November, 1941–July, 1942: Articles, Stories and Eye-Witness Accounts by Soviet War Correspondents. London, 1943.

Sevastopol': Putevoditel'. Simferopol, 2004.

Shavshin, Vladimir. *Bastiony Sevastopolia, Pamiatniki i polia srazhenii Krymskoi voiny.* Simferopol, 2000.

Smirnov, I.A. *Smolensk: Gorod-geroi.* Moscow, 1988.

———. *Smolensk: Gorod russkoi slavy.* Moscow, 1982.

Smolensk: Putevoditel'. Moscow, 1974.

Smolensk: Spravochnik-putevoditel'. Smolensk, 1960.

Tolstoy, Lev. *Sevastopol Tales.* Moscow, 1982.

Venikeev, E.V. *Arkhitektura Sevastopolia: Putevoditel'.* Simferopol, 1983.

———. *Sevastopol' i ego okrestnosti.* Moscow, 1986.

Voitekhov, Boris. *The Last Days of Sevastopol.* Translated by Ralph Parker and V.M. Genne. New York, 1943.

Zaitsev, I.A., and I.I. Kushnir, *Ulitsy Novgoroda: Spravochnik.* Leningrad, 1975.

Secondary Sources

Ackerman, Phyllis. "The Symbolic Sources of Some Architectural Elements." *Journal of the Society of Architectural Historians* 12, no. 4 (1953): 3–7.

Adam, Robert. *Classical Architecture: A Comprehensive Handbook to the Tradition of Classical Style.* New York, 1991.

Agrest, Diana, and Mario Gandelsonas. "Semiotics and the Limits of Architecture." In *A Perfusion of Signs,* edited by Thomas A. Sebeok, 90–120. Bloomington, 1977.

Anderson, Benedict. *Imagined Communities: Reflections on the Origin and Spread of Nationalism.* London, 1983.

Arnheim, Rudolf. *Dynamics of Architectural Form.* Berkeley, 1977.

Barber, John, and Mark Harrison. *The Soviet Home Front, 1941–1945: A Social and Economic History of the USSR in World War II.* New York, 1991.

Barkhina, G. *G. B. Barkhin.* Moscow, 1981.

Bittner, Stephen V. *The Many Lives of Khrushchev's Thaw: Experience and Memory in Moscow's Arbat.* Ithaca, 2008.

Blackwell, Martin J. "Regime City of the First Category: The Experience of the Return of Soviet Power to Kyiv, Ukraine, 1943–1946." PhD diss., Bloomington, 2005.

Blake, Peter. "The Soviet Architectural Purge." *Architectural Record* 106 (September 1949): 127–29.

Bradley, Joseph. *Muzhik to Muscovite: Urbanization in Late Imperial Russia.* Berkeley, 1985.

Brandenberger, David. *National Bolshevism: Stalinist Mass Culture and the Formation of Modern Russian National Identity, 1931–1956.* Cambridge, MA, 2002.

Brodersen, Per. "Am weitesten im Westen. Werden und Sein einer sowjetischen Stadt: Kaliningrad 1945–1971." PhD diss., Dusseldorf, 2005.

Brooks, Jeffrey. "*Pravda* Goes to War." In *Culture and Entertainment in Wartime Russia,* edited by Richard Stites, 9–27. Bloomington, 1995.

———. *Thank You Comrade Stalin! Soviet Public Culture from Revolution to Cold War.* Princeton, 2000.

Brubaker, Rogers. *Nationalism Reframed: Nationhood and the National Question in the New Europe.* New York, 1996.

Brubaker, Rogers, and Frederick Cooper. "Beyond 'Identity.'" *Theory and Society* 29, no. 1 (February 2000): 1–47.

Brumfield, William Craft, ed. *Reshaping Russian Architecture: Western Technology, Utopian Dreams.* Washington, DC, 1990.

Bucher, Greta. *Women, the Bureaucracy and Daily Life in Postwar Moscow, 1945–1953.* Boulder, 2006.

Bullock, Nicholas. *Building the Post-War World: Modern Architecture and Reconstruction in Britain.* London, 2002.

Burton, Chris. "Medical Welfare during Late Stalinism: A Study of Doctors and the Soviet Health System, 1945–1953." PhD diss., Chicago, 2000.

Clark, Katerina. *The Soviet Novel: History as Ritual.* Chicago, 1981.

Colton, Timothy. *Moscow: Governing the Socialist Metropolis.* Cambridge, MA, 1995.

Confino, Alon. *The Nation as a Local Metaphor: Württemberg, Imperial Germany, and National Memory, 1871–1918.* Chapel Hill, NC, 1997.

Cook, Catherine, ed. *Russian Avant-Garde Art and Architecture.* London, 1983.

Corney, Frederick. "Rethinking a Great Event: The October Revolution as Memory Project." In *States of Memory: Continuities, Conflicts, and Transformations in National Retrospection,* edited by Jeffrey K. Olick, 17–42. Durham, NC, 2003.

Cottam, Kazimiera Janina. *Women in War and Resistance: Selected Biographies of Soviet Women Soldiers.* Nepean, Ont., 1998.

Cottam, Kazimiera Janina, and Nikoloai Vissarionovich Masolov. *Defending Leningrad: Women behind Enemy Lines.* Nepean, Ont., 1998.

Cubitt, Geoffrey. *History and Memory.* Manchester, UK, 2007.

Czaplicka, John, Nida Gelazis, and Blair Ruble, eds. *Cities after the Fall of Communism: Reshaping Cultural Landscapes and European Identity.* Baltimore, MD: Johns Hopkins University Press and Woodrow Wilson Center Press, 2009.

Davies, Sarah. *Popular Opinion in Stalin's Russia: Terror, Propaganda and Dissent, 1934–1941.* New York, 1997.

Diefendorf, Jeffry. *In the Wake of War: The Reconstruction of German Cities after World War II.* New York, 1993.

Diefendorf, Jeffry, Carola Hein, and Yorifusa Ishida, eds. *Rebuilding Urban Japan after 1945.* New York, 2003.

Dimaio, Alfred John. *Soviet Urban Housing: Problems and Policies.* New York, 1974.

Dunham, Vera. *In Stalin's Time: Middleclass Values in Soviet Fiction.* Durham, NC, 1990.

Dunmore, Timothy. *Soviet Politics, 1945–1963.* New York, 1984.

Dunstan, John. *Soviet Schooling in the Second World War.* New York, 1997.

Duskin, Eric J. *Stalinist Reconstruction and the Confirmation of a New Elite, 1945–1953.* New York, 2000.

Edele, Mark. "A 'Generation of Victors?': Soviet Second World War Veterans from Demobilization to Organization, 1941–1956." PhD diss., Chicago, 2004.

Edelman, Murray. *The Symbolic Uses of Politics.* Urbana, IL, 1985.

Ellman, Michael. "The 1947 Soviet Famine and the Entitlement Approach to Famines." *Cambridge Journal of Economics* 24, no. 5 (September 2000): 603–30.

Erickson, John. *The Road to Berlin: Continuing the History of Stalin's War with Germany.* Boulder, 1983.

———. *The Road to Stalingrad.* London, 1974.

Erickson, John, and David Dilks, eds. *Barbarossa: The Axis and the Allies.* Edinburgh, 1994.

Esping-Andersen, Gosta. *The Three Worlds of Welfare Capitalism.* Princeton, 1990.

Ewing, E. Thomas. *The Teachers of Stalinism: Policy, Practice, and Power in Soviet Schools of the 1930s.* New York, 2002.

Filtzer, Donald. *Soviet Workers and Late Stalinism: Labour and the Restoration of the Stalinist System after World War II.* Cambridge, UK, 2002.

———. *Soviet Workers and Stalinist Industrialization: The Formation of Modern Industrial Relations, 1928–1941.* Armonk, NY, 1986.

Fitzpatrick, Sheila. "Postwar Soviet Society: The 'Return to Normalcy,' 1945–1953." In *The Impact of World War II on the Soviet Union,* edited by Susan J. Linz, 129–56. Totowa, NJ, 1985.

———. "Readers' Letters to *Krest'ianskaia Gazeta,* 1938." *Russian History/Histoire russe* 24, nos. 1–2 (Spring–Summer 1997): 149–70.

———. "Signals from Below: Soviet Letters of Denunciation of the 1930s." *Journal of Modern History* 68 (1996): 831–66.

———. "Supplicants and Citizens: Public Letter-Writing in Soviet Russia in the 1930s." *Slavic Review* 55 (1996–97): 78–105.

Fortier, John. *Fortress of Louisbourg.* Toronto, 1979.

Fürst, Juliane, ed. *Late Stalinist Russia: Society between Reconstruction and Reinvention.* New York, 2006.

———. "Prisoners of the Soviet Self? Political Youth Opposition in Late Stalinism." *Europe-Asia Studies* 54, no. 3 (2002): 353–75.

Gallagher, Matthew P. *The Soviet History of World War II: Myths, Memories, and Realities.* New York, 1963.

Gellner, Ernest. *Nations and Nationalism.* Ithaca, 1983.

Gillis, John R. *Commemorations: The Politics of National Identity.* Princeton, 1994.

Glantz, David. *When Titans Clashed: How the Red Army Stopped Hitler.* Lawrence, KS, 1995.

Goodsell, Charles T. *The Social Meaning of Civic Space: Studying Political Authority through Architecture.* Lawrence, KS, 1988.

Gorlizki, Yoram, and Oleg Khlevniuk. *Cold Peace: Stalin and the Soviet Ruling Circle, 1945–1953.* Oxford, 2004.

Gorsuch, Anne E., and Diane P. Koenker, eds. *Turizm: The Russian and East European Tourist under Capitalism and Socialism.* Ithaca, 2006.

Gutman, Amy, ed. *Democracy and the Welfare State.* Princeton, 1988.

Harris, James. *The Great Urals: Regionalism and the Evolution of the Soviet System.* Ithaca, 1999.

———. "Resisting the Plan in the Urals, 1928–1956." In *Contending with Stalinism: Soviet Power and Popular Resistance in the 1930s,* edited by Lynne Viola, 201–28. Ithaca, 2002.

Harrison, Mark. *Accounting for War: Soviet Production, Employment, and the Defence Burden, 1940–1945.* Cambridge, UK, 1996.

Heinzen, James. "The Art of the Bribe: Corruption and Everyday Practice in the Late Stalinist USSR." *Slavic Review* 66, no. 3 (2007): 389–412.

———. "Informers and the State under Late Stalinism: Informant Networks and Crimes against 'Socialist Property,' 1940–53." *Kritika* 8, no. 4 (2007): 789–815.

Hobsbawm, Eric. *Nations and Nationalism since 1780: Programme, Myth, Reality.* New York, 1990.

Hoffmann, David L. *Peasant Metropolis: Social Identities in Moscow, 1929–1941.* Ithaca, 1994.

Holmes, Larry. *The Kremlin and the Schoolhouse: Reforming Education in Soviet Russia, 1917–1931.* Bloomington, 1991.

———. Stalin's School: *Moscow's Model School No. 25, 1931–1937.* Pittsburgh, 1999.

Holquist, Peter. "'Information Is the Alpha and Omega of Our Work': Bolshevik Surveillance in Its Pan-European Context." *Journal of Modern History* 69 (1997): 415–50.

———. *Making War, Forging Revolution: Russia's Continuum of Crisis, 1914–1921.* Cambridge, MA, 2002.

———. "New Terrains and New Chronologies: The Interwar Period through the Lens of Population Politics." *Kritika* 4, no. 1 (Winter 2003): 163–75.

Hoppe, Bert. *Auf Den Trümmern von Königsberg. Kaliningrad 1946–1970.* Munich, 2000.

Howard, Ebenezer. *Garden Cities of Tomorrow.* London, 1902.

Hudson, Hugh. *Blueprints and Blood: The Stalinization of Soviet Architecture, 1917–1937.* Princeton, 1994.

Johnston, Timothy. "Subversive Tales?: War Rumours in the Soviet Union 1945-1947." In Fürst, *Late Stalinist Russia,* 62–78.

Jones, Jeffrey W. *Everyday Life and the "Reconstruction" of Soviet Russia during and after the Great Patriotic War, 1943–1948.* Bloomington, 2008.

Kelly, Catriona. *Comrade Pavlik: The Rise and Fall of a Soviet Boy Hero.* London, 2005.

Kenez, Peter. "Black and White: The War on Film." In Stites, *Culture and Entertainment in Wartime Russia,* 157–75.

Khan-Magomedov, Selim Omarovich. *Pioneers of Soviet Architecture: The Search for New Solutions in the 1920s and 1930s.* Translated by Alexander Lieven. New York, 1987.

Koenker, Diane P. *Republic of Labor: Russian Printers and Soviet Socialism, 1918–1930.* Ithaca, 2005.

Kojevnikov, Alexei. "Rituals of Stalinist Culture at Work: Science and the Games of Intraparty Democracy Circa 1948." *Russian Review* 57 (January 1998): 25–52.

Kopp, Anatole. *Constructivist Architecture in the USSR.* London, 1985.

Kosenkova, Iuliia. *Sovetskii gorod 1940-kh–pervoi poloviny 1950-kh godov: Ot tvorcheskhikh poiskov k praktike stroitel'stvo.* Moscow, 2000.

Koshar, Rudy. *German Travel Cultures.* New York, 2000.

——. "'What Ought to be Seen': Tourists' Guidebooks and National Identities in Modern Germany and Europe." *Journal of Contemporary History* 33, no. 3 (July 1998): 323–40.

Kotkin, Stephen. *Magnetic Mountain: Stalinism as a Civilization.* Berkeley, 1995.

——. "1991 and the Russian Revolution." *Journal of Modern History* 70 (June 1998): 384–425.

Krivosheev, G.F. *Soviet Casualties and Combat Losses in the Twentieth Century.* London, 1997.

Kuromiya, Hirokai. *Stalin's Industrial Revolution: Politics and Workers, 1928–1932.* Cambridge, UK, 1988.

Landsberg, Alison. *Prosthetic Memory: The Transformation of American Remembrance in the Age of Mass Culture.* New York, 2004.

Lasswell, Harold D. *The Signature of Power: Buildings, Communication and Policy.* New Brunswick, NJ, 1979.

Linz, Susan J., ed. *The Impact of World War II on the Soviet Union.* Totowa, NJ, 1985.

Lowenthal, David. *The Past Is a Foreign Country.* Cambridge, UK, 1985.

Manley, Rebecca. "The Evacuation and Survival of Soviet Civilians, 1941–1946." PhD diss., Berkeley, 2004.

——. "'Where Should We Resettle the Comrades Next?' The Adjudication of Housing Claims and the Construction of the Post-war Order." In Fürst, *Late Stalinist Russia,* 233–47.

Martin, Terry. "Modernization or Neo-traditionalism? Ascribed Nationality and Soviet Primordialism." In *Russian Modernity: Politics, Knowledge, Practices,* edited by David Hoffmann and Yanni Kotsonis, 161–82. New York, 2000.

McReynolds, Louise. "Dateline Stalingrad: Newspaper Correspondents at the Front." In Stites, *Culture and Entertainment in Wartime Russia,* edited by Richard Stites, 28–43.

Mosse, George. *Fallen Soldiers: Reshaping the Memory of the World Wars.* New York, 1990.

Motorin, Dmitrii. *Vozrozhdennyi Sevastopol': Ocherki o vosstanovlenii goroda 1944–1953 gg.* Moscow, 1984.

Murray, John. *Politics and Place-Names: Changing Names in the Late Soviet Period.* Birmingham, UK, 2000.

Nakachi, Mie. "Population, Politics and Reproduction: Late Stalinism and Its Legacy." In Fürst, *Late Stalinist Russia,* 23–45.

Nekrich, Alexander. *The Punished Peoples: The Deportation and Fate of Soviet Minorities at the End of the Second World War.* Translated by George Saunders. New York, 1978.

Nove, Alec. *An Economic History of the USSR.* New York, 1976.

Pennington, Reina. "Wings, Women and War: Soviet Women's Military Aviation Regiments in the Great Patriotic War." Master's thesis, University of South Carolina, 1993.

Pethybridge, R.W. *A History of Postwar Russia.* New York, 1966.

Petrone, Karen. *Life Has Become More Joyous, Comrades: Celebrations in the Time of Stalin.* Bloomington, 2000.

Platt, Kevin, and David Brandenberger, eds. *Epic Revisionism: Russian History and Literature as Stalinist Propaganda.* Madison, 2006.

Pollock, Ethan. *Stalin and the Soviet Science Wars.* Princeton, 2006.

Prezios, Donald. *The Semiotics of the Built Environment: An Introduction to Architectonic Analysis.* Bloomington, 1979.

Qualls, Karl D. "Local-Outsider Negotiations in Sevastopol's Postwar Reconstruction, 1944–53." In *Provincial Landscapes: The Local Dimensions of Soviet Power,* edited by Donald J. Raleigh, 276–98. Pittsburgh, 2001.

Raleigh, Donald J. "Languages of Power: How the Saratov Bolsheviks Imagined Their Enemies." *Slavic Review* 57, no. 2 (1998): 320–49.

Ruble, Blair A. "Moscow's Revolutionary Architecture and Its Aftermath: A Critical Guide." In *Reshaping Russian Architecture: Western Technology, Utopian Dreams,* edited by William Craft Brumfield, 111–44. Washington, DC, 1990.

Salisbury, Harrison. *Russia on the Way.* New York, 1946.

Sartorti, Rosalinde. "On the Making of Heroes, Heroines, and Saints." In Stites, *Culture and Entertainment in Wartime Russia,* 176–93. Bloomington, 1995.

Savchenko, Vyacheslav. "Crimea Is Shaken by President-Parliament Clash," *Current Digest of the Soviet Press* 12 October 1994, 5.

Scott, James C. *Seeing Like a State: How Certain Schemes to Improve the Human Condition Have Failed.* New Haven, 1998.

Siegelbaum, Lewis. *Stakhanovism and the Politics of Productivity in the USSR, 1935–1941.* Cambridge, UK, 1988.

Sevastopol': Entsiklopedicheskii spravochnik. Sevastopol, 2000.

Sezneva, Olga. "Living in the Russian Present with a German Past: The Problems of Identity in the City of Kaliningrad." In *Socialist Spaces: Site of Everyday Life in the Eastern Bloc,* edited by David Crowley and Susan E. Reid, 47–64. Oxford, 2002.

Shvidkovskii, O.A. *Building in the USSR, 1917–1932.* New York, 1971.

Slezkine, Yuri. "The USSR as a Communal Apartment, or How a Socialist State Promoted Ethnic Particularism." *Slavic* Review, 53, no. 2 (Summer 1994): 415–52.

Starr, S. Frederick. "The Revival and Schism of Urban Planning in Twentieth-Century Russia." In *The City in Russian History,* edited by Michael Hamm, 222–42. Lexington, 1976.

——. "Visionary Town Planning During the Cultural Revolution." In *Cultural Revolution in Russia, 1928–1931,* edited by Sheila Fitzpatrick, 207–40. Bloomington, 1978.

Steinmetz, George. *Regulating the Social: The Welfare State and Local Politics in Imperial Germany.* Princeton, 1993.

Stites, Richard, ed. *Culture and Entertainment in Wartime Russia.* Bloomington, 1995.

——. "Iconoclastic Currents in the Russian Revolution: Destroying and Preserving the Past." In *Bolshevik Culture: Experiment and Order in the Russian Revolution,* edited by Abbott Gleason, Peter Kenez, and Richard Stites, 1–24. Bloomington, 1985.

——. *Revolutionary Dreams: Utopian Vision and Experimental Life in the Russian Revolution.* Oxford, 1989.

Tarkhanov, Alexei, and Sergei Kavtaradze. *Architecture of the Stalin Era.* New York, 1992.

Timasheff, Nicholas. *The Great Retreat: The Growth and Decline of Communism in Russia.* New York, 1946.

Titmuss, Richard. *Essays on the Welfare State.* New Haven, 1959.

Tomoff, Kiril. *Creative Union: The Professional Organization of Soviet Composers, 1939–1953*. Ithaca, 2006.

Tzonis, Alexander, and Liane Lefaivre. *Classical Architecture: The Poetics of Order.* Cambridge, MA, 1986.

Vale, Lawrence J., and Thomas Campanella, eds. *The Resilient City: How Modern Cities Recover from Disaster.* New York, 2005.

Varga-Harris, Christine. "Constructing the Soviet Hearth: Home, Citizenship and Socialism in Russia, 1956–1964." PhD diss., University of Illinois, 2005.

——. "Green Is the Color of Hope? The Crumbling Facade of Postwar Byt through the Public Eyes of *Vechernaia Moskva.*" *Canadian Journal of History* 34, no. 2 (1999): 193–219.

Verdery, Katherine. *What Was Socialism? And What Comes Next?* Princeton, 1996.

Viola, Lynne, ed. *Contending with Stalinism: Soviet Power and Popular Resistance in the 1930s.* Ithaca, 2002.

Vitruvius. *The Ten Books on Architecture.* Translated by Moris Hicky Morgan. New York, 1960.

Weiner, Amir. *Making Sense of War: The Second World War and the Fate of the Bolshevik Revolution.* Princeton, 2000.

——. "The Making of a Dominant Myth: The Second World War and the Construction of Political Identities within the Soviet Polity." *Russian Review* 55, no. 4 (October 1996): 638–60.

Weiner, Douglas. *A Little Corner of Freedom: Russian Nature Protection from Stalin to Gorbachev.* Berkeley, 1999.

Wertsch, James V. *Voices of Collective Remembering.* Cambridge, UK, 2002.

Winter, Jay, and Sivan Emmanuel, eds. *War and Remembrance in the Twentieth Century.* Cambridge, UK, 1999.

Wortman, Richard. *Scenarios of Power: Myth and Ceremony in Russian Monarchy.* 2 vols. Princeton, 1995, 2000.

Yekelchyk, Serhy. "Diktat and Dialogue in Stalinist Culture: Staging Patriotic Historical Opera in Soviet Ukraine, 1936–1954." *Slavic Review* 59, no. 3 (Fall 2000): 597–624.

——. *Stalin's Empire of Memory: Russian-Ukrainian Relations in the Soviet Historical Imagination.* Toronto, 2004.

Zima, V.F. *Golod v SSSR 1946–1947 godov: Proiskhozhdenie i posledstviia.* Moscow, 1996.

Zubkova, Elena. *Obshchestvo i reformy 1945–1964.* Moscow, 1993.

——. *Poslevoennoe sovetskoe obshchestvo: politika i povsednevnost, 1945–1953.* Moscow, 1999.

——. *Russia after the War: Hopes, Illusions, and Disappointments, 1945–1957.* Translated by Hugh Ragsdale. Armonk, NY, 1998.

Zubkova, E. Iu., L.P. Kosheleva, G.A. Kuznetsova, A.I. Miniuk, L.A. Rogovaia, eds., *Sovetskaia zhizn' 1945–1953.* Moscow, 2003.

INDEX

Note: Page numbers in *italics* indicate figures; those with a *t* indicate tables.

abortion rates, 117–19, 118*t*
Academy of Architecture, 57
accommodation, 2–7, 38, 48–55, 61–67, 76–77, 80–124, 156, 192–93
Ackerman, Phyllis, 150n45
Adam, Robert, 150n46
aesthetics, Soviet, 8, 9, 47, 54–55, 132, 147–49
Afghanistan, 170
agitational space, 5–6, 48–51, 55, 124–47, 156
Agrest, Diana, 143n33
agricultural policies, 3, 4, 70, 102, 106, 123. *See also* famine
Akademgorodok, 87
Alabian, K., 57n29
Aleksandr Nevskii, 27, 132n13, 161

Alëshina, Tamara, 67–70, 78–79, 89, 115
All-Union Society of Proletarian Architects (VOPRA), 51–53
Almazova, S. D., 106n75, 113
Amelchenko, Mikhail, 74–79, 81–82
Andreev-Khomiakov, Gennady, 97n42
Arabadzhy, Volodymyr, 189
Aref'ev, A. V., 74–75, 78, 79, 82
Arkin, David, 85
Arnheim, Rudolf, 149n44
Artemenko, A., 188n66
Artillery Bay, *xviii,* 99
Artiukhov, Valentin, 63n44
Ashkhabad earthquake, 70, 147
Association of New Architects (ASNOVA), 50–52

avant-garde architecture, 50n8
Aviators of the Black Sea Navy, Monument to, 141, 169

Baburov, V. V., 66
Baida, Maria, 34–36, 38
Bakhchisarai, 176, 177
Balaklava, 69, 134n20, 172
Barber, John, 48n5
Barkhin, Grigorii, 56n27, 112, 155–56; criticisms of, 63–66, 68, 129–30, 135–36; Sevastopol's reconstruction plans of, 57, 59–61, 66, 67, 78, 127–29
Bashkiria, 80, 84
Battle for Sevastopol (film), 33, 42–43
Belogortsev, I., 161n2
Bittner, Stephen V., 5n6
Blake, Peter, 57n29
Bogatyr, Ivan, 34
Bol'shaia Morskaia Street, 114, 143, 144; commercialization of, 178–81, *179–81;* map of, *xviii*
Borger, Julian, 184n55
Borisov, Boris, 17n7, 18, 141
Borisova, Irina, 157, 162n8
Boudreaux, Richard, 184n54
Bradley, Joseph, 50n11
Brandenberger, David, 12n1, 132n14, 155n50, 161n4
Brezhnev, Leonid, 159, 169
Briullov, A. P., 137
Briullov, Karl, 137
Brodersen, Per, 8n12, 71n68
Brooks, Jeffrey, 44n64
Brubaker, Rogers, 8n13, 191–92
Bucher, Greta, 36n43, 87n4
Bugaichuk, F., 114n99
Burton, Chris, 86n1
Bush, Jason, 170n29

Callimachus, 152
Campanella, Thomas, 4n5, 6
Catherine the Great, 24, 32, 131, 176, 193
cemeteries, 16, 111, 127, 134n20, 139–41
censorship, film, 121

Chankvetadze, K., 139–40
Chaus, Anastasia, 37
Chebaniuk, Zakhar, 162–69
Chechnya, 183
Chersonesus. *See* Khersones
Christ the Savior Cathedral (Moscow), 54n20, 136
Chufut-Kale, 177
cinema, 20*t*, 111–14, 133, 145, 150; censorship of, 121; German propaganda and, 22–23, 39–41; Soviet propaganda and, 28, 30, 33, 38, 41–43; wartime newsreels and, 8–9, 28, 38–43, 132, 162
City Planning Commission, 68, 69
Clark, Katerina, 41n59
collective farms, 3, 70, 102, 106, 123
Colton, Timothy, 74n73
commercialization, 171–72, 178–82, *179–81*
Committee on Architectural Affairs (KA), 48, 83; creation of, 55–56, 133; historic preservation plans of, 134–35; Sevastopol's reconstruction plans of, 57–60, 66, 81
Commune Square, 128, 144
Communist Underground Organization in the German Rear (KPOVTN), 16–17
Confino, Alon, 7
Constitution of 1936, 86, 93
constructivist architects, 50–52, 57, 146
Cooper, Frederick, 8n13, 191–92
Corney, Frederick, 8n11
Cottam, Kazimiera Janina, 36n43
Council of Ministers, 70–72, 75, 80
Council of People's Commissars (Sovnarkom), 55–56, 59; reconstruction directive of, 64, 122, 133
Count's Wharf, *xviii,* 42, 58–59
Crimean Administration for Architectural Affairs, 142
Crimean Autonomous Republic, 183–84
Crimean Khanate, 175–77. *See also* Tatars

Crimean War, 12, 25, 29–33, 193; in guidebooks, 161, 163–65; heroines of, 34–36; monuments to, 22, 127–30, 137, 163, 169; Tolstoy's writing on, 11–12, 25–26, 29–31, 43; World War II and, 25, 30–31, 38, 144, 155–56
Crimean War Panorama. *See* Panorama of the Great Defense
Cubitt, Geoffrey, 7n8

Davies, Sarah, 154n48
Defenders of Sevastopol Monument, 169
demographics, of Sevastopol, 19, 20*t*, 101, 194n74
Dilks, David, 14n3
Dimaio, Alfred John, Jr., 100n49
diphtheria, 2, 103*t*
Directorate for the Restoration of Sevastopol (UVS), 72, 93–94
Directorate of Architecture, 78
Directorate of Deputy Ministers of the Russian Federation, 78
Dobry, Aleksandr, 157, 162n8, 166, 169
Doronina, Emiliia, 139n27, 140n28, 162–64, 166–70
Dunaev, M., 161n3
Dunham, Vera, 4n4, 71n70, 86n2
Dunstan, John, 70n65
Duskin, Eric, 4n4
dysentery, 2, 101, 102, 103*t*, 104–5

Edele, Mark, 88n6
Edelman, Murray, 126n3
education, 70n65, 116, 119–21, 142; postwar plans for, 21–22, 22*t*, 69–70; trade schools and, 91, 94–95
Ehrenburg, Ilya, 37, 44
Eisenstein, Sergei, 24–25
Ellman, Michael, 109n85
Erickson, John, 14n3, 55n21
Esping-Andersen, Gosta, 86n1
ethnicity, 125, 145–47, 157–58, 165, 174–78, 182–83, 194n74
European Union (EU), 183, 186
Ewing, E. Thomas, 70n65

famine, 4, 91, 102, 105, 109. *See also* agricultural policies
Fete clothing store, 179–80, *180*
Filippov, V. I., 76
film. *See* cinema
Filtzer, Donald, 18n14, 71n69, 91–92, 109n85, 114n103
Five Black Sea Men, 33–34, 167–68
Fortier, John, 126n2
Fraternal Cemetery, 16, 127, 134n20, 141
French Revolution, 7
Friendship and Cooperation Treaty, 184
Frunze, Mikhail, 143
Frunze Street, 128
functionalist architecture, 50, 51, 146
Fürst, Juliane, 122n128

Gallagher, Matthew, 31n32, 35n42
Gandelsonas, Mario, 143n33
Garmash, Petr, 162n5
GASK. *See* State Architectural-Construction Inspectorate
Gassko, Igor, 162n5
Georgia, 118, 187
Ginzburg, Moisei, 50–51, 57–60, 127, 129
Glantz, David, 14n3, 55n21
Golli, Valentin, 79
Gol'ts, Georgii, 56n24, 57n29
Golubets, Ivan, 34, 140–41
Goodsell, Charles T., 150n45
Gorispolkom, 142n30, 146
Gorplan, 68, 69
Gosbank, 89, *90,* 150
Gosplan, 48, 68
Greek port. *See* Khersones
guidebooks, 159–74

hagiographies, heroic, 26–27, 32–37, 42, 132, 168, 169. *See also* historiography
Harris, James, 15, 73n71, 87n4
Harrison, Mark, 48n5
hero-cities, 3, 11–12, 28, 42, 124, 171n30, 192; architecture for, 58, 60, 169; definition of, 60n35
Heroes of the Defense Monument, 169

Hero of the Soviet Union obelisk, 141
Historical Boulevard, *xviii,* 111–12, 127–29, 137
historiography, 7–8, 131–32, 159–74. *See also* hagiographies
Hockstader, Lee, 184n55
Hoffmann, David L., 50n11
Holmes, Larry, 70n65
Holquist, Peter, 96
Hotel Sevastopol, *xviii,* 146, 152, *154*
House of Pioneers, 112, 146
housing concerns, 87–99, *90, 98,* 100–101, 148, 151, 185
Howard, Ebenezer, 50
Hudson, Hugh, 51n14, 52

Iakovleva, Tamara, 139n27, 162n7, 170n26
Iarskaia-Smirnova, Elena, 62n39
identification, urban, 8–10, 13, 124–30, 142–47, 154–56, 191–95
Il'inichna, Zoia, 90
infant mortality, 109–10, 110*t. See also* public health concerns
influenza, 101, 103*t*
Interdepartmental Commission for the Examination of Projects for Construction, 78
Iofan, Boris, 57n29
Iraq, 187
Irin, L., 56n25
Islam, 145–46, 176
Israel, 145
Istomin, V. I., 129, 135
Ivanov, A. N., 129, 133–35, 142
Ivan the Terrible, 161

Jews, Karaite, 125, 145, 152, 158, 175, 177, 194n74
Johnston, Timothy, 106n77
juvenile delinquency, 114, 121

KA. *See* Committee on Architectural Affairs
Kaganovich, L. M., 53
Kalinin, Mikhail, 56n25, 132

Kandinsky, Vasilii, 51
Karaites. *See* Jews
Kavtaradze, Sergei, 148n43
Kazarskii, Aleksandr I., 30, 34, 162–63, 168; monument to, *xviii,* 137, *138,* 139, 162, 171
Kelly, Catriona, 27n24
Kenez, Peter, 41n60
Khanate, Crimean, 175–77. *See also* Tatars
Khan-Magomedov, Selim, 50n8
Khapaev, V., 162n9
Khersones, 23–24, *24,* 72, 140, 147, 149, 155; Archaeological Preserve of, 116, 146, 177; school trips to, 119, 142; St. Vladimir's Cathedral at, 127, 135–36, 177, 185–86
Khmelnitsky, Bogdan, 34–35
Khrushchev, Nikita, 176; agricultural policies of, 4; historiography under, 165; transfer of Crimea to Ukraine by, 3, 158, 183, 190
Khrushelnycky, Askold, 176n45
Kirgizstan, 118
Kiselev, A. D., 139
Klebanov, S., 37
Kojevnikov, Alexei, 77n79
Kolobov, Evgenii, 141
Komsomol, 3, 125, 142n30
Kopp, Anatole, 50n8
Korchinskaia, Lilia, 89
Korean War, 4, 80
Kornilov, V. A., 32, 129, 135
Korobkov, F., 141
Koshar, Rudy, 160n1
Koshka, Petr (Petro Kishka), 32, 141, 165
Kosmodemianskaia, Zoia, 27, 169
Kostner, Klim, 190n72
Kotkin, Stephen, 41n59, 55n22, 86n1, 86n2
KPOVTN. *See* Communist Underground Organization in the German Rear
Krivosheev, G. F., 2n1, 14n3, 55n21
Krylova, E., 95n35
Kuchma, Leonid, 183, 185–86
Kurban-Bairam (Muslim holiday), 176
Kuromiya, Hirokai, 114n103

Kushnir, I. I., 161n3
Kutuzov, Mikhail, 132n13
Kuznetsov, Aleksandr, 79, 80

Lasswell, Harold D., 143n33
Lavrov, V. A., 56n24
Lazarev Square, *xviii,* 144
Lefaivre, Liane, 150n46
Leningrad, 52, 122, 123, 192
Leningrad Affair, 79–80
Lenin Street, *xviii,* 89, 143, 150
Lenin, Vladimir I., 82; monuments to,
    xviii, 41, 127–29, 141, 157
Levchenko, I. P., 62n39, 100n49
Levitan, Iurii, 42–43
Liakhovich, Aleksandr, 140n28
Lomagin, Georgii, 56n27, 57, 60, 129,
    130; successor of, 62, 63n44
Lowenthal, David, 126n2
Lunacharskii Theater, *xviii,* 112, 115–16,
    146, 148, 152, *153*
Luzhkov, Iurii, 185, 186, 190, 193

Malakhov Kurgan, 22, 86, 127, 129, 150,
    151, 163, 164
malaria, 2, 69, 101, 102, 103*t*
Manley, Rebecca, 88n5
Manstein, Erich von, 15
Marshall Plan, 4, 97
Marx, Karl, 128, 143–44
Masolov, Nikoloai, 36n43
McDonald's restaurant, 178, 181, 187, 189
McReynolds, Louise, 44n64
Megasport sporting goods store, 178–79,
    179
memory, 6–8; collective, 7, 194; meaning
    and, 21–28, 131–33, 137–42
Meshkov, Iurii, 183
Michmanskii Boulevard, 64, 65
Mingorstroi. *See* Ministry of City Building
Ministry of City Building (Mingorstroi),
    75, 77
Mironov, Mikhail, 23n20, 89
mnemonic practices, 7–8
modernist architecture, 49–52, 55, 146
Moldova, 91, 105, 125, 194n74

Morozov, Pavlik, 27
Moscow Architecture Institute, 57
Moscow Plan (1935), 8, 53–54, 62, 66
Moscow State University, 5, 146, 149
mosques, 145–46
Mosse, George, 47n3, 137n26, 160n1
Motorin, Dmitrii, 18n11
Murmansk, 56n25
Murray, John, 143n33
Museum of the Black Sea Fleet, 151
Muslims, 145–46, 176
Muzika, Nikolai, 141
Mycio, Mary, 185n56

Nakachi, Mie, 117n112
Nakhimov Prospect, *xviii, 98,* 143, 152,
    154
Nakhimov, P. S., 32, 135, 137; monument
    to, *xviii,* 129, 144, 188
Nakhimov Square, *xviii,* 144, 186–88
Napoleonic wars, 24, 27, 161, 165
NATO. *See* North Atlantic Treaty
    Organization
Nekrich, Alexander, 176n45
neoclassical architecture, 40, 54–55, 143,
    146–55, *151–54*
newsreels, wartime, 8–9, 28, 38–43, 132,
    162
Nicholas I, tsar, 25, 162
Nightingale, Florence, 32–33
North Atlantic Treaty Organization
    (NATO), 183, 184, 186, 189, 190, 192
Nove, Alec, 47n4
Novgorod, 56, 161

obelisks, 45, 56, 58–59, 131, 139–41, 169
Odessa, 184, 192
Okhitovich, Mikhail, 52
Oktiabrskii, F. S., 31, 36, 130, 141–43
Olick, Jeffrey K., 8n10
Olshevskii, Vitalii, 162n5
Orange Revolution, 157, 186–90
Orlov, Nikolai, 162n5
OSA. *See* Union of Contemporary
    Architects
Ostriakov, N., 141

Ostrovsky, Alexei, 190
Ottoman empire, 24, 30, 137, 161, 162, 193. *See also* Crimean War
Ozerov, L., 35

Palace of Pioneers, 152, *153*
Palace of Soviets, 54, 66
Panorama of the Great Defense, 58, 65, 129, 137, 140, 150, *151,* 163–65, 171; in *Battle for Sevastopol,* 42; map of, *xviii*
parks, 5–6, 88, 99, 111
Pavlichenko, Ludmilla, 33, 34–35
Pennington, Reina, 36n43
Pereislav, Treaty of, 183
Peremyslov, A., 85
Peter and Paul Cathedral, 136, 148, 150
Pethybridge, R. W., 47n4
Petrone, Karen, 41n59
Pioneer camps, 104, 142
Platt, Kevin, 12n1, 155n50, 161n4
Pobeda cinema, *xviii,* 112–14, 150
Pogodin, N., 106n76
Pokhodaev, Iurii, 161n3
Pokrovskii Cathedral, *xviii,* 40, 148
Poliakov, N., 62n38
Potemkin (film), 25. *See also* Russian Revolution of 1905
Potemkin-Tavricheskii, Prince, 32
Potemkin villages, 46, 53, 93–94
Pozhenian, G., 33n36
Prezios, Donald, 143n33
Primorskii Boulevard, 22, 47, 64, 65, 78, 111–12, 146, 187
prisoners of war (POWs), 43, 92–93, 97, 125
public health concerns, 1–2, 69, 99–106, 103*t*; abortion rates and, 117–19, 118*t*; famine and, 4, 91, 102, 105, 109; infant mortality and, 109–10, 110*t*; mobilized workers and, 91; parks and, 5–6, 88; school children and, 21–22; with workers' housing, 94
purges, Stalin's, 4, 5, 57, 176
Pushkin, Aleksandr, 175
Putin, Vladimir, 185–86

Raleigh, Donald J., 116n110
rationalist architects, 50–52, 54–55
Razumovsky, F., 161n3
realism, socialist, 26–27, 35, 61
Remnick, David, 176n45
revolution, 7. *See also* Russian Revolution of 1917
Riabkov, G. T., 161n2
Rimsky-Korsakov, Nikolai, 23
Rosseikin, Boris, 162n5
Rostov-on-Don, 56n25, 57n29, 63
Rubanenko, Boris, 56
Ruble, Blair A., 53n17
Rudnev, Lev, 57n29
Russian Orthodox Church, 26, 132n13, 148, 177, 185–86
Russian Revolution of 1905, 8, 25, 131, 144, 165
Russian Revolution of 1917, 25, 31, 82, 138–39; historiography of, 7–8, 165–67
Russian Soviet Federated Socialist Republic (RSFSR), 56, 64, 75, 133
Russocentrism, 10, 128, 143, 155, 158, 191
Russo-Turkish wars, 24, 30, 137, 161, 162, 193. *See also* Crimean War
Ryabchikov, Lev, 185n58

Sabsovich, Leonid, 52
Sadovskii, M. A., 138
Saint Michael's Admiralty Church, 135
Saint Vladimir Cathedral, *xviii,* 127, 135–36, 177, 185–86
Saints Peter and Paul Cathedral, 136, 148, 150
Salisbury, Harrison, 89
Sapun Gora, 140, 169, 177
Sartorti, Rosalinde, 27n25, 33n38
Savchenko, Vyacheslav, 183n52
Sazhin, Petr, 33n36
scarlet fever, 102, 103*t*
Scott, James C., 57n30
Scuttled Ships monument, *xviii, 134,* 135, 163, 171, 182
Sechenov Institute of Physical Therapy, *xviii,* 106, 111–12, 146, 152, *153*

Semenov, V. N., 45n67, 57n29, 63n41, 131n11
Semin, Georgii, 162n5
Sevastopolskaia, Dasha, 32–34, 36, 38, 137
Shavshin, Vladimir, 185n61
Shchusev, Aleksei, 57n29
Shkvarikov, V. A., 78, 129
Shmidt, P. P., 138
Shvetsov, P. M., 113–14
Siegelbaum, Lewis, 27n23
Simferopol, 67, 69, 188
Simonov, G. A., 57n29
Simonov, Konstantin, 42, 44
Sladkov, I. D., 139
Smirnov, I. A., 161n2
Smolensk, 56, 57n29, 161
Sobolev, Leonid, 46, 65
socialist realism, 26–27, 35, 61
Sofinskii, I., 161n2
Sosnitskii, Sergei, 78–79
Soviet Street, *xviii*, 90, 157
Sovnarkom. *See* Council of People's Commissars
space: agitational, 5–6, 48–51, 55, 124–47, 156; commercialization of, 178–82, *179–81;* politicized, 186–90; redefinition of, 174–78
Stakhanov, Aleksei, 26–27
Stalin, Joseph, 10, 52, 70–72, 81, 114; agricultural policies of, 70, 102, 106, 123; Constitution of 1936 and, 86, 93; death of, 6; historiography under, 161, 165–66; monuments to, 47, 59, 127–29; purges of, 4, 5, 57, 176; telegram to Sevastopoltsy by, 11, 12, 26
Stalingrad, 47, 48, 56, 75, 192
Starr, S. Frederick, 49n6
State Architectural-Construction Inspectorate (GASK), 115
Steinmetz, George, 86n1
Stepanenko, M., 141
Stetsenko, I., 188n67
Stites, Richard, 82n87
Suvorov, Alexander, 132n13
Suvorov Square, *xviii*

Tarkhonov, Alexei, 148n43
Tatars, 27, 125, 145–46, 158, 175–77, 194n74
Tchaikovsky, Petr, 23
Tennyson, Alfred, 25
Tikhii, A., 187n65
Timasheff, Nicholas, 86n2
Titmuss, Richard, 86n1
Tolstoy, Lev, 23, 137, 165; *Sevastopol Tales,* 11–12, 25–26, 29–31, 43; as Soviet hero, 12; Voitekhov on, 36
Tolstoy Library, 150
Totleben, Eduard Ivanovich, 23, 43, 129, 135
tourism, 158–74; commercialization and, 178–82, *179–81;* ethnicity and, 174–78
traditionalist architects, 51–52, 54–55
Trautman, Iurii, 56n27, 72, 115, 155–56; Alëshina and, 67; appointment of, 62, 63n44; criticism by others of, 73–74, 76–77; criticism of Barkhin by, 63–66; newspaper articles by, 142; reconstruction plans of, 66–70, 81; removal of, 74, 78, 80; renaming of streets by, 143–44; on Tatar mosque, 146
Trotsky, Leon, 166
Tsingalenok, V., 79
tuberculosis, 2, 101, 103t, 106
Turkey. *See* Ottoman empire
Turkmenistan, 70, 118, 147
Turovsky, M., 37, 38
typhus, 2, 101, 103t, 104
Tzonis, Alexander, 150n46

Ukraine, 182–86; conscripted laborers from, 91, 125; economic development projects of, 170–71; EU membership and, 183, 186, 187; independence of, 158, 182; Iraq participation by, 187; NATO and, 183, 184, 186, 187, 189, 190, 192; Orange Revolution of, 157, 186–90; Russian conflicts with, 158, 184–86, 192–93; Sevastopol's identity and, 8–10, 165, 174, 182–86, 190–95; transfer of Crimea to, 3, 10, 158, 183–84, 190

Union of Architects, 63
Union of Contemporary Architects (OSA), 51–52
Union of Soviet Socialist Republics (USSR), 27–38, 41–43; aesthetics and, 8, 9, 47, 54–55, 132, 147–49; collapse of, 156, 159–60, 170–76, 183; propaganda films of, 28, 30, 33, 38, 41–43; Revolution of 1917 and, 7–8, 25, 31, 82, 165–67; urban planning in, 8, 53–62, 66. *See also* Stalin, Joseph
urban identification, 8–10, 13, 124–30, 142–47, 154–56, 191–95
urban planning, 8, 53–62, 66
Ushakov Square, *xviii,* 144, 151
Uspenskii Monastery, 177
UVS. *See* Directorate for the Restoration of Sevastopol
Uzbekistan, 118

Vale, Lawrence, 4n5, 6
Varga-Harris, Christine, 88n6, 94n27
Vasyukov, Vadim, 185
Velikanov, A., 65
Venikeev, E. V., 146n41, 185n61
Verdery, Katherine, 4n3
Victory Monument, 140, 169
Viola, Lynne, 87
Vitruvius, Marcus, 150n46
Vladimir Cathedral, *xviii,* 127, 135–36, 185–86

Vladimir the Great, 177, 185, 186
Voitekhov, Boris, 15–16, 36, 89
Voronin, N., 56n24
Voroshilow, Kliment, 124

Weiner, Amir, 27n26, 155
Weiner, Douglas, 47n2, 114n98
Weitz, Richard, 189n69
whooping cough, 101, 103*t*
Williams, Carol J., 185n57
World War II, 1–2, 13–23, 20*t*, 27–38, 47–48; Crimean War and, 25, 30–31, 38, 144, 155–56; media coverage of, 22–23, 28–29, 32–34, 38–43; memorials to, 131–36, 139–42, 167–70, 177
Wortman, Richard, 26n22, 32n33, 143n33

Yalta, 62, 69, 171n30, 172, 174
Yanukovich, Viktor, 188
Yekelchyk, Serhy, 35n40
Young People, Monument to, 169
Yushchenko, Viktor, 187–90, 193

zabota (care or concern), 77, 85, 86
Zaitsev, I. A., 161n3
Zaitsev, Vasilii, 34
Zima, V. F., 109n85
Zolotarev, M., 162n9
Zubkova, Elena, 3n2, 4n4, 86n2, 122n128, 154n48